My Shakespeare

The Authorship Controversy

MY SHAKESPEARE

The Authorship Controversy

EXPERTS EXAMINE THE ARGUMENTS FOR BACON, NEVILLE, OXFORD, MARLOWE, MARY SIDNEY, SHAKSPERE, AND SHAKESPEARE.

Edited by William Leahy

Professor of Shakespeare studies at Brunel University London, and Chairman of the Shakespearean Authorship Trust

EER Edward Everett Root, Publishers, Brighton, 2018.

EER

Edward Everett Root, Publishers, Co. Ltd.,
30 New Road, Brighton, Sussex, BN1 1BN, England.
www.eerpublishing.com
edwardeverettroot@yahoo.co.uk

My Shakespeare: The Authorship Controversy
First published in Great Britain in 2018

ISBN 9781911454540 Paperback
ISBN 9781911454557 Hardback
ISBN 9781911454564 eBook

Cover designed by John Tollett.
Typesetting by Head & Heart Book Design
Printed in Great Britain by Lightning Source UK, Milton Keynes.

Contents

The Contributors

Alan H. Nelson is Professor Emeritus in the Department of English at the University of California, Berkeley. His specializations are palaeography, bibliography, and the reconstruction of the literary life and times of medieval and Renaissance England from documentary sources. He is author of *Monstrous Adversary: The Life of Edward de Vere, Seventeenth Earl of Oxford* (Liverpool University Press 2003). He has contributed essays to "Shakespeare Documented", an online project sponsored by the Folger Shakespeare Library, Washington, D.C.

Diana Price is the author of *Shakespeare's Unorthodox Biography: New Evidence of An Authorship Problem* (Greenwood Press 2001), the first book on the subject to be published in a peer-reviewed series; the updated paperback edition was released in 2013. Price's bibliography can be found at her website at <http://www.shakespeare-authorship.com>.

Alexander Waugh is the author of several books including *Fathers & Sons* (2004) and *The House of Wittgenstein* (2008). He is Senior Visiting Fellow of the University of Leicester; General Editor of a 43-volume scholarly edition for the Oxford University Press; co-editor of several books on Shakespeare; Honorary President of the Shakespeare Authorship Coalition and Chairman of the De Vere Society.

Ros Barber is a lecturer at Goldsmiths, University of London, and Director of Research at the Shakespearean Authorship Trust. Publications include *Shakespeare: The Evidence* (leanpub.com/shakespeare), *30-Second Shakespeare* (2015) and *The Marlowe Papers* (2012). She is twice joint winner of the Calvin Hoffman Prize for a distinguished work on Christopher Marlowe.

John Casson retired after 30 years' practice as a psychotherapist. His ground-breaking research, *Drama, Psychotherapy and Psychosis: Dramatherapy and Psychodrama with People who Hear Voices*, was published in 2004 by Routledge. He began researching Henry Neville in 2005 and has published four books culminating in 2016 with *Sir Henry Neville was Shakespeare: The Evidence* (with W. D. Rubinstein, Amberley).

William D. Rubinstein was Professor of History at Deakin University and at the University of Wales Aberystwyth, and is currently an Adjunct Professor at Monash University in Melbourne. He was the co-author, with Brenda James, of *The Truth Will Out* (2005), which first made the case for Sir Henry Neville as Shakespeare.

David Ewald is a Shakespeare scholar specifically engaged in research supporting the Neville/Shakespeare authorship. He contributed to the book, *Sir Henry Neville Was Shakespeare: The Evidence* by John Casson and William D. Rubinstein, especially with his discovery of the Ring Composition in Shakespeare's Sonnets.

Robin Williams spent twenty-five years writing computer books, then formalized her lifelong immersion in Shakespeare with a Master's degree and a Ph.D. in Shakespeare studies from Brunel University London. She cofounded the International Shakespeare Centre and is Director of iReadShakespeare.org and the ISC Press in Santa Fe, New Mexico. She is founder and president of the Mary Sidney Society.

Barry Clarke has published journal articles in Shakespeare studies and quantum mechanics, as well as an academic treatise *The Quantum Puzzle* (2017). Columns in *The Daily Telegraph* and *Prospect* magazine have furnished mathematics and logic puzzle books for Cambridge University Press and Mensa. His PhD explored Bacon's contribution to three Shakespeare plays. His book *The Bacon-Shakespeare Connection: A Scholarly Study* [with a Preface by Sir Mark Rylance], will be published by Edward Everett Root Publishers in 2018.

William Leahy is Professor of Shakespeare studies at Brunel University London. His book *Elizabethan Triumphal Processions* appeared in 2005. He has published widely on the Shakespeare Authorship Question, most notably in his 2010 edition of collected essays *Shakespeare and his Authors: Critical Perspectives on the Authorship Question* and as co-editor of *The Many Lives of William Shakespeare*, a special edition of the *Journal of Early Modern Studies* (2016).

Introduction

The Wonderful Doubt of Galileo

William Leahy

In scene 3 of Bertolt Brecht's *Life of Galileo*, in response to Galileo's desire, having invented the telescope to convince the Church of his revolutionary discoveries concerning the universe, his friend Sagredo says: "Do you imagine the Pope will hear the truth when you tell him he is wrong, and not just hear that he's wrong?" (1980, 33). In many ways, this could sum up the overarching reality of the field of study generally known as the Shakespeare Authorship Question, where excellently researched theories are often dismissed out of hand not because of their lack of plausibility or robustness of approach but because they contend that long held truths are highly questionable and built upon myth, anecdote and supposition. A book such as this current one, constituted as it is by a number of different versions of the author of the plays and poems traditionally attributed to William Shakespeare of Stratford-upon-Avon and which are each presented as equal, is naturally founded in a rather different reality, one which could be defined by something Brecht's Galileo says of himself later in the play in scene 9: "My object is not to establish that I [am] right but to find out if I am" (80-81). It is in this spirit that *My Shakespeare* is presented to its readers, along with a defining principle that great research is made up of much more than its conclusion: it is defined by its journey and not by its destination. Given this, many versions of the author can be presented as they are here and each can be regarded as equally describing interesting and useful journeys. This situation demonstrates, among other things that the study of the Shakespeare Authorship Question has come a long way.

It is now just over twelve years since my own first public intervention in this fascinating field of authorship studies. This intervention took the form of a short article in the *New Statesman* in which I argued that there is no such thing as a Shakespeare Authorship Question and that those who believed there is were rebelling against the authoritarian forces of the orthodox Shakespeare community and the chocolate-box fantasy world of Stratford-upon-Avon. My next intervention was more open-minded than this as I made myself more aware of the various issues and then, within a couple of years I became convinced there are any number of problems with the traditional narrative of Shakespeare as the author of the plays and poems attributed to him and that research in this field of study was worth pursuing. Indeed, the attraction of a field of study in which so much is unresolved became too much to resist.

In those twelve years there has been so much change, perhaps most evidently registered in the publication in 2016 of the new edition of *The New Oxford Shakespeare: The Complete Works* by the Oxford University Press and edited by Gary Taylor *et al.* As I explain in my own chapter here, in this *Complete Works* these orthodox Shakespeare scholars clearly and unambiguously claim that the works of Shakespeare were written by many authors, some of whom they do not know. In essence, these orthodox scholars of great distinction show that they do not know what is going on in terms of the authorship of the Shakespeare canon and that the authorship issue is indeed unresolved. This is an incredible admission and one that would not have been possible twelve years ago.

I would claim that many of the authors in this current collection have been instrumental on all sides of this debate and many have helped effect this change in the field of Shakespeare authorship studies. In the first chapter, Alan Nelson provides us with much evidence that demonstrates, in his view that the case for Shakespeare of Stratford-upon-Avon as the author of the plays and poems traditionally attributed to him is beyond question. Nelson is perfectly placed to make such a case and it is for this reason that his version of Shakespeare is presented first. Diana Price, whose contribution forms chapter two, draws upon her years of research questioning the traditional narrative of Shakespeare and, while not postulating a defined alternative shows why, in her view the man from Stratford could not have been the author. The next five chapters then argue for individual alternative authors; Alexander Waugh argues that Edward De Vere, the seventeenth Earl of Oxford wrote the plays and poems; Ros Barber that it was Christopher Marlowe; John Casson *et al* argue that it was Henry Neville and Robin

Williams that it was Mary Sidney. Barry Clarke's approach in chapter seven is somewhat different, arguing that evidence only allows him to postulate the contribution of Francis Bacon to a number of plays traditionally attributed to Shakespeare rather than enabling him to make an overarching case for Bacon as the hidden author of the entire canon. In the final chapter, a slightly different approach enables a case to be made for an "amalgamated" author. I owe each of these contributors a great debt of thanks for their incredible efforts.

Naturally, all of these versions of the author cannot be right. However, if there is one single unified argument here, it is this: there is a real issue with the idea that the literary works traditionally attributed to William Shakespeare were written by the man from Stratford (alone) and that the truth can only be discovered if we open ourselves to that reality. In other words, much like Gary Taylor *et al*, the single and most important argument this book makes is that the authorship issue is *unresolved*. Given this, the excellent and compelling work that appears in this collection joins with the work by many orthodox scholars and, in combination seeks resolution of the authorship issue. It seeks answers to the same question in the same spirit of endeavour, integrity and the pursuit of truth. That the authorship is unresolved is not a problem. Indeed, the lack of resolution is exciting and inspiring. But that all of this pursuit of truth occupies the same territory and is driven by the same intellectual curiosity is where progress lies. It brings us all together in a spirit which we share with Galileo; not to establish we are right, but to find out if we are.

Chapter 1

William Shakespeare of Stratford-upon-Avon and London

Alan H. Nelson

On June 12, 1593, Richard Stonley, a clerk of the Exchequer of Receipt, the tax-gathering branch of the royal treasury, purchased two recently-published books for a total of twelve pence: *The Survey, or Topographical Description of France* (1592), and *Venus and Adonis* (1593), a long poem which had been entered in the London "Stationers Register" (see Arber 1875-94, ref 22354; entries referenced in Pollard and Redgrave 1976-91) on April 18, 1593. Though no author's name graces the title page of either book, the dedication of *Venus and Adonis* is signed "William Shakespeare". Stonley logically inferred that the poem was written by Shakespeare — or, as he wrote in his own hand, mixing Latin and English: "Per Shakspere".[1] Did Stonley know 'Shakspere' personally? He was well-read, the owner of over 400 books by 1599, and London's population was small by modern standards, perhaps 200,000. But a poet, especially the author of a first publication, was not necessarily a public figure. In 1594 a second poem appeared, *The Rape of Lucrece*, again with a dedication signed "William Shakespeare". Both poems sold well, and

1 Most documents referenced in this essay are standard for Shakespeare biographies. Photographs and reference numbers of documents are available on the "Shakespeare Documented" website <http://www.shakespearedocumented.org/>, Folger Shakespeare Library, Washington D.C., for which the author has supplied many of the relevant essays. Keywords are the most efficient finding-aid. Footnotes are supplied only where additional information or explanations have been deemed necessary. I am grateful to Michael L. Hayes for reading this essay in draft and giving advice.

both were quickly praised in print. But would their author have been recognized on the street?

"William Shakespeare" was also the name of a player on the public stage. On March 15, 1595, he and two other members of the Lord Chamberlain's company, William Kemp and Richard Burbage, accepted payment from the royal treasury for two court performances over the 1594-95 Christmas season. On the same day, and for the same season, three members of the Lord Admiral's company, Edward Alleyn, Richard Jones, and John Singer, received payment for three court performances. All six recipients were players. Evidence that Shakespeare was a player even earlier than Christmas 1594-95 survives in a copy of the play *George a Greene, Pinner of Wakefield* (1599), now in the Folger Shakespeare Library, Washington, D.C (see Nelson 1998). Like most plays of its day, *George a Greene* announced the name of its publisher on its title-page, but not the name of the playwright. The play had been entered into the Stationers Register in 1595, again without the name of the playwright. Owner of the Folger copy was Sir George Buc, slated to succeed Edmund Tilney as Master of the Revels — the royal officer with supervisory authority over all play texts and performances, whether in public or at court. Buc made a practice of identifying authors of anonymous plays. To discover the author of *George a Greene* he conducted personal interviews with "W. Shakespeare" and "Edward Juby". Juby's thespian career is well-documented over the years 1594 to 1618. Shakespeare's career, up to the time of the interview, which cannot have been earlier than 1599, was roughly similar. Juby told Buc that the play was by Robert Greene, while Shakespeare said that it was by "a minister, who acted the pinner's part in it himself." A contemporary document known as "Henslowe's Diary" reveals that *George a Greene* was performed at the Rose Playhouse on December 29, 1593, and on January 2, 8, 15, and 22, 1594 (Foakes 2002, 21-2).[2] It is likely that Juby and Shakespeare both knew *George a Greene* because they had both acted in it, or at least visited the Rose in the post-Christmas season of 1593-94. Indeed, the play which immediately followed *George a Greene* at the Rose, on January 23, was *Titus Andronicus*. Although *Titus* was published in the same year, 1594, its author was, as usual, not named on the title page. In 1598, however, Francis Meres, in his *Palladis Tamia*, attributed the play to Shakespeare.

2 Some scholars think the days are off by one weekday; of importance here are not the particular days but the sequence. See also the Henslowe Alleyn website compiled and edited by Grace Ioppolo: <http://www.henslowe-alleyn.org.uk/>.

Ben Jonson, in his 1616 *Workes*, lists ten "principall Comœdians" in the 1598 first performance of *Every Man In His Humour*, all members of the Lord Chamberlain's Men, beginning with "Will Shakespeare". Jonson similarly lists eight "principall Tragœdians" in the 1603 first performance of *Sejanus*, all members of the King's Men (as the Lord Chamberlain's Men were called following the accession of King James), including "Will. Shake-Speare". In the years leading up to 1603 William Shakespeare became involved with the College of Arms, London, where he was characterized, perhaps derisively, as "Shakespeare ye player". Until recently this designation had been known only from a late manuscript copy (circa 1700). Now an earlier manuscript has been identified, roughly datable as "early 17th century", probably 1642 at the latest.

On March 13, 1602, John Manningham, a member of the Middle Temple, one of the four major legal societies in London, recorded an anecdote which he heard from his roommate Thomas Curle. The narrative concerns a 'citizen' — slang for the wife of a member of a London livery company — and two players:

> Vpon a tyme when Burbidge played Richard 3 there was a citizen [gone] soe farr in liking with him, that before shee went from the play shee appointed him to come that night vnto hir by the name of Richard the 3 / Shakespeare ouerhearing their conclusion, went before, was intertained, and at his game ere Burbidge came. Then message being brought that Richard the 3d was at the dore, Shakespeare caused returne to be made that William the Conquerour was before Richard the 3.

Manningham added (for clarification): "Shakespeares name William". While this anecdote may well have been apocryphal (it is perhaps too clever to be true), it confirms that Burbage was a leading player whose identity required no explanation, and that Shakespeare was another player of similar renown. Since a complete appreciation of the jest assumes knowledge of Shakespeare's first name, Manningham supplies it. The jest would be even more pointed for anyone who knew that Burbage's first name was Richard, or if Burbage had been referenced as "Richard the Second", since he was second in line for the lady's attentions. Apparently, however, Burbage was more firmly identified in the public mind with the notorious Richard the Third.

William Shakespeare's name heads a list of nine "Players" among more than a thousand royal servants who received red or scarlet cloth for the royal entry of James I into London, March 15, 1604. The source document contains three lists of players, one for the King's Men, one for the Queen's Men, and one for the Prince's Men. The lists comprise a roster of twenty-eight players in three companies, all of them active in the early years of James I. Though Shakespeare was the top player of the top company, he was not necessarily the most skilled actor — Edward Alleyn and Richard Burbage would doubtless have won the Oscars of their day. But he was the acknowledged leader of his company, which could not have happened if he had not also been an accomplished actor. Shakespeare was not only a player however, but a "sharer" and a "fellow" in his company. A "sharer" held a financial stake, while a "fellow" in this context was a senior member who held, in Hamlet's words, "a fellowship in a cry of players".[3] Shakespeare was named first among five players who, on February 21, 1599, bought a half-share of the lease of the site of the future Globe playhouse on Bankside, Southwark. Though the original lease does not survive, it is referenced in some eleven documents dated May 17, 1599, to 1635. The other owners of the same half-share were John Heminges, Augustine Phillips, Thomas Pope, and William Kemp, all players. The other half-share was held by the brothers Richard and Cuthbert Burbage, sons of the recently deceased James Burbage. Richard was a player, as James had been also, while Cuthbert's interest was purely financial.

When Shakespeare's company received its royal license from King James in 1603, the first three "servants" (out of a total of nine) were named as Lawrence Fletcher, William Shakespeare, and Richard Burbage. Fletcher may have been listed first because of an earlier acquaintance with King James in Scotland. But Shakespeare is second, taking precedence over Richard Burbage. When the Blackfriars playhouse lease was signed in 1608, the order was different: Richard Burbage, John Heminges, William Shakespeare, Cuthbert Burbage, Henry Condell, and Thomas Evans (Evans, like Cuthbert Burbage, was not a player). In his own *First Folio*, published in 1623 by his fellow players John Heminges and Henry Condell, "William Shakespeare" is listed as the first of twenty-six "Names of the Principall Actors in all these Plays". When Cuthbert Burbage recalled the long history of the Globe playhouse in 1635, "Shakspere" came to his mind as the first of

3 Noted in my essay on "fellow" on the "Shakespeare Documented" website.

"those deserving men" who joined the enterprise founded by his father and continued by his brother Richard and himself.

"William Shakespeare" was also a playwright. The name first appeared on the title pages of printed plays in 1598: *Love's Labour's Lost* ("By W. Shakespere"), and *Richard II* and *Richard III* ("By William Shake-speare"). All three were second editions. Extant first editions of *Richard II* and *Richard III*, dated 1597, do not carry the name of the author. An early, now lost first edition of *Love's Labour's Lost* may be inferred from the full title of the 1598 edition: *A pleasant conceited comedie, called Loues labors lost As it was presented before her highnes this last Christmas. Newly corrected and augmented by W. Shakespere.* In 1599 *1 Henry IV* was "Newly corrected by W. Shakespere"; in 1600, four more plays by "William Shakespeare" appeared: *2 Henry IV*; *Merchant of Venice*; *A Midsummer Night's Dream*; and *Much Ado About Nothing.* More plays by William Shakespeare would be published as the years wore on, culminating in the *First Folio* of 1623. Thus, by 1598, three "Shakespeares" were known to the London public: the poet (confirmed from 1593), the player (confirmed from 1595), and the playwright (confirmed from 1598). Did three William Shakespeares inhabit late Elizabethan London, or were all three the same individual?

Spelling and hyphenation are of no help in establishing identities from this period. Variant spelling is routine for all English surnames before 1700. To take two examples: Ben Jonson's surname was often spelled "Johnson", while Christopher Marlowe's only known signature reads "Marley". Though "Shakespeare" is taken today as the 'correct' spelling for the poet and playwright, nineteenth-century scholars often preferred "Shakspeare" as more authentic. In truth, the simple principle of variation is more authentic than any particular spelling. As for hyphenation, "Shakespeare" is but one of many compound surnames sometimes hyphenated or written as two words between 1550 and 1650, along with All-de, Bridge-good, Camp-bell, De-bre, Fair child, Full of love, Good-all, Good-inch, Hard-castle, Harm-wood, Harrow-good, Hold craft, Horn blow, Mount clear, Old-castle, Penny-ale, Red head, Walde-grave, and White head.[4] An even closer match is "Break-speare", a name cited frequently in early English printed books because Pope Adrian IV (d. 1199), the only English pope, was born Nicholas Breakspeare. English historians and printers

4 The *Short Title Catalogue* records many instances of All-dee, Camp-bell, Walde-grave. Other names in this list are taken from the registers of St. Saviour's parish, Southwark, 1561-1650: London Metropolitan Archive, MSS P92/SAV/2001-2.

contemporary with Shakespeare spelled Breakspeare with or without a hyphen, showing no apparent preference for one form over the other.[5] The point is made even clearer in an essay on English surnames by William Camden in his *Remains concerning Britain* (1605, 111), who cites names based on what men presumably carried: "Long-sword, Broad-speare, Fortescu, that is, Stong-shield, and in some such respect, Break-speare, Shake-Speare, Shotbolt, Wagstaffe". Camden (or his printer) hyphenates some compound names and not others, apparently at random. Plays from 1598 are attributed on their title pages to "Shakespeare" and to "Shake-speare"; one and the same player in Ben Jonson's *Folio* of 1616 is called "Shakespeare" and "Shake-Speare". *King Lear* (1608) is attributed to "Shakespeare" in the Stationers Register, but to "Shak-speare" on the printed title page, while the *Sonnets* (1609) are entered in the Stationers Register as "Shakespeares" but printed as "Shake-speares". Hyphenation occurs with the same irregularity, and with the same insignificance, as variation in spelling.

That Shakespeare the poet and Shakespeare the playwright were one and the same is confirmed by similarities of vocabulary, style, and metrical development. Though Shakespeare the poet may have been an unknown quantity in 1593, he had every opportunity to achieve personal fame through the publication of his works. By 1610 William Shakespeare's *Venus and Adonis* and *The Rape of Lucrece* had appeared in a total of fifteen editions; the appearance of *Shake-speares Sonnets* in 1609 made for a total of sixteen. How many copies were printed of each edition? As one historian of printing cites the number 1250 (Bennett 1965, 298), let us take an excessively conservative estimate of a 500 copy print-run for each edition. This estimate makes for an eventual total of 8000 copies of Shakespeare's poems, with his name attached, circulating in and around London, beginning in 1593 and with a fresh infusion nearly every year thereafter. The number of play-texts attributed on their title pages to William Shakespeare, calculated at the same rate, and not counting editions which may have been mere printers' variants, is also sixteen, making another 8000 copies. The grand total is 16,000 copies of poems and plays openly attributed to William Shakespeare, to which more could be added by counting books such as *Love's Martyr, or Rosalins Complaint* (1601), which also name William Shakespeare as an author.

5 Observations are derived from putting the names Breakspeare and Shakespeare with and without the hyphen into the "Keyword" box of "Early English Books Online", limiting dates of publication as desired.

The same literate public which could purchase Shakespeare's poems and plays on London's book-stalls could attend plays at the Theatre through 1598, or at the Globe beginning in 1599. In the uncurtained early-modern stage, reimagined as Shakespeare's Globe in today's London, each individual actor was thoroughly exposed to the public's gaze. Which player was merely a player and which (if any) was also the playwright, or at least capable of being a playwright, could be determined with ease. Indeed, the individual identities of actors and actor-playwrights were well-known to the London public. For this we have the explicit testimony of Sir Richard Baker, author of *A Chronicle of the Kings of England ... unto the raigne of our Soveraigne Lord King Charles.* Baker, who was born in 1568, a mere four years after Shakespeare, was a personal witness to the major cultural events of his time. Baker died in 1645, but his *Chronicle* was published in 1643. In a chapter entitled "The Raigne of Queen Elizabeth" he considered "Men of Note in her time". After naming men of power and authority, he continues:

> After such men, it might be thought ridiculous to speak of Stage-players; but seeing excellency in the meanest things deserve remembring, and [R]oscius the Comedian is recorded in History with such commendation, it may be allowed us to do the like with some of our Nation. Richard Bourbidge and Edward Allen, two such actors, as no age must ever look to see the like: and, to make their Comedies compleat, Richard Tarleton, who for the Part called the Clowns Part, never had his match, never will have. For Writers of Playes, and such as had been Players themselves, William Shakespeare, and Benjamin Johnson, have specially left their Names recommended to posterity (120).

Baker's assertion is as authoritative as it is explicit: William Shakespeare and Ben Jonson had been stage-players and also playwrights. The index of the volume adds yet another detail: "William Shakespeare an excellent writer of Comedies".

About 1601 students of St. John's College, Cambridge, wrote and staged *The Return from Parnassus* (Part II), a play which survives in both manuscript and print. The play was entered in the Stationers Register on October 16, 1605, and printed in two successive editions in 1606. The manuscript supplies both a title and a date: "The progresse to Parnassus as it was acted in St Iohn's Colledge in Cambridge Anno 1601." The scribal date matches the 1601-2 Christmas season of college plays. Act IV Scene III of *The Return from Parnassus: or the Scourge of Simony*, contains a scene between "Dick" Burbage and "Will" Kemp — the very men who had gone with William Shakespeare to the royal treasury in Westminster on March 15, 1595. Two Cambridge students audition to become professional players in London. While Burbage is hopeful, Kemp disparages habits the young men may have picked up at Cambridge:

> *Burbidg/* Now Will Kempe, if wee can entertaine these schollars at a low rate it will bee well, they oftentimes have a good conceite in a parte/
>
> *Kempe/* Its true indeed honest Dick; but ye slaves are somewhat prowde, & besides tis good spoorte in a parte to see them never speake in their walke, but at ye end of ye stage, just as though in walking with a fellowe wee should never speake but at a stile, a gate or a ditch, where a man can goe no farther; I was once at a Commedye in Cambridge & there I saw a parasite make faces & mouthes of all sortes on this fashion/

Presumably the actor playing Kemp makes a grotesque face. Burbage hopes that the former students will double as playwrights, but Kemp is again doubtful:

> *Burb:* A little teaching will mend those faultes, & it may bee besides they will be able to penne a parte.
>
> *Kempe/* Few of ye Vniuersitye men penne plaies well, they smell too much of yat writer Ouid, & yat writer Metamorphoses, & talke too much of Proserpina & Iupiter: why heeres our fellowe Shakspeare putts them all downe, [aye], and Ben Iohnson too: O yat Ben Iohnson is a pestilent fellowe, hee brought vpp Horace giuing ye poetts a pill; but our fellowe shakespeare hath given him a purge yat made him beraye his creddитt.
>
> *Burbage* Its a shrewd fellowe indeed: I wonder these schollers stay so longe, they appointed to bee heare presentlye yat we might trye them; O heere they come …

Here Kemp fears that men brought up in the university will never make good playwrights because they are too steeped in classical literature: as counter-example he points to "our fellowe Shakspeare" who "puts them all downe", and to Ben Jonson, another non-university playwright. The *Parnassus* plays, to be sure, are fiction; but as with any satire, the humour depends on real and well-recognized circumstances. The player Kemp's explicit identification of Shakespeare as "our fellowe" prefigures Augustine Phillips's will of 1605, which lists Shakespeare first among eight players from the King's Men, seven of whom Phillips calls "my fellow". Though Ben Jonson is also mentioned in the *Parnassus* play, he is not called "our fellowe", as indeed he was not, since he had not succeeded as an actor, and, so far as is known, was never a formal member of the Lord Chamberlain's Men. Kemp alludes to a rivalry between Jonson and Shakespeare in which the latter had the best — reflecting Shakespeare's easy ascendancy in a perceived competition between London's two leading playwrights of the late 1590s.

The authorship of contemporary plays was known above all to Edmund Tilney, Master of the Revels, and his staff. A notebook which Tilney submitted for royal inspection in 1605 contains a table in three columns, listing (1) playing companies; (2) play titles, dates, and venues; and (3) "The poets w*hi*ch mayd the plaies". Ten court entertainments over the 1604-5 Christmas season were performed by "the Kings Maiesties plaiers" or "his Maiesties plaiers". Three of the company's plays are assigned (correctly, in view of all external evidence) to "Shaxberd": "Mesur for Mesur", "The Plaie of Errors", and "The Marchant of Venis". The last of these plays was acted twice, the second performance "Againe Com*m*anded By the Kings Ma*ies*tie". The perfect match between play and playwright reveals that "Shaxberd" is "Shakespeare" in the peculiar orthography of Tilney's secretary William Honnyng. Other plays are assigned to other playwrights with equal precision. Not only Edmund Tilney, but all three of his assistants appended signatures testifying to the accuracy of their joint report.

Shakespeare's connection to both his poems and his plays was openly acknowledged in contemporary publications. The anonymous author of *Willobie his Avisa* (1594) wrote: "And Shake-speare, paints poor Lucrece rape." The next year the Cambridge scholar William Covell, in *Polimanteia* (1595), associated "Sweet Shakspeare" with both *Venus and Adonis* and *Lucrece*. However, towering above all contemporary authors mentioning Shakespeare is Francis Meres, whose *Palladis Tamia* (1598) constitutes a virtual "Who's Who" of contemporary English poets and playwrights. Meres names Shakespeare on nine separate occasions (but not as often as Michael Drayton, who must count as Meres's most admired author):

> [1] ... The English tongue is mightily enriched, and gorgeouslie inuested in rare ornaments and resplendent abiliments by sir *Philip Sidney, Spencer, Daniel, Drayton, Warner, Shakespeare, Marlow* and *Chapman.*

On the same page, "Brunswerd" is commended for his Latin verse; this was John Brownswerd (d. 1589), former schoolmaster at the Free Grammar School of Stratford-upon-Avon (see *DNB* 2004).

> [2] As the soule of *Euphorbus* was thought to liue in *Pythagoras:* so the sweete wittie soule of *Ouid* liues in mellifluous & hony-tongued *Shakespeare,* witnes his *Venus* and *Adonis,* his *Lucrece,* his sugred Sonnets among his priuate friends, &c.

> [3] As Plautus and Seneca are accounted the best for Comedy and Tragedy among the Latines: so Shakespeare among ye English is the most excellent in both kinds for the stage; for Comedy, witness his Gentelmen of Verona, his Errors, his Loue Labors lost, his Loue labours wonne, his Midsummers night dreame, & his Merchant of Venice; for Tragedy his Richard the 2, Richard the 3, Henry the 4, King John, Titus Andronicus and his Romeo and Iuliet.

> [4] As Epius Stolo said, that the Muses would speake with Plautus tongue, if they would speak Latin: so I say that the Muses would speak with Shakespeares fine filed phrase, if they would speake English.

> [5] *As* Ouid saith of his worke . . . as *Horace* saith of his so say I seuerally of sir *Philip Sidneys, Spencers, Daniels, Draytons, Shakespeares,* and *Warners workes* ...

> [6] As *Pindarus, Anacreon* and *Callimachus* among the Greekes; and *Horace* and *Catullus* among the Latines are the best Lyrick Poets: so in this faculty the best

> among our Poets are *Spencer* (who excelleth in all kinds) *Daniel, Drayton, Shakespeare, Bretton...*
>
> [7] These are our best for Tragedie, the Lorde *Buckhurst,* Doctor *Leg* of Cambridge, Doctor *Edes* of Oxforde, maister *Edward Ferris,* the Author of the *Mirrour for Magistrates, Marlow, Peele, Watson, Kid, Shakespeare, Drayton, Chapman, Decker,* and *Beniamin Johnson....*
>
> [8] The best for Comedy amongst us bee, *Edward* Earle of Oxforde, Doctor *Gager* of Oxforde, Maister *Rowley* once a rare Scholler of learned Pembrooke Hall in Cambridge, Maister *Edwardes* one of her Maiesties Chappell, eloquent and wittie *John Lilly, Lodge, Gascoyne, Greene, Shakespeare, Thomas Nash, Thomas Heywood, Anthony Mundye* our best plotter, *Chapman, Porter, Wilson, Hathway,* and *Henry Chettle....*
>
> [9] These are the most passionate among us to bewaile and bemoane the perplexities of Loue, *Henrie Howard* Earle of Surrey, sir *Thomas Wyat* the elder, sir *Francis Brian,* sir *Philip Sidney,* sir *Walter Rawley,* sir *Edward Dyer, Spencer, Daniel, Drayton, Shakespeare, Whetstone, Gascoyne, Samuell Page* sometimes fellowe of *Corpus Christi* Colledge in Oxford, *Churchyard, Bretton.*

It will not have escaped the attentive reader that under tragedy Meres lists both "Marlow" and "Shakespeare"; under comedy, both "*Edward* Earle of Oxforde" and "Shakespeare". By the testimony of Francis Meres in 1598, therefore, Marlowe, Oxford, and Shakespeare were three different individuals, each with a particular reputation: Marlowe for tragedy, Oxford for comedy, Shakespeare for both. By the same token, Shakespeare was not Sir Edward Dyer or Thomas Sackville Lord Buckhurst, who are praised for works of their own. Meres further reveals that by 1598 Shakespeare's sonnets, as yet unpublished, were circulating among his "private" — or personal — friends. From the fact that Meres accurately describes the sonnets as "sugred" we may infer that he himself was one of those private friends. If Meres had limited himself to information available in print by 1598, he would have been able to attribute only three of twelve play-titles to Shakespeare; clearly, therefore, he had independent knowledge of the playwright and his works. His sources, whether direct or indirect, must have included the Theatre in Shoreditch, where most if not all of Shakespeare's plays would have been performed through 1598, not once only, but again and again (as was demonstrably the case with *Titus Andronicus* at the Rose in January 1594). *Palladis Tamia* thus provides incontrovertible evidence that by 1598 Shakespeare was known to the English public as a poet and playwright of remarkable accomplishment.

Francis Meres sheds further light on Shakespeare's identity by the order in which he names English poets and playwrights, for his lists are arranged not by literary merit, but by social rank. Paragraph [1] begins with Sir Philip Sidney (knight), and then moves to Spenser, Daniel, Drayton, Warner, Shakespeare, Marlowe and Chapman. Paragraphs [2-4] mention Shakespeare only. Paragraph [5] begins with Sir Philip Sidney, then moves to Spenser, Daniel, Drayton, Shakespeare, and Warner. Paragraph [6] includes untitled poets only: Spenser, Daniel, Drayton, Shakespeare, Bretton. The remaining three lists begin with ranks higher than that of knight. Paragraph [7] begins with Thomas Sackville Lord Buckhurst, a baron; Thomas Leg of Cambridge and Richard Edes of Oxford, both academic doctors; Edward Ferris, a Master of Arts; then the untitled Marlowe, Peele, Watson, Kid, Shakespeare, Drayton, Chapman, Decker, and Ben Jonson. Paragraph [8] begins with Edward de Vere, Earl of Oxford; William Gager of Oxford, an academic doctor; Rowley and Edwards, both Masters of Arts; then the untitled John Lyly, Lodge, Gascoigne, Greene, Shakespeare, Thomas Nash, Thomas Heywood, Anthony Munday, Chapman, Porter, Wilson, Hathway, and Henry Chettle. Paragraph [9] begins with Henry Howard, Earl of Surrey; then Thomas Wyat the elder, Francis Brian, Philip Sidney, Walter Raleigh, and Edward Dyer, all knights; then the untitled Spencer, Daniel, Drayton, Shakespeare, Whetstone, Gascoigne, Samuel Page, Churchyard, and Bretton. In sum, Meres always ranks Shakespeare with untitled commoners.

After the publication of *Palladis Tamia*, Shakespeare was lauded or at least mentioned in print almost annually for the rest of his life:

> Richard Barnfield, *The Encomium of Lady Pecunia* (1598), "A Remembrance of some English Poets": "Shakespeare, [whose works] Thy Name in fames immortall Booke haue plac't"
>
> John Weever, *Epigrammes in the Oldest Cut* (1599), "Ad Gulielmum Shakespeare"

John Bodenham, *Bel-védere, or The Garden of the Muses* (1600) (see below)

A mournefull Dittie (1603), "brave Shakspeare, Johnson, Greene …"

John Cooke, *Epigrames* (1604), "As he that caled to Shakespeare, Johnson, Greene / To write of their dead noble Queene"

Anthony Scoloker, *Diaphantus* (1604), "Friendly Shake-speares Tragedies"

William Camden, *Remaines concerning Britaine* (1605), "William Shakespeare"

William Barksted, *Mirrha the mother of Adonis* (1607), "His Song was worthie merrit, Shakspeare hee"

John Davies of Hereford, *The scourge of Folly* (1610), "To our English Terence Mr. Willi: Shake-speare"

John Webster, *The White Devil* (1612), "M. Shake-speare"

Richard Carew, "The Excellencie of the English Tongue', in the second edition of Camden" (1614), "Shakesphere and Barlowes [=Marlow's] fragment"

Thomas Freeman, *Rubbe, and a Great Cast* (1614), "To Master W: Shakespeare"

John Stowe [continuation by Edmund Howes], *The Annales, or a generall great Chronicle of England* (1615) (see below).

The third of these authors, John Bodenham (1600), lists some forty poets, again by social rank. "Edward, Earl of Oxford" occurs near the top of the list, in the company of another earl; far below, among commoners, are "Christopher Marlow, Beniamin Iohnson, William Shakspeare". The four men were clearly distinct individuals, all known from contemporary sources: one is a well-documented aristocrat, and three are well-documented commoners.

Edmund Howes's continuation of John Stowe's *Annales*, in its fifth edition of 1615, adds a lengthy note on Elizabethan and more recent English poets:

> Our moderne, and present excellent Poets which worthely florish in their owne workes, and all of them

> in my owne knowledge lived togeather in this Queenes raigne, according to their priorities as neere as I could, I have orderly set downe (viz) *George Gascoigne* Esquire, *Thomas Churchyard* Esquire, Sir *Edward Dyer* Knight, *Edmond Spencer* Esquire, Sir *Philip Sidney* Knight, Sir *Iohn Harringion* Knight, Sir *Thomas Challoner* Knight, Sir *Frauncis Bacon* Knight, & Sir *Iohn Davie* Knight, Master *Iohn Lillie* gentleman, Maister *George Chapman* gentleman, M. *W. Warner* gentleman, M. *Willi. Shakespeare* gentleman, *Samuell Daniell* Esquire, *Michaell Draiton* Esquire, of the bath, M. *Christopher Marlo* gen., M. *Benjamine Iohnson* gentleman, *Iohn Marston* Esquier, M. *Abraham Frauncis* gen., master *Frauncis Meers* gentle., master *Iosua Siluester* gentle., master *Thomas Deckers* gentleman, M. John Flecher gentle., M. *Iohn Webster* gentleman, M. *Thomas Heywood* gentleman, M. *Thomas Middleton* gentleman, M. *George Withers* (811).

As with other lists, rank is more important than merit. While esquires occur throughout, knights always take precedence over gentlemen. William Shakespeare is called both "Master" and "gentleman", a double-barreled appellation shared with John Lyly, George Chapman, William Warner, Christopher Marlowe, Ben Jonson, Abraham Francis, Francis Meres, Joshua Silvester, Thomas Decker, John Fletcher, John Webster, John Heywood, and Thomas Middleton. All were securely middle-class. The title is spelled out for John Lyly and a few others as "Master", and for George Chapman as "Maister". Neither here nor in any other document does William Shakespeare rise even to the rank of "esquire", unlike the better situated George Gascoigne, Thomas Churchyard, Edmund Spenser, Samuel Daniel, Michael Drayton, and John Marston (the title "Master" is always dropped for esquires). Bringing up the rear is George Withers, not even a "gentleman". Howes, like Meres and Bodenham, is very explicit about who Shakespeare was not: he was not "Sir *Frauncis Bacon* Knight" or "M. *Christopher Marlo* gen"; he was, rather, "M. *Willi(am) Shakespeare* gentleman".

Shakespeare was privately mentioned, and sometimes lauded, by contemporary owners of books. When Richard Stonley purchased *Venus and Adonis*, he immediately identified "Shakspere" as its author. About 1601 Gabriel Harvey, now remembered only as a pedant, noted in his personal copy of Chaucer: "The younger sort takes much delight in Shakespeares Venus, & Adonis: but his Lucrece, & his tragedy of Hamlet, Prince of Denmark, have it in them, to please the wiser sort." As this was written prior to the first publication of *Hamlet* in 1603, Harvey must have known Shakespeare's tragedy, including its full title, from the public stage. In a second memo Harvey suggests that Sir Edward Dyer's *Amaryllis* and Sir Walter Raleigh's *Cynthia* are worthy of emulation by "Spenser, Constable, Fraunce, Watson, Daniel, Warner, Chapman, Sylvester, Shakespeare, & the rest of our flourishing metricians." Harvey clearly thinks that run-of-the-mill poets should take instruction from their social superiors.

Edward Pudsey was a private Londoner who began compiling a commonplace book in 1600. His practice was to write the name of a poem or play, and its author, in the 'header' line of a page, and to transcribe lines of verse in the 'text block'. To take two examples, on folio 41 recto he writes at the top (abbreviations expanded): "Play", "Shakespeare", "Johnson"; then, below, lines from "Merchant of Venice / Shakespeare", and from "Every Man Out of his Humour, Johnson". On a leaf now in the Shakespeare Birthplace Trust, Stratford, he writes at the top: "Play", "Romeo and Juliet", "Richard 2", "Shakespeare", "Richard 3"; then, below, lines from each play. Elsewhere he similarly cites John Marston, Thomas Dekker, John Lyly, Thomas Nash, George Chapman, Thomas Heywood, Cyril Tourner, and John Webster.

William Drummond recorded (in a notebook) that he read several plays in 1606. Among them was "Romeo and Julieta Tragedie", published in three editions in Shakespeare's lifetime (1597, 1599, 1609) but never with his name on the title page. Drummond added the name of the playwright to his personal copy of the 1599 edition: "Wil[liam] Sha[kespeare]". Sometime later Drummond wrote: "[t]he authors I have seen on the Subject of Love, are the Earl of Surrey, Sir Thomas Wyat (whom, because of their Antiquity, I will not match with our better Times) Sidney, Daniel, Drayton, and Spenser. The last we have are Sir William Alexander and Shakespear, who have lately published their Works".

As William Alexander was knighted in 1608 or 1609, and *Shakespeares Sonnets* was published in 1609, Drummond's comments were evidently penned in late 1609 or early 1610. Drummond implies that both were alive and active at the time of their recent publication, and gives the knight priority over the commoner. In 1619 Ben Jonson visited Drummond in Scotland, where the Londoner said of his old friend and rival: "That Shakspear wanted Arte." This comment is buried in a page of observations on contemporary poets and playwrights, including

Samuel Daniel, Michael Drayton, Sir John Harington, William Warner, John Donne, John Fletcher, George Chapman, Edward Sharpham, John Day, Thomas Dekker, and John Minsheu. Shakespeare was only one of many contemporary authors, of whom few escaped the sharp edge of Jonson's tongue. Jonson made additional comments on Shakespeare in notes published posthumously (1640-41) as "Timber, or Discoveries" (see Walker 1953, 52).[6] Here, in notes perhaps written about 1630, Jonson famously declared of Shakespeare: "… I loved the man and do honour his memory (on this side idolatry) as much as any. He was, indeed, honest and of an open and free nature …."

Sir John Harington, translator of *Orlando Furioso* (1591) and author of *The Metamorphosis of Ajax* (1596), compiled several lists of books in 1609. One list is of plays in his possession, gathered into volumes, including the recently published (1608) "K. Leir of Shakspear". Edward Alleyn, probably the most famous player of his day, maintained a small library. In or shortly after 1609 he bought a copy of *Shake-speares Sonnets*, recording his purchase as "a book Shaksper Sonets 5d". Humphrey Dyson, who was born in late 1581 or early 1582, owned a copy of *Troilus and Cressida* (1609) which he inscribed with his own name, as owner. On the title page was printed: "By William Shakespeare". Sometime between publication of the *First Folio* in 1623 and his death in January 1633, Dyson added, in his own hand: "and printed amongst his works". Dyson must necessarily have leafed through a copy of the *First Folio*, as *Troilus and Cressida* is notoriously missing from its table of contents. Dyson clearly accepted both the 1609 quarto and the 1623 *Folio* as the work of William Shakespeare. Dyson had reason to know, for he was personally aquatinted with Henry Condell, John Heminges, and Nicholas Tooley *alias* Wilkinson, all members of the King's Men; he also knew Richard Field, who had printed Shakespeare's earliest poems. Pudsey, Drummond, Harington, Alleyn, Dyson, Jonson, and others, all had a chance to correct the printed record in the seclusion of their studies; instead, like contemporaries back to Richard Stonley in 1593, they endorsed printed attributions to William Shakespeare. William Shakespeare, in brief, was acknowledged in public, and confirmed in private, as a poet, playwright, and player. Much of the same evidence which establishes his full identity simultaneously demonstrates that he was not Edward de Vere, earl of Oxford; Thomas Sackville, Lord Buckhurst; Sir Francis Bacon; Sir Edward Dyer; or Christopher Marlowe.

6 First published in Ben Jonson, *Works*, 2nd ed., 3 vols. (1640-41), pp. 97-8 (separately paginated section at the end of volume 2).

Having examined evidence which tracks the multifaceted William Shakespeare in London, I now turn to documents which track him back to the town of his birth.

The single surviving letter addressed to "Mr William Shakespere", dated October 25, 1598, was written by Richard Quiney of Stratford-upon-Avon, who calls his correspondent "countryman". Like many letters of its time, it included no street address. It was, however, directed "from the Bell in Carter Lane", a public house near St. Paul's Cathedral where Quiney lodged when conducting business in London. Two additional Quiney letters not addressed to Shakespeare connect him to Stratford-upon-Avon.

While the Shakespeare coat of arms was originally sought by John Shakespeare of Stratford-upon-Avon, "Shakespeare the player" was included in the eventual grant. From Stratford records we know that John and William Shakespeare were father and son. The brief appearance of Edmund Shakespeare, "player", in London and Southwark records of 1607, establishes a link by inference, for William's brother Edmund had been baptised in Stratford in 1580, the (fourth) son of "Mr John Shakespeare".

The Bellott-Mountjoy lawsuit, which includes a deposition by "William Shakespeare of Stratford vpon Aven in the Countye of Warwicke gentleman of the Age of xlviij [i.e., 48] yeres or thereabouts", dated May 11, 1612, reveals that ten years earlier, about 1602, the deponent had lodged with Christopher and Marie Mountjoy in the parish of St. Olave Silver Street, London (the qualifier "or thereabouts" occurs in all depositions and does not imply ignorance or doubt). The lawsuit not only links William Shakespeare of London to William Shakespeare of Stratford, and to 1564, the exact year of his birth (he had just turned forty-eight), but connects Shakespeare to George Wilkins, the playwright who collaborated with him on *Pericles*, a play entered in the Stationers Register on May 20, 1608 and published in 1609. Another link appears in an indenture for the purchase of Blackfriars gatehouse, London, in March 1613, and in an accompanying mortgage, both naming "William Shakespeare of Stratford vpon Avon in the countie of Warrwick." The Bellot-Mountjoy lawsuit and the purchase of Blackfriars gatehouse yield three of Shakespeare's six known signatures. The other three signatures occur on Shakespeare's will of 1616, which ties our subject not only to the town of his birth ("I, William Shakespeare of Stratford upon Avon in the county of Warwick, gent."), but to "the Blackfriars in London near the Wardrobe", and to the testator's three London associates, "my fellows John Heminge, Richard Burbage, and Henry Condell". Like most signatures on early modern official documents, all six Shakespeare signatures are attested by witnesses.

Yet another connection between London and Stratford occurs through Leonard Digges, born in 1588, the offspring of a mathematician and an astronomer. After Leonard's father died in 1595, his mother, who owned property in the parish of St. Mary Aldermanbury, London, married Thomas Russell, esquire, of Alderminster, a village located some five miles from Stratford-upon-Avon. In 1616 Shakespeare appointed the same "Thomas Russell esquire" an overseer of his will. Leonard Digges, Thomas Russell's step-son, happened to be in Madrid in 1613, when his friend and mentor James Mabbe purchased a book of sonnets by Lope de Vega Carpio, which he sent to William Baker, an acquaintance in Oxford. Digges penned a note onto the flyleaf: "Will Baker: Knowinge that Mr Mab: was to sende you this Booke of Sonets, which with Spaniards here is accounted of their Lope de Vega as in Englande wee sholde of our Will Shakespeare. I colde not but inserte thus much to you, that if you like him not, you muste neuer neuer reade Spanishe Poet. Leo: Digges". Digges thus recommends the sonnets of Lope de Vega by comparing them to those of "our Will Shakespeare", obviously referencing *Shake-speares Sonnets* (1609). Digges elevates both de Vega and Shakespeare to the status of national poets. Digges later composed two highly informed poems on Shakespeare, one printed in the 1623 *First Folio*, with an explicit reference to "thy Stratford monument", the other printed posthumously in the 1640 edition of Shakespeare's *Poems*. As Sidney Lee wrote of Digges in the *DNB*, "few contemporaries wrote more sympathetically of Shakespeare's greatness."

The Shakespeare funeral monument in Holy Trinity Church, Stratford-upon-Avon — referenced by Digges as "thy Stratford monument" — shows a balding man leaning, entirely conventionally, on a cushion, his right hand hovering over a sheet of paper, with a hole between forefinger and thumb to receive a pen. The monument is correspondingly literary: a Latin inscription compares Shakespeare to ancient writers and philosophers, while an English text refers explicitly to "all that he hath writ". The installation of the monument, which must have occurred approximately a year after the burial on April 25, 1616, triggered a famous elegy written by William Basse, entitled, in its most prominent manuscript source: "On Mr Wm Shakespeare / He dyed in April 1616." Basse's elegy is referenced by Ben Jonson in the

First Folio of 1623, evidence of its early composition and circulation (any reader in 1623 was expected to have known it). The *First Folio* was edited by John Heminges and Henry Condell, two of the three "fellows" Shakespeare named in his will of 1616 (the third fellow, Richard Burbage, died in 1619.) The *First Folio* refers not only to the author's "Stratford monument", but to two rivers, Stratford's Avon and London's Thames. The *First Folio* contains dedicatory poems signed by Ben Jonson, Leonard Digges, and James Mabbe.

In or about 1619, about four years before the publication of the *First Folio*, John Weever, a native of Preston, Lancashire, who had praised Shakespeare in his *Epigrammes* of 1599, visited Stratford-upon-Avon while gathering notes for his magisterial *Ancient Funeral Monuments* (1631). In Holy Trinity Church he transcribed verses from the tombs of both William Shakespeare and John Combe, identifying "William Shakespeare" in a marginal note as "the famous poet". A popular jest-book registered and first printed in 1630 characterizes Stratford-upon-Avon as "a Towne most remarkeable for the birth of famous *William Shakespeare.*" Four years later, in 1634, a military officer surnamed Hammond noted in his description of the same town: "A neat Monument of that famous English Poet, Mr Wm Shakespeere; who was borne heere." Richard Hunt, an Oxford graduate and minister of Bishop's Itchington, 15 miles distant, praised Shakespeare as "our Roscius" (meaning "player") in a private inscription lauding him as the most recent of three men who had made Stratford-upon-Avon famous. Hunt's inscription is undated, but must have been written between 1621 and 1661.

Though most of Shakespeare poems and plays are set in remote times and places, a few relate to the author's personal identity, home, and personal experiences. Establishing his identity beyond all question are three "Will" sonnets (135, 136, 143) published in 1609, especially sonnet 136: "My name is Will." Less certain — and less probative — is the possible pun in Sonnet 145 on "hate away", his wife's maiden name being "Hathaway". The surnames of two characters in *Henry V*, one common (Fluellen), the other rare (Bardolph), occur one after the other in a 1592 Warwickshire recusant list which also contains the name of Shakespeare's father John. The Induction to *The Taming of the Shrew* names "Burton-heath" and "Cicily Hacket the fat ale-wife of Wincot": Barton-on-the-Heath and Wilmcote are both situated near Stratford-upon-Avon, and Hackett was a local surname.[7] Highly technical

7 Will of Luke Hackett, Farmer of Saint John Bedwardine, Worcestershire; 7 July 1587: The National Archives PROB11/71; Luke's wife was Margaret, his daughter, Margery.

references to gloves (*Merry Wives of Windsor* 1.4.423; *Twelfth Night* 3.1.1246) and to wool (*Winter's Tale* 4.3.1756) recall the professional skill and jargon of John Shakespeare, glover.

Further evidence for the identification of William Shakespeare of Stratford-upon-Avon with William Shakespeare of London lies in his simultaneous rise from plain William to "Master" and "Gentleman" in Stratford and in London. The crucial years are 1597 to 1602. When he purchased New Place, Stratford-upon-Avon, in 1597, William Shakespeare was identified by his personal name only, while the seller, William Underhill, is called "gentleman"; in 1602, however, when the purchase was renewed, both Underhill's son Hercules and William Shakespeare are *generosus* — Latin for "gentleman". William Shakespeare is cited by name only in a *post-mortem* of May 17, 1599, referencing the Globe-site lease of March 21, 1599, but in enrolled indentures dated October 7 and 10, 1601, both William Shakespeare and Richard Burbage are called "gentlemen".

Early in October 1598, fishing for a substantial loan, Adrian Quiney wrote to his son Richard in London, discussing a possible "bargain with 'William Shakespeare". The same letter contains a more deferential reference to "Mr [John] Combe". On the 25th of the same month Richard addressed a letter directly "To my Loveinge good ffrend & contreyman Mr Wm Shakespere", while a follow-up letter (now illegible) from Abraham Sturley dated 4 November references "Mr Wm Shakespeare". In effect, when his countrymen discussed him behind his back, the prospective lender was "William Shakespeare"; but when they approached him directly he became, perhaps by courtesy, perhaps by flattery, Mr. William Shakespeare.

In London, in 1598, three plays were attributed to "William Shakespeare" or to "William Shake-speare". On August 23, 1600 two play-titles were entered into the Stationers Register: "Entred for their copies vnder the handes of the wardens Twoo Bookes. the one called *Muche a Doo about nothinge*. Thother *the second parte of the history of kinge Henry the IIIJth with the humours of Sir John ffallstaff*: Wrytten by Mr Shakespere." *Much Ado about Nothing* and *2 Henry IV* were both advertised on their title pages as "Written by William Shakespeare". On November 26, 1607, John Busby registered *King Lear* under the name of "Mr William Shakespeare"; the play was printed in 1608 under the name of "M. William Shak-speare".

Cambridge students, in their *Parnassus* plays of 1598-1601, applied the title "Master" to Shakespeare with abandon: "O sweete Mr Shakspeare,

Ile haue his picture in my study at the courte"; "Let mee heare Mr Shakspears veyne"; "Ile worshipp sweet Mr Shakspeare, and to honoure him will lay his *Venus and Adonis* vnder my pillowe." Shakespeare is called "Mr." in print by John Davies of Hereford in 1610, by John Webster in 1612, and by Edmund Howes in 1615. The *First Folio* was twice advertised for the Frankfurt book fair, in 1622 as by "Mr. William Shakespeare", in 1624 as "Master *William Shakesperes* workes." It was entered in the Stationers Register (1623) as "Mr William Shakspeers Comedyes Histories & Tragedyes", and published the same year as *Mr. William Shakespeares Comedies, Histories, & Tragedies*. The entire world knew, in effect, that the author was of the social level designated by the title "Master". He was thus a man of personal distinction, and of modest social rank.

Documentation which we have now explored in detail, combined with information to be found in most conventional biographies, creates a fully coherent portrait of the man, the player, the poet, and the playwright.

William Shakespeare, baptized April 26, 1564, in Holy Trinity Church, Stratford-upon-Avon, was the son of John Shakespeare, an illiterate glover who served on the Stratford common council, including one year as bailiff, local equivalent of mayor. Householders of the town supported a Free Grammar School to ensure that their sons would be better educated than themselves. Schoolmasters employed by the townsmen were over-qualified Masters of Arts from Oxford University. The schoolmaster at the time of Shakespeare's birth, John Brownswerd, was the most gifted Latin poet in England — though not Shakespeare's mentor. Pupils learned Latin as their sole course of study. A successful pupil would gain sufficient fluency for entrance into Oxford University. William Shakespeare's marriage at the age of eighteen precluded any possibility of admission to a university. By 1593 he had begotten a daughter, then twins; moved to London; joined a company of players; written several plays; and published his first poem — through the offices of Richard Field, a London printer who likewise haled from Stratford-upon-Avon. 1594 saw the publication of his second poem (again printed by Field) and his first play (but without his name attached). By 1595 the player-playwright acted as one of three financial trustees for his company, along with William Kemp and Richard Burbage. Shakespeare's son Hamnet died in 1596. For some time before 1597 Shakespeare was a resident of the parish of St. Helen's Bishopsgate, London, evidently moving to the district of the Clink in Southwark, which two years later would become the site of the Globe playhouse. In 1597 Shakespeare purchased New Place in Stratford-upon-Avon. Shakespeare's father John died in 1601, his mother in 1608, while his wife Anne lived until 1623.

Shortly after the death of Queen Elizabeth on March 24, 1603, James I (or his surrogates) granted Shakespeare's company a patent which allowed them to perform as the King's Men. Under this rubric and in this same year Ben Jonson's *Sejanus* was first performed, with William Shakespeare as one of eight named players; under this rubric Shakespeare and eight fellow-players received red cloth for the coronation procession of the new king; under this rubric Shakespeare's company made ten appearances at court over the 1604-5 Christmas season, eight with his own plays, three of which the office of Edmund Tilney, Master of the Revels, attributed to him by name. A year later, in 1605, William Shakespeare received a testamentary bequest as a "fellow" of the actor Augustine Phillips, and in 1608 he became one of six shareholders in the refounded Blackfriars playhouse in London. On May 11, 1612 he walked (or rode) to the church of St. Mary de Arcubus, Cheapside, London, to give his formal deposition in the case of Bellott vs. Mountjoy. On March 10 and 11, 1613, he met in London with Henry Walker, seller, William Johnson and John Jackson, trustees, to sign documents for the purchase of Blackfriars Gatehouse. Absent from the gathering was John Heminges, intended as a third trustee; but Heminges signed a subsequent indenture in 1618. Comparison with signatures in the parish register of St. Mary Aldermanbury for 1608-10 demonstrates that this was Shakespeare's fellow player.

Meanwhile, Shakespeare's poems and plays continued to be published, for a total of at least 16,000 copies for sale on London bookstalls, and subsequently in the hands of its literate elite, between 1593 and 1610. Shakespeare was lauded in print at the approximate rate of one publication per year. As he revised his will at home in the days before his death in April 1616, he specifically remembered his London associates: "my fellows John Heminge, Richard Burbage, and Henry Condell". Far from being forgotten at the time of his death, William Shakespeare was memorialized as no other poet or playwright had been or would be for many years. He was given the monument of a literary super-star in Holy Trinity Church, Stratford-upon-Avon; lauded with a poem explaining why he was buried there and not with other poets and playwrights in Westminster Abbey; remembered with the so-called "Pavier Quartos" in 1619; identified as "William Shakespeare the famous poet" by John Weever about the same year; and remembered again, this time with permanent effect, with the *First Folio* of 1623, now recognized as the most important non-scientific book ever published in English, rivaled only by the 1611 "King James Bible".

The documentation which supports conventional biographies of William Shakespeare is not speculative, nor is the evidence a chain of facts no stronger than its weakest link. It is a dense fabric of interwoven threads which, while not as complete as one might desire (who would not wish for a memo recording Shakespeare's thoughts while he was writing *Hamlet*?), contains not a single internal contradiction. The only way to challenge this coherent picture is through the nihilism of denigrating the man, disparaging Stratford-upon-Avon and its grammar-school, and contesting the validity of hundreds of individual pieces of evidence, one by one by one.

Before I conclude I wish to address 'non-Stratfordian' objections to traditional biographies of William Shakespeare.

Some Shakespeare skeptics have adopted the practice of dismissing any and all evidence later than the death of Shakespeare in 1616. No legitimate historian, however, could possibly endorse such a practice, which would even rule out obituaries and memorial recollections. I am 78 years old as I write these words. I distinctly recall the latter years of WWII, including, as if it were yesterday, the death of Franklin Delano Roosevelt in April 1945. My actual memory is of my best friend's mother sitting in a lawn chair, weeping. I asked my mother why my friend's mother was crying. It was then my mother told me the President had died. No reasonable biographer could claim that my recollection, or any recollection about FDR from after his death (my recollection of his death was certainly from after his death!), should be automatically excluded from a biography, or excluded as evidence. Sir Richard Baker, author of *A Chronicle of the Kings of England* (1643), had to cast his mind back less than half of his life-time to report: "For Writers of Playes, and such as had been Players themselves, William Shakespeare, and Benjamin Johnson, have specially left their Names recommended to posterity."

It has been objected that a man of provincial rather than metropolitan birth, a man without a university education, could not have written the works of Shakespeare. Genius may certainly be associated with higher education and even, though less often, with aristocracy: consider Wolfgang von Goethe, Lord Byron, Le Comte Antoine-Laurent de Lavoisier. But many of the very greatest geniuses have been autodidacts of extremely humble origin: consider Michael

Faraday, Thomas Edison, or Bill Gates (who dropped out of Harvard). The educationally deficient Abraham Lincoln became one of the finest modern masters of English prose. Or consider, from Shakespeare's day, Christopher Marlowe, son of a Canterbury shoemaker, who gained a university education; or Ben Jonson, the adopted son of a London bricklayer, who did not. As for Shakespeare's knowledge of geography, which in any case is deeply flawed (his Venice has no canals, his Bohemia has a sea-coast), even the best-travelled Elizabethan had not visited Caesar's Rome or Cleopatra's Egypt; nor had Christopher Marlowe, for all his university education, walked in the footsteps of Tamburlaine, or flown through the heavens with Dr. Faustus. Whatever stories and whatever geographical knowledge were needed for the sake of a poem or a plot could be — and were — obtained from books.

I conclude with my one and only purely polemical argument. Assuming that the Shakespeare poems and plays could only have been written by a man of elevated birth, rank, education, and travel, why were they attributed, over a period of thirty years, from 1593 to 1623, to a man much in the public eye who had none of these supposedly necessary qualifications? It is suggested, to be sure, in the film *Anonymous*, that the Earl of Oxford allowed his plays to be attributed to an illiterate fool, but this is surely one of the film's least persuasive fictions. If a nobleman chose more reasonably to attribute a work of literature to a person who could have written it, that same person cannot be rejected as someone who could not have written it. In sum, both evidence and logic dictate that the poems and plays attributed to him in his lifetime and after his death were written by Mr. William Shakespeare of Stratford-upon-Avon in the county of Warwick, gent.

Chapter 2

My Shakspere: "A Conjectural Narrative" Continued

Diana Price

My Shakspere is not a writer.[1] His biography is supported by a considerable amount of evidence, but his is not a literary life. Biographers face the seemingly insurmountable problem of constructing a narrative of Shakspere's supposed career as the dramatist based on the documentary evidence. Although the facts about Shakspere are nonliterary, they present a coherent and consistent character. Those same facts lose their coherency when combined with the facts that emerge from the literary works themselves. Andrew Hadfield had numerous documents with which to prepare his literary biography of the poet Edmund Spenser, but elsewhere, he apologizes for the absence of documentary evidence in the genre of literary biography, bemoaning the "little information [that] survives, as is the case with virtually all modern lives" (Hadfield 2014, 377). But that is not the case with Spenser or Ben Jonson or William Shakspere.

My thesis is simple: *if* Shakspere is the author the title pages proclaim him to be, then he was, by definition, a professional writer. Therefore, there should be no difficulty identifying the professional

1 In this chapter, the spelling "Shakespeare" designates the dramatist, whoever he was. The spelling "Shakspere" designates the man from Stratford who was the shareholder in the Lord Chamberlain's / King's Men and the Globe and Blackfriars theatres. Some sections have been adapted from my *Shakespeare's Unorthodox Biography* and article on "Hand D" in *JEMS*. Line numbers are from the Arden Three editions of *Romeo and Juliet*, *2 Henry IV* and *King Lear*.

evidence that he left behind that can support one simple statement: he was a writer. But Shakspere's literary biography is unique. He is the only alleged writer from the time period for whom one must rely on posthumous evidence to make the case for his writing career. And twice, as of this writing, Stanley Wells has acknowledged that this thesis is correct, even though he deems the singular deficiency of contemporaneous "literary paper trails," as I call them, to be "irrelevant" to the orthodox biography (Wells 2013).

The Shakspere that I find in the documentary record was a member of the commercial class and a real estate investor. The evidence suggests that he was a shrewd negotiator at the bargaining table and sometimes involved in questionable business practices. His principal residence was Stratford-upon-Avon, but he spent considerable time in London conducting business. Shakspere rented and owned properties in the city. He was a tax delinquent. He made a lot of money. He was numerate if not literate, and was viewed by others as a source of capital. That documentation, augmented and extended by satirical allusions, supports the career of an entrepreneur who traded in commodities, frippery, loans, a marriage, and probably an *impresa* assignment.

The theatrical documentation shows that, like Christopher Beeston or Philip Henslowe, Shakspere was a financier and business agent who bought and sold theatrical paraphernalia, including costumes, properties, and playbooks. In the absence of any evidence to show that Shakspere was paid as a writer, one can only speculate on what money he may have made from trading in plays, regardless of whether he wrote them, "corrected" them, brokered or otherwise "supplied" them. Shakspere's vocation as play broker and *Batillus* (an ancient Roman who took credit for verses written by Vergil) could account for a number of plays, known today to be somebody else's, but published over the name of William Shakespeare (however spelled) or over the initials "W. S.". E. A. J. Honigmann observed that in the 1600s, "unscrupulous men used [Shakespeare's] name to sell plays that, as all the world now agrees, could not have come from his pen" (Honigmann 1982, 46). The evidence suggests that one of those unscrupulous men was William Shakspere.

Non-Stratfordian Alden Brooks describes a character in *Histrio-mastix* who provides a basis for his interpretation of Shakspere: Post-hast is "a would-be poet" who "wishes to pass as a gentleman," who "furnishes plays, plays of others"; "haggles over prices"; "can only rhyme extempore doggerel, . . . misuses words, shows business acumen, and controls the disposal of the company's playing apparel" (Brooks 1943,

69, 71). That Shakspere conjures up the familiar images of *Groatsworth of Wit's* "gentleman player," the acquisitive Ant whose "thrift is theft," and the paymaster of playwrights. The characterization of the Ant whose "thrift is theft" in 1592 should raise questions. What prompted the satire at that early date? Was Shakspere, the "gentleman player," merely hiring a Robert Greene or a Samuel Rowley for the purpose of "rewriting the plays of other companies," such as *King John*, *Taming of the Shrew*, and *Richard III* (Honigmann 1954, lv, lvi; see also Knutson 1997, 469-70). Are the two parts of the 1591 *The Troublesome Reign of King John* possibly bad quartos of a rip-off of *King John*?

There is no question that Shakspere, the theatrical shareholder, was in physical proximity to the Shakespeare plays. Andrew Gurr supposes that Shakspere was adroit enough to retain ownership of his playbooks during the early and "lost" years and "eventually handed them over to the Chamberlain's [Men], perhaps as the price of his 'share' in the new company" (Gurr 2009, 208). Gurr's suggestions are not only plausible, they are logical inferences based on the evidence. Yet the publishing circumstances of the Shakespeare plays are puzzling. Quite a few of them were first published in what many critics have deemed as unauthorised texts, such as those of *Romeo and Juliet* and *Hamlet.* Any financial interest in play scripts that Shakspere retained as a theatre shareholder or as an owner, was subverted by the theft of the Shakespeare plays. Shakspere therefore stood to lose hard cash from any unauthorized sale of the Shakespeare plays — *unless Shakspere himself stood to gain by that sale.* In other words, either this aggressive businessman with a financial stake in the Shakespeare plays inexplicably did nothing to stop the "underhand brokerage," or he figured out a way to profit from an unauthorized sale.

I adopt as my starting point what I consider to be the strongest circumstantial evidence for Shakspere as dramatist, the title-page attributions to William Shakespeare (however spelled). If Shakspere was not the writer the title pages claim him to be, then his name appears on those title-pages for some other reason. In my conjectural narrative, his name on a title-page may signify ownership, or as likely, Shakspere's willingness to take credit for someone else's work. The play *King Lear* has been the subject of recent controversy, especially concerning the manuscripts that served as printer's copy. Nobody knows how the 1608 text of *M. William Shak-speare: His True Chronicle Historie of the life and death of King* LEAR was obtained by the King's Men, who procured it and how it came to be printed. Nobody knows the nature of the manuscript that served as printer's copy. A dramatist wrote a play about King Lear.

Thereafter, every single link in the chain of transmission is unknown. It got into performance. How? It got into print. How? My conjectural narrative proposes that Shakspere of Stratford is present in one or more links, and this chapter attempts to find him in the vicinity of some of those links, if not *in flagrante*.

"Foul papers," Hand D, and printer's copy

In the spring of 2016, the British Library announced a project concerning its manuscript collections. One of its manuscripts is the collaborative play *Sir Thomas More*, which includes three pages of Additions written by a penman referred to as "D," whose handwriting is referred to as "Hand D." According to the Library's website, those Additions comprise the "only surviving literary manuscript" in Shakespeare's handwriting. That remarkable, not to say alarming claim, was still on the Library's website as of August 2017 and is only the most recent effort to transform the Hand D Additions into Shakspere's authorial manuscript. There is no evidence to support the claim (see Hays 2016; Price 2016). The identification of Hand D as Shakspere's is critical for the orthodox biographical narratives, because if an authorial manuscript of a Shakespeare play had survived, there would not *be* an authorship question. So if Hand D can be proved to be Shakspere's, then the Hand D Additions to *Sir Thomas More* could constitute the first "foul papers" from the time period ever discovered. They also fill the unique evidentiary gap, constituting a personal literary paper trail for Shakspere — and an excellent one at that. And according to Hugh Craig, the claim that Hand D is Shakspere's is "now beyond reasonable doubt" (Craig 2012, 23). That claim is integrally related to Shakspere's "foul papers". What exactly are "foul papers"?

By 1927, the eminent bibliographer W.W. Greg had conceived of his definition of "foul papers" after coming across the term in an annotation made by Edward Knight on a transcript of John Fletcher's *Bonduca* (Werstine 2013, 2, 6-7). Greg formulated his definition of "foul papers," most specifically Shakespeare's "foul papers" (as authorial drafts might vary in their respective features from playwright to playwright), as a theoretical construct capable of explaining why "good quartos" contained certain types of errors and imperfections. Another objective of the exercise was, theoretically, to get as close as possible to the dramatist's handwritten manuscript (see Murphy 2010,

70), ideally to make the case that the printer's copy for a quarto was Shakspere's autograph manuscript, thereby conferring upon a particular text his authority. It is a seductive exercise. However, in his *Early Modern English Playhouse Manuscripts*, Paul Werstine demonstrates that Greg's theory is fatally flawed. No useful printer's copy from the time period survives.[2] None of the playhouse manuscripts that survive fulfills Greg's hypothetical definition of "foul papers," and his decades-long search for any "foul papers" by any playwright of the time period failed. He came up empty-handed, yet he continued to use the term. And over time, the term "foul papers" became embedded in various textual and bibliographical studies.

Nowadays, the term "foul" is often employed without reference to Greg's original formulation and without acknowledgement that there are no extant manuscripts that fit his formulation (Werstine 2013, 34-38). The editors of, for example, the *Oxford Textual Companion* offer a general definition of "foul papers" as "an author's first complete draft of a play" (Wells *et al* 1987, 9). They claim that Shakespeare's handwriting in his "foul papers" is "implied by errors in printed editions" and with reference to D's handwriting (124, 510; see also John Jowett 2007, 99, 101; 2011, 440-41). The Arden Three editor of *Much Ado About Nothing* identifies in the text the dramatist's "characteristic lightness of punctuation" and "characters designated variously both by function and by given name," among other idiosyncratic elements contained in Shakespeare's "foul papers" (McEachern 2006, 128-29). Thus, an editor may claim that certain printed features and imperfections can be explained by Shakespeare's "foul papers," even though nobody knows what they looked like, and the identity of the penman who inscribed the Hand D Additions remains unknown. In her essay for the 2012 *Oxford Companion to Shakespeare*, Grace Ioppolo lists no fewer than sixteen Shakespeare texts that were "almost certainly" printed from "foul papers" (93), including the First Quarto (Q1) of *King Lear*. Her count is easily corroborated in critical editions published over the past several decades. Yet none of the manuscripts in her discussion of "foul papers" can be shown to have served as printer's copy and many characteristics in her definition, including duplication and "confusions in character names" are also present in other types of manuscripts, including transcripts for playhouse use (Werstine 2013, 9, 204-5; Mowat 1998, 133).

2 Peter W. M. Blayney cites a surviving "titlepage layout of 1611 and . . . half a book of 1613" (1982, 10).

Hand D and "foul papers" are intertwined in today's scholarship, despite considerable confusion and contradictions. Jowett agrees with the paleographers who describe the Hand D pages "as showing a writer in the immediate process of composition" (2011, 440). Ioppolo proposes that the Hand D additions are authorial "fair copies" (2012, 94). Gerald E. Downs makes the case for a scribal transcript (2000, 24). They cannot all be correct. If Ioppolo is correct to classify the Hand D Additions as authorial fair copy, then either all arguments asserting or implying that D's Additions are Shakespeare's only surviving "foul papers" are mistaken, or, alternatively, a definition of "foul papers" is a matter of choice. Ultimately, the good quartos (further discussed below) cannot be proved to be based on "foul papers," because without the Hand D Additions to point to, no "foul papers" survive that would allow for comparison and judgment. Each surviving playhouse manuscript that Werstine examined — including the manuscript of *Sir Thomas More* and the Hand D Additions — fails to exhibit the characteristics enumerated by Greg in his hypothetical definition. And as we will see, the theory of "foul papers" bears directly on the biographical narratives.

Good and bad quartos

In 1909, A.W. Pollard categorized early printed plays of Shakespeare as "good quartos" and "bad quartos" (see Greg 1955, 88). As mentioned above, the theory of "foul papers" was originally proposed by Greg to explain features and imperfections in the "good" quartos. Various theories have been proposed to explain the corruptions in the "bad" quartos, among them theories of printer's copy originating from memorial reports and memorial reconstruction, as well as playhouse scripts shortened for touring.[3] According to Leo Kirschbaum, at least nine early printed Shakespearean plays are "bad" quartos.[4] In his 1938 article "A Census of Bad Quartos", Kirschbaum defines the term: "the simplest way to describe a bad quarto is to state that it cannot possibly represent a written transcript of the author's text" (20). This definition still strikes me as a useful working definition, being broad enough to accommodate imperfect texts resulting from

3 Paul Werstine demonstrates that there is no evidence to support the theory that playhouse texts were truncated for touring (1998).

4 His list of twenty complete plays includes *2 Henry VI (First Part of the Contention), 3 Henry VI (True Tragedy), Richard III, Romeo and Juliet, Merry Wives, Henry V, Hamlet, King Lear* and *Pericles.*

any type of flawed or unauthorized transmission, and broad enough to encompass all manner of errors introduced in any link in the chain of transmission. Unfortunately, since Kirschbaum published, the term "bad quarto" has gone from a term of utility to a pejorative unbefitting a Shakespearean text (even though most of Kirschbaum's designated "bad" quartos are non-Shakespearean plays, such as *Philaster* or *George a Greene*). More recently, the concept of a bad quarto has been somewhat deconstructed by Laurie E. Maguire, who introduced the term "suspect texts." She outlined her diagnostics to identify those texts that might have been typeset from manuscripts that were the result of memorial reconstruction (MR), defined below.

Maguire's verdict on the "suspect" 1609 quarto of *Pericles* is instructive: "Wrecked verse is the only possible indication of MR. . . . If a reported text, it is a very good one" (1996, 295). Her verdict calls into question the very meaning of the words "good" and "bad." Perhaps Maguire is confining her verdict of "good" in a narrow way, strictly to describe the relative performability of the recovered text, but it is impossible to describe Q1 *Pericles* in any way, shape, or form as "good." In her Arden Three edition (2004), Suzanne Gossett describes *Pericles* in terms such as "a uniquely damaged text" (1); the only Shakespeare play "of which we have only a 'bad' text, a quarto markedly damaged or defective" (8); that contains "dialogue that makes little or no sense" (11); "involving … reporting of the script by actors, dictation, possibly involving shorthand" (27). Gossett suggests that there are "complex, multipartite" explanations for Q1 *Pericles*, and therefore "it is unlikely that we can infer the play's history from the surviving quarto" (15-16). In other words, to paraphrase Kirschbaum, Q1 *Pericles* is based on a manuscript that cannot possibly represent what the author(s) intended. In Maguire's analysis, the origin of Q *Pericles* is "possibly MR" and therefore not completely eliminated from her "suspect" classification. But Maguire has shifted the nomenclature from "bad quartos" to "suspect texts." Further, those texts judged to be "Not MR" — that is, not originating with a memorial reconstruction, are implicitly eliminated from the "suspect" category. The shift may seem insignificant, but the shift subtly invests formerly "bad" quartos with more goodness and avoids the broader category of memorial reports.[5]

5 While Maguire finds that the manuscript of *John of Bordeaux* is "Not MR," Gerald E. Downs argues that *Bordeaux* is indeed the unpublished "bad" quarto that Harry R. Hoppe thought it was (2007-8).

Memorial reconstruction or memorial report?

In 1942, W.W. Greg theorized that Q1 *Merry Wives of Windsor* was based on a text reconstructed by the "actor who took the part of mine Host" (1951, 60). In 1999, Paul Werstine concluded that Greg's theory of memorial reconstruction was "an undemonstrable hypothesis" (1999, 329). Nevertheless, in 1996, Laurie Maguire proceeded to define memorial reconstruction as "the reproduction of a playtext in whole or in part by someone who had at some stage substantial knowledge of the original play as written or performed" (224-25). Her definition is problematic. She acknowledges that her study does not seek to "identify the agent behind reconstruction" (225), but the identification of the "agent behind reconstruction" goes beyond actor(s) or theatrical personnel likely involved in reporting or dictating. Textual reconstruction and transmission must also take into account the *method* by which text moves from point A to point B.

A *memorial report* records a performance, a speech, a sermon, or some other verbal delivery, live and (ideally) *verbatim*, almost as though the reporter had access to a modern-day tape recorder. [6] Such a report may be recorded using shorthand or some form of speedwriting. A memorial report of a play, performed live onstage by actors who have "substantial knowledge of the play" is not the same as a Memorial Reconstruction, because the dialogue is recorded at a live performance, not recalled or remembered at some later time. The dialogue can reflect words as originally written or as somewhat corrupted by, for example, actors' imperfect memories or flawed performances. In contrast, memorial reconstruction recovers a text recalled from memory sometime subsequent to performance, in a setting in which errors may be corrected. Because Maguire omits the agent(s) of transmission, including a reporter who takes down words at the speed of speech, any text categorized by Maguire as "Not MR" may nevertheless have as its origin a memorial report. Maguire concludes that Q1 *Lear* is "not MR," i.e., not memorial reconstruction. If Q1 *Lear* is "not MR", then that text is absolved, at least in semantic terms, of its "suspect" or "bad" status, and that reclassification opens the door to reconsidering the possibility that authorial "foul papers" or an immediate transcript served as printer's copy.

In her sections about speed writing systems, Maguire considers

6 Even John Jowett admitted that "no one to date has advanced coherent explanations of all the 'bad' quartos that do away with memorial transmission entirely" (Jowett 1999, 77; see also Weis, 105 and Craik, 20-21).

the evidence for recording live performances but marginalizes that evidence as "complicated and/or ambiguous" (98-107). Her diagnosis of "Not MR" is therefore misleading, because it rules out printer's copy based on text recovered later by memory, *as well as* a text reported from a live performance.[7] And there's the rub. If printer's copy for Q1 *Lear* is instead a memorial report of a live performance, taken down in shorthand, and then transcribed into longhand for use in the printing house, then Q1 *Lear* cannot be based on authorial "foul papers." Instead, as a memorial report, the text is subject to actor error, shorthand error, transcription error, compositor error, in short, any errors introduced into any link in the chain of transmission. As Downs has demonstrated with respect to the play *John of Bordeaux*, actor errors are faithfully recorded in the manuscript (2007-8, 122-23, 124). If Q1 *Lear* is based on "foul papers," then the dramatist is a direct and late link in the chain of transmission. But if Q1 *Lear* is a memorial report, then the dramatist is *not* a late link in the chain. The impact on the orthodox biography is significant. Supposing that some of Maguire's "not MR" plays, such as *Lear* and Q1 *Romeo* turn out to be based instead on memorial reports, then the biographer is faced with the disconcerting question: where was Shakespeare?

A memorial reconstruction is surely more palatable as an explanation of a "suspect" quarto, because the hapless actors can be imagined to be reconstructing a previously performed text that they no longer have access to and recall imperfectly. A memorial report, on the other hand, generally injects presumably unauthorized agents, those of an entrepreneur and a stenographer, possibly one and the same. The forty-one plays listed in Maguire's Table (227, 324-325) are grouped by category, that is, her verdicts of possible transmission by Memorial Reconstruction. The majority of her verdicts, thirty-one, are "Not MR", with two more "probably not" MR. However, many of those texts may have been transmitted not by Memorial Reconstruction but by a memorial report using shorthand, in which case, her verdicts suggest numerous false negatives. *John of Bordeaux* is certainly one of the false negatives, and the first quartos of *King Lear*, *Romeo and Juliet*, and *Hamlet* are probably others.

Bryan Crockett points out that "the theory of shorthand origins of some Shakespeare playtexts has been out of vogue since the mid-

---

7 Similarly, Adam G. Hooks incorporates the concept of "memorial reconstruction" in his section on "Bad Shakespeare" specifically "bad quartos". He criticizes both unnamed opportunistic actors and the integrity or professionalism of the printers but overlooks the category of memorial reports (2014, 138-39).

twentieth century" (2015, 263). There are possible explanations that come to mind for such a theory being "out of vogue." Biographers, editors, and critics naturally gravitate to the narrative that puts Shakespeare, whoever he was, as close as possible to the printing of his plays. "Foul papers" are therefore preferred as printer's copy, rather than any manuscript copy at one or more removes from the author. The verdict of "not memorial reconstruction" serves to diminish the badness of a text and potentially move the dramatist closer to the printed play. Werstine demonstrated fatal flaws in the case for memorial reconstruction in the case of Q *Merry Wives*, but theories about "memorial reconstruction" continue to exert an influence on the textual studies of, in particular, the Shakespeare texts that contain many mistakes and corruptions. The preferred narrative, then, may be contradicted by the probable means of textual transmission of many Shakespearean quartos.

Shorthand reports as printer's copy?

Among the Shakespeare plays that some editors suppose may have been based in whole or in part on memorial reports are early quartos of *Hamlet*, *Richard III*, *Romeo and Juliet*, *Merry Wives of Windsor*, *Henry V*, *Pericles*, and *King Lear*. In an 1898 issue of *Shakespeare Jahrbuch*, Curt Dewischeit apparently proposed that *all* the early Shakespeare quartos were pirated, "having been procured, during performances, by stenographers using [Timothy Bright's] *Characterie*" (cit. by Duthie 1949, 73; see also Hoppe 1948, 66-67). Not only is Dewischeit not readily available in English, he has also dropped out of sight in most bibliographies. Even if Bright's system proves inadequate to the task of recording a performance at the speed of speech, we know that other systems existed, even if they remained unpublished, and one of them was good enough to produce the manuscript of *Bordeaux*. Downs describes features found in bad quartos in his close study of the *Bordeaux* manuscript, and it includes, most persuasively, instances of actor error onstage recorded by the shorthand reporter (Downs finds such error also in Q1 *Hamlet*; 2007-8, 124 n42).

The origin and presentation of speech prefixes are also important factors when considering questions of textual transmission. In *Romeo* Q1 (1597) and Q2 (1599), "Capulet's wife" is never named in a speech prefix. Her character appears variously as "Old La[dy]" or "Wife" or "Mo[ther]". Most editors and critics would agree with Jowett's claims that these inconsistent speech prefixes are "generally accepted as authorial in complexion" (2007, 99-100). René Weis assumes the compositors of Q2 relied on "foul papers" for text not found in Q1, and that the varying speech prefixes represent authorial choice (2012, 99; see also Greg 1955, 230-34). "Capulet" appears by name but also as "Oldeman" and "Fa[ther]". Inconsistent speech prefixes can be explained in any number of ways besides authorial choice, for example, by a theatrical bookkeeper's "interventions" (Werstine 2013, 204-5). They could also be explained by a shorthand reporter who recorded spoken dialogue only, transcribed his notes into longhand, and then added in speech prefixes (and perhaps stage directions) as best he could, taking his cues from the dialogue. In any case, the presence of inconsistent or varying speech prefixes cannot be explained with any certainty as being a feature or habit typical of Shakespeare's authorial "foul papers", since no such "foul papers" have ever been discovered.

"Foul papers" proponents defend the inconsistent and generic speech prefixes as authorial in both Q1 and Q2 *Romeo*, yet one of J. Dover Wilson's arguments in his essay about Hand D was his assumption that the dramatist maintained the utmost respect for the particular spelling of a character, specifically in the case of Justice "Scilens" in *2 Henry IV*. Wilson could scarcely contain his excitement when he found the word "scilens," same spelling, in the Hand D Additions (Pollard 1923, 128-29). But Wilson made a selective comparison, because in the quarto of *2 Henry IV*, the word *Silence* is spelled "Scilens" in just under half of the occurrences. It is surely ironic that Wilson's assumption about the sacrosanct spelling of a character's name is today contradicted by claims concerning the alleged authorial origins of inconsistent and generic speech prefixes. Wilson's essay was published in the 1923 collection of essays that officially launched the theory that Hand D was Shakspere's into the academic mainstream. The inconsistent speech prefixes in the Hand D Additions are cited by Jowett to make his case for authorial origins of the Q2 *Romeo* speech prefixes (2007, 99-100). Weis explains authorial choices such as spelling and stage directions with reference to Hand D, that is, "as we know from *Sir Thomas More* and other foul papers" (100). Despite the ongoing contradictions and unsupported assertions, the consensus positions on Hand D and "foul papers" serve to situate the dramatist in a late link in the chain of textual transmission.

The two-text *King Lear* theory

The play *King Lear* has come down to us in two different versions, quarto [Q] and Folio [F]. Q1 *Lear* is imperfect, containing many corruptions. The second quarto of 1619 (Q2) essentially reprints Q1, but the text in the 1623 *First Folio* differs from Q1, containing additions, omissions, and variant readings. For many years, critics and editors considered both Q1 and F *Lear* to have been based on the same copy-text, with Q1 a corrupt version, and the *Folio* text, while flawed, closest to the author's intentions. Most early editors therefore chose the best lines from both Q1 and F *Lear* to create a conflated text. Their goal was to determine which words Shakespeare wrote, and which were corruptions from the printing house or the theatre, by a non-authorial agent, or introduced in the process of reported transmission. In other words, early editors did not think that Q1 was based on an authorial manuscript or an immediate transcript. According to Charlton Hinman, "Greg described [Q1 *Lear*] succinctly in 1942 as 'a report, probably stenographic, of a performance or somewhat cut version' of the play . . . It bears many of the stigmata associated with reports. It abounds in various kinds of memorial errors, some lines are assigned to the wrong speakers, and there are many confused and even quite unintelligible passages" (Hinman 1965, 9). Q1 *Lear* has almost no punctuation except for a lot of commas, and that was another feature that led Greg to postulate a "shorthand report" (1951, 95).

However, in 1978, Michael Warren proposed that Q1 and Folio *Lear* should be treated as two distinct authorial texts; his essay was followed a few years later by *The Division of the Kingdoms*, a collection of essays most of which reject *King Lear* as a single work of which we have variant versions. Instead, the contributors argued that Q1 *Lear* represents the dramatist's first effort, and the *Folio* text represents his deliberate revision. This theory acknowledges errors, omissions, or contamination from compositors, theatre personnel, and other meddling hands, but it insists that both texts derive directly from the author, Q1 from his so-called "foul papers," and F from his deliberate revisions to that quarto as subsequently transcribed (Taylor 1983, 365). Various critics point out that the only significant changes made in the *Folio* revision are cuts (see, for example Thomas 1984). Cutting a text will inevitably affect plot or character, but cuts are not necessarily authorial. They could as easily be theatrical or editorial cuts. An author who deliberately revises a text will surely compose new lines and re-write dialogue. Further, the two-text theorists cannot explain the multitude of corruptions, especially in Q1 but also in the supposed revised version, each of which is supposedly authorial. Why didn't the author correct *all* the errors and nonsense passages in Q1 *Lear* for the revised version? Why did the author rely on a corrupt and, in some instances, incoherent text in the first place to begin his revisions?[8] Nevertheless, since 1983, this two-text theory has been hardening into orthodoxy.

In his Introduction to *The Division of The Kingdoms*, Stanley Wells cited the then-forthcoming second volume of Peter W. M. Blayney's *The Texts of 'King Lear' and their Origins*:

> The publication of Blayney's second volume, which will directly address the problem of the printer's copy for the Quarto, and its relationship to the Folio, must be awaited with the keenest interest. But already, even in advance of the publication and assessment of Blayney's evidence, it is fair to claim that those who regard the Quarto as a reported text have, by their own admission, not yet offered a satisfactory explanation of how such a report came into being (13).

Wells was writing in 1983, and Blayney's second volume has never been published. However, since then, research by, for example, Adele Davidson and Bryan Crockett has further advanced the case for transmission of the text of Q1 *Lear* by shorthand. The present chapter will set forth a conjectural narrative as to "how such a report came into being."

Q1 *King Lear* is one of the plays that Kirschbaum categorised as a "bad quarto," and he described the problematic text: "the general impression left by the Quarto is that the printer had before him copy that was entirely undivided metrically and altogether without punctuation. There is, indeed, some slight bibliographical evidence to this effect. Such copy would normally result from a shorthand report, and I do not know what else would produce it" (1938, 26-27; see also Chambers 1930, 1:182). Consider Regan's protestations of filial love in 1.1.69-76:

8 Taylor himself poses the question: "Why would anyone setting out to rework *King Lear* begin from a copy of Q1?" (1983, 365) and proposes his explanation. In his review of *Division of the Kingdoms*, Knowles points out some difficulties with Taylor's explanations (117-119).

REGAN Sir, I am made
Of the self-same metal that my sister is,
And prize me at her worth. In my true heart
I find she names my very deed of love;
Only she comes too short: that I profess
Myself an enemy to all other joys,
Which the most precious square of sense possesses;
And find I am alone felicitate
In your dear highness' love.

How do editors explain the line "Which the most precious square of sense possesses"? If you were the actress performing Regan or the director, you might want to cut that line. The speech makes more sense without it. Most critical editions consulted for this chapter provide glosses for that line, none of them satisfactory. For example, Wells glosses "square of sense" as "variously explained; the general sense is 'area' or 'criterion' (from the carpenter's square) of sensibility; there may be a hint of "genital area" (Wells 2000, 103 n68). Many of the glosses go back to the 1880 *Variorum* edition (Furness, 12-13n). But as that edition was released, a distinguished critic, Richard Grant White, raised commonsense questions about the corrupt line: "What is a precious square? What is a square of sense? How can a square of sense profess? . . . What can it mean? … [D]oes any one of these paraphrases satisfy the intelligent Shakespeare lover whose mind is clear and unmuddled by the study of various readings, — the most distracting and bewildering of all mental occupations, one which tends to idiocy? I will venture to say that it does not" (White 1880, 827).

Such a blatant corruption, and it is not the only one (see P. W. K. Stone's appendices, esp. 190-200) severely weakens the two-text theory. Gary Taylor proposes that the dramatist wrote out his revisions on a copy of the corrupt Q1 *Lear*, but if he did, he evidently failed to correct errors and unintelligible dialogue such as "precious square of sense." On the other hand, analysis of shorthand transmission error in Q1 *Lear* can lead solutions to stubborn cruxes. Adele Davidson is able to suggest a resolution to the famous *Lear* crux at 4.1.10: "Who's here, my father parti, eyd" or "poorlie led", proposing instead the more satisfying "bloody-eyed" (2009, 203), and she did so by testing the assumption that the text was transmitted by stenography (though in her argument, not of a live performance). Davidson's technique of reverse engineering a corrupt phrase or passage by using phonetics, synonyms, first letters, interchangeable consonants, absence of vowels, and other stenographic diagnostics led to a better textual solution.[9]

In 2016, Brian Vickers's book, *The One King Lear*, challenging the two-text theory set off a firestorm. *Times Higher Education* took note of the firestorm, including Holger S. Syme's scathing review in *The Los Angeles Review of Books* followed by hundreds of hostile tweets. It is obvious that Vickers's book touched a nerve. His theory is essentially that F *Lear* restores text omitted from Q1 *Lear* for reasons of paper constraints. If additions printed in the Folio text are restorations, not revisions, then the theory that the dramatist took up a copy of Q1 *Lear* to inscribe his deliberate revisions is no longer tenable. Vickers's theories may or may not withstand scrutiny, but he has demonstrated that the two-text theory remains vulnerable. Perhaps the ongoing controversy can lead to more productive discussions about the possible origins of Q1 *Lear*. However, the possibility that the quarto originated in a memorial report again puts the orthodox biography at risk, because the dramatist would be at many removes from printer's copy. As Harold Bloom famously asked, how could there "have been a writer for whom the final shape of *King Lear* was a careless or throwaway matter" (1994, 52).

Profiting from a "bad" quarto

The motive behind every quarto, bad, less bad, or good, was presumably to make money. In the Stationers' Registers (SR) are entries for both good and bad quartos; sometimes there was no entry. Stationers purchased copy without much investigation into a manuscript's provenance or authority, with or "without its author's knowledge or consent," as long as the transaction seemed legal (see Blayney 1997, 394-95). The play *King Lear* was entered in the SR in November 1607.

Suppose Shakspere decided to sell a play to a printer. If Shakspere owned a particular play, or if he had already either sold or rented it to the acting company, why would he hire a stenographer to record a performance of the play? Why would he not just hire a scribe to copy the existing manuscript to sell to a printer? He would be cutting out the stenographer's fee and going straight to the scribal transcript in longhand. But a printed quarto of a play still in repertory would then be available to competing companies in London. E. K. Chambers

9 The inapt and extra-metrical "Abraham" in Q1 *Romeo* at 2.1.13 is a proper name, and it starts with the letter "A" — which may be significant if Q1 is based on a shorthand report; perhaps "Amor: Cupid" was intended, with a possible pun on "aimer" "he that shot so true."

supposed that "the acting companies did not find it altogether to their advantage to have their plays printed . . . Presumably the danger was . . . that other companies might buy the plays and act them" (Chambers 1923, 3:183). In that case, an entrepreneur attempting to sell a playbook might be seen as subverting his company's best interests. Chambers is considering a relevant factor that Evelyn May Albright dubbed "stage-right." Back then, according to Albright, "stage-right" was to acting companies what copyright was to stationers. Stage-right confers the unique right of an acting company to perform a particular play that it owns. The concept is based on a single discrete sale from author to theatrical buyer. Pamphleteer Thomas Nashe sarcastically referred to Robert Greene's double sale of *Orlando Furioso* to the "queenes players for twenty nobles. And then when they were in the country, sold the same play to Lord Admiral's men, for as much more? Was not this plain coney-catching?" (Albright 1927, 223). The Induction scene to John Marston's *Mal-Content* contains dialogue attesting to a breach of stage-right, the practice of selling a play to one, and only one acting company. However, a double sale could be made, not just to another acting company, but also to a printer. In 1608, Thomas Heywood criticized those playwrights who "have used a double sale of their labours, first to the stage, and after to the press" (Albright, 234). Heywood's 1608 claim squares with the Whitefriars theatrical contract of 1607/8, to which poet and dramatist Michael Drayton was a party, and which stipulates that no sharer "shall at any time hereafter put into print . . . any manner of playe booke now in use" (Albright, 239). Years later, in his address "To The Reader" from *The English Traveller* (1633), Heywood referred to some of his plays that "are still retained in the hands of some actors, who think it against their peculiar profit to have them come in print" (Albright, 238). Blayney cites Albright as his source for the Whitefriars contract (Blayney 1997, 418n 21), although he does not bring forward the term "stage-right." The term has encountered resistance. In his negative review of Albright's book, Greg found it "impossible to believe that the more difficult matter of stage-right was sustainable . . . at common law". Yet Greg himself points out that "infringements of stage rights in London were comparatively rare . . . to trespass on another's was to invite retaliation" (95). His statement rather supports the *de facto* concept of stage-right. In any case, Albright does not insist on a legal framework for "stage-right" but allows for "a common-sense business attitude toward respecting a neighbor's common-law property rights"

(223). Putting a name to "stage-right" is useful in a discussion about play ownership and protocols in Shakespeare's London.

Richard Dutton suggests that "Shakespeare contrived somehow to hold on to [the early Shakespeare playbooks]" that were produced by other companies prior to the formation of the Lord Chamberlain's Men, later the King's Men, adding that "such a collection of plays would have been ideal collateral for a founding shareholder" (Dutton 1989, 49). At the point of formation, and with "stage-right" in mind (and anticipating the Whitefriars codifications), the shareholders collectively may have decided to take physical custody of the stock of playbooks by placing them in secure storage until needed for production. Such an arrangement would make the original manuscript, whether authorial or scribal, inaccessible to Shakspere or any other shareholder without express company approval. Such an arrangement may or may not have been specified in writing. No governing documentation comparable to that for the Whitefriars company survives for the Chamberlain's or King's Men. C. J. Sisson cites the title page of John Rastell's interlude (ca 1519) of *The Four Elements* as "designed almost exclusively for the attention of practical men of the theatre, giving them information and directions necessary for men in search of a play to act" (Sisson 1942, 131, see also 133). According to Sisson, acting companies were "a primary market" for printed play texts for good reason: "It is evident that to their eyes the use of a *printed* play as prompt-copy [i.e., a performing script] was equivalent to a license from the Master of Revels and gave them *complete protection*" (142) [emphasis added].

Could selling a memorial report to a printer be one of Shakspere's sidelines to increase his cash flow? Such a transaction would breach stage-right, because the printed playbook would then be available to competing companies in London, but respect for stage-right may be the reason we do not know about performances of *Lear* by other London companies. In her discussion of stage-right, Albright acknowledges that "if there were no other means of getting copy, it could certainly be acquired by shorthand" (223). Even supposing that the text for Q1 *Lear* was acquired by shorthand, the circumstances concerning acquisition and sale to the printer are unknown. However, we *do* know that a copy of Q1 *King Lear* (1608) was the playbook used for performances by Sir Richard Cholmesley's Men on tour in Yorkshire in 1609 (Mowat 1997, 213-14); also in their possession was a copy of *Pericles* (1609), another bad quarto. This company traveled with at least one copy of each printed quarto, which therefore served as authorized texts that would satisfy any persnickety local magistrates. According to Sisson, "over and over again it is stated that the actors played only from *printed* books. Richard Simpson [an actor] stated, for example, that 'that booke by which he and the other persons did act the said play . . . was a *printed* booke, And they onelie acted the same according to the contents therein *printed*, and not otherwise. . . . And such as were acted in Common and publicke places and Staiges. . . and such as were *played publicly* and *prynted* in the books'" (Sisson, 138) [emphasis added]. The testimony that Q1 *Lear* (and *Pericles*) was the playbook for a company on tour in 1609, shortly following publication, suggests a possible motive behind obtaining a stenographic report of a live performance in London. The companies going on tour represented a ready market in the short-term, and playbooks used for out-of-town performances that did not compete with the company's London repertory may have constituted a technical breach of stage-right but one that was not worth pursuing.

In the Cambridge student satire ca. 1601-2, *The Return to Parnassus*, the writer Ingenioso is offered "40 shillings [£2]; and an odd pottle of wine" (Smeaton 1905, 1.3.10) by a printer for his book. With respect to the sale of *Lear*, one possibility is that Shakspere negotiated with the printer for complimentary printed copies in *lieu* of the pottle of wine; he could then sell his copies to touring companies, such as Sir Richard Cholmesley's. The translator Richard Robinson usually received 26 copies instead of a fee from the stationer; he then sold his copies at inflated prices to friends and patrons to make his money (Miller 1959, 160-61). In my conjectural narrative, Shakspere could net a small profit — after paying the shorthand note-taker for both the report and the transcription into longhand — either by selling the manuscript outright to a printer for around £2 (see Blayney 1997, 396) or negotiating for a lower fee plus some quantity of copies to sell on to other companies planning to tour; he might sell his copies at no less than the going rate of sixpence apiece, but knowing Shakspere, he probably got more.

Non-authorial transmission

In 1633, Thomas Heywood complained that some of his plays were recorded by shorthand stenographers, who sold them to the press, with the result that the printed texts were "scarce one word true." He was referring to his play *If You know Not Me*, published in 1605 in a bad quarto from a shorthand report (Greg 1951, 57-58). The cover of *Shakespeare Quarterly*'s fall 2015 issue reproduces a page of John Willis's

The Art of Stenographie; the inside caption reads in part "This example of shorthand notation from Willis's text has been superimposed upon the kind of small writing tablebook in which shorthand notetakers might have recorded transcriptions of live performances" (250). In the lead article, Bryan Crockett extends the discussion concerning memorial reports and their potential roles in the origins of at least two of the "bad" Shakespeare quartos. His analyses and arguments describe some of the diagnostics that his predecessors have considered (although Hoppe, Stone, and Downs are not cited), and he examines the case for transmission of a memorial report, taken in shorthand, and transcribed into longhand for manuscripts serving as printer's copy for a sermon and two "bad" quartos. He finds sufficient presence of certain types of errors consistent with shorthand transmission to suggest that a memorial report was indeed a factor in producing printer's copy for the quartos of *Romeo and Juliet* and *King Lear*. If these texts had their origins in a memorial report, then the dramatist is not a late link in the chain.

It is encouraging to see the theory of shorthand reports coming back "in vogue," and it is one of several significant developments in textual studies. The consequences of Paul Werstine's research on Greg's theory of "foul papers" and the firestorm over Vickers's book challenge to the two-text *Lear* theory reveal an Achilles's heel in Shakespearean textual studies and biography. Despite claims to the contrary with respect to the penman and nature of the Hand D Additions, no "foul papers" survive. No printer's copy for the Shakespeare plays survive. Greg's imaginary "foul papers" have been serving as potential surrogates for documentation needed to support Shakspere's supposed literary life, but they are not substitutes for the missing literary paper trails. Unfortunately, such issues remain not only controversial, they have become politicized. In the case of *The Division of The Kingdoms*, Gary Taylor proclaimed the launch of the two-text *Lear* theory a "palace coup" (Rosenbaum 2006, 38-39). The palace guard is today threatened by Vickers's book, because Vickers questions that two-text theory, which in turn threatens theories of authorial revision and "foul papers".

There has been another related development in textual studies, albeit one that has not been in the headlines. Until recently, most editors have followed Greg's proposal that printer's copy for *2 Henry IV* was "foul papers" (Humphries 1966, lxviii). However, James C. Bulman, the Arden Three editor, challenges the "foul papers" as well as the "Scilens/Hand D" arguments and instead proposes that a theatrical playbook served as printer's copy (2016, 439-440). As Bulman argues, Q *2 Henry IV* may contain features consistent with a theatrical playbook, but as discussed above, some of those features may also be consistent with a memorial report. The speech prefixes in Q may also be significant (cf. Bulman, 434-35; Humphries, lxviii n4). In Act 1, the Earl of Northumberland is named in the speech prefixes as "Earle" until he self-identifies as "Northumberland" in the dialogue at 1.1.152, after which the speech prefixes specify "Northumberland". By questioning "foul papers" as underlying Q *2 Henry IV*, Bulman is going against the current. Even if the tide is starting to turn, it will undoubtedly take years to dismantle the entrenched positions. An acknowledged collapse of the "foul papers" narrative would necessarily send editors back to the drawing board, and the theory that Hand D is Shakspere's would collapse with it. And that puts the dramatist at many removes from the printed texts.

The willingness of the Shakespearean community to accept "foul papers" as printer's copy and Hand D as Shakspere's is certainly understandable. Every Shakespeare lover wants to get as close as possible to Shakespeare's original manuscript and authorial intent. But if the theory of "foul papers" is finally rejected as a hypothetical construct because no such papers survive, and errors in the good quartos cannot be explained by demonstrable authorial transmission, then *none* of the Shakespeare plays carries authority. This is surely one of orthodoxy's worst nightmares, that none of the texts that we have of Shakespeare's plays are based on the dramatist's original manuscripts. Yet none of the so-called "good quartos" are really good. If they were, Greg would not have formulated the features in his hypothetical definition of "foul papers" that could explain the errors that they contain (see Werstine 2013, 13, 38, 41, 98).

Transmission through non-authorial agents, whether actors, stenographers, scribes, editors, revisers, playhouse personnel, or compositors has serious consequences for the orthodox concept of Shakspere. Non-authorial transmission chips away at Shakspere as a hands-on playwright and it contradicts his concern for a literary legacy, a concern expressed in many of the sonnets. But "My Shakspere" moves easily into the conjectural narratives of textual transmission to the acting company and into print, including transmission of texts that cannot possibly represent what the author intended. These unresolved questions of textual transmission raise many doubts about Shakespeare's authorship. My Shakspere is more likely than the playwright, whoever he was, to be found in the chains of transmission at and after the point of procurement. He is likely to be an entrepreneur who figures out that commissioning a memorial report to then sell as printer's copy was a practical, if less than honorable solution to the problem of an inaccessible manuscript. If the printed playbook was full of corruptions, it was of no concern to him. He can assure his colleagues that the better script is still in their possession and being performed onstage in London. As for the touring companies, who cares that the printed play is full of errors? The actors can ad lib to minimise corruptions in the text, and the touring company's major objective is met with the printed book. They have a script sufficiently authorized to satisfy the local officials. In my conjectural narratives, I find Shakspere, the entrepreneur and play broker, either in plain sight or lurking in the shadows. He is someone who would have had no scruples about taking credit for works written by somebody else, and as the financier and business agent for the Lord Chamberlain's Men, he is the one trading in theatrical commodities, including playbooks. The presence of his name, however spelled, on title-pages is entirely consistent with that narrative.

Some of the questions that take on increased significance as one tries to fill in some of the blanks in Shakspere's activities and character are those that relate to dubious dealings and non-authorial transmission. For example, how did Thomas Middleton's fragment of a play *Yorkshire Tragedy* get printed with an attribution to Shakespeare? Is *Locrine* "by W.S." the Tilney play, and if so, why did George Buc comment, rather dismissively, that "some fellow has published it"? When he was questioned by Buc about the authorship of *George a Greene*, why did Shakspere pretend he could not remember who wrote the play? *George a Green* was written ca. 1587-93 and printed in a bad quarto in 1599, about which Shakspere feigns ignorance. How many other bad quartos contain signs of a shorthand memorial report in their origins? In this chapter, I have considered possible links in the chain of transmission of certain Shakespearean play texts, none of which get us any closer to the dramatist. In fact, the distances between the playwright and the plays as performed or as printed, only increases. On the other hand, we get closer to *my* Shakspere, the entrepreneur and play-broker found in my conjectural narratives. Amongst the bad quartos, good quartos that are not good, and mis-attributed texts, I find some faint footprints left by my Shakspere. The question remains: Where was Shakespeare?

Chapter 3

My Shakespeare Rise!

Alexander Waugh

1. Enter Oxford

The precocious, madcap, scandal-ridden and brilliantly learned poet-playwright, Edward de Vere, 17th Earl of Oxford (1550-1604) was born into a play-loving family — one of the first in England to keep its own company of actors. His grandfather was a great patron of theatre for whom the eminent dramatist, John Bale, wrote at least fourteen plays, including *King Johan,* identified as the major source of Shakespeare's *King John.* Orthodox scholars have never explained how Shakespeare found himself in possession of Bale's old, unpublished manuscript (Moray 1994, 327-31).[1] Among Oxford's uncles were Arthur Golding, the translator of Ovid's *Metamorphoses* (a major source for many passages in Shakespeare), Henry, Earl of Surrey, a pioneer of the so-called "Shakespearean sonnet" and Edmund Sheffield, a sonneteer after the Italian fashion and a skilled musician.

Oxford was tutored by Thomas Smith, Regius Professor of Civil Law, and by Lawrence Nowell, the celebrated legal historian. Lawyers lived with his family from his earliest years and he continued his father's habit of hospitality to lawyers throughout his adult life (see Byrd 1580

1 According to Jesse Harris, "Bale's heading to the catalog of fourteen plays in the *Anglorum Heliades* (1536) states that he composed them especially for Master John Vere, the Earl of Oxford. Apparently the statement is inclusive and means that all fourteen of the plays were written for the earl of Oxford" (1940, 68).

and Nashe 1592).[2] At the age of sixteen he entered Gray's Inn to study law. Since the 18th century it has been noted how Shakespeare naturally, frequently and accurately placed legal metaphors into his poems and plays. Lord Penzance, Baron of the Exchequer, believed Shakespeare "to have thought in legal phrases", while Shakespearean scholar Richard Grant White observed how "legal phrases flow from his pen as part of his vocabulary and parcel of his thought" (White 1859, 102).

In 1562, when the 16th Earl died, his twelve-year-old son was made a ward of the Queen and placed under the guardianship of the Master of Wards and Lord Treasurer, Sir William Cecil (later Lord Burghley), who, nine years later would become his father-in-law. Among Burghley's private peculiarities was his habit of returning home after a long day's work, laying down his official robe and saying to it: "Lie there, Lord Treasurer". In Shakespeare's *Tempest* the magician, Prospero, "lays down his mantle" and commands it to "Lie there, my Art!" (I.ii). In 1869 George Russell French identified Shakespeare's Ophelia as a portrait of Oxford's wife, Anne Cecil, and Polonius (her father) as a caricature of Lord Burghley, an identification accepted by many scholars since (see French 1869, 301-06; Gollancz 1898; Phillips 1936; Jolly in Malim 2004, 173-4). In the first quarto of *Hamlet* Polonius is called Corambis (meaning "double-hearted"), teasing Burghley's armorial motto, *cor unum, via una* ("One heart, one way"). Like Burghley, Polonius is cast as Senior Advisor to the Queen and like Burghley, who sent servants to spy on his son, Polonius sends servants to spy on his son; like Burghley, who gave the boy ten moral "Precepts" to memorize, Polonius requires his son to memorize ten moral precepts which, in tone and substance, closely ape those of Burghley. Hamlet calls Polonius a "fishmonger" in apparent mockery of Burghley's zealous promotion of a bill to make fish-eating compulsory on Wednesdays[3] and "Jephthah" in apparent mockery of Burghley's active campaigning for the "Assassins Charter" in the mid-1580s (see Beane 2016, 23-30).

2 Samuel Byrd, in *A friendlie communication or dialogue betweene Paule and Damas* (1580), records that Oxford's father "kept Lawiers in his house". Nashe, in his dedication to *Strange Newes* (1592), records Oxford being among "men of judgment in both laws [i.e., civil and canon law] everie day". The Alleyns' lawyer, Hugh Swift, was one of the lawyers who graced Oxford's table.

3 For extracts from Burghley's parliamentary speech advocating Wednesday as a second compulsory fish-day entitled "Arguments to prove that it is necessary for the restoring of the navy of England to have more fish eaten and therefore one day more in the week ordained to be a fish day, and that to be Wednesday rather than any other", see <www.historyofparliamentonline.org/volume/1558-1603/member/cecil-sir-william-1521-98> (accessed 19 May 2017)

Acknowledging these coincidences, E. K. Chambers (1930) asked: "Can Polonius have resembled some nickname for Burghley?" (1930, 418). "Polonius", when attached to a name, means a Pole (i.e., a native of Poland) and Oxford was present at New College, Oxford, on 2 September 1566 when poet, George Coryat, gave an oration in which Lords Burghley and Leicester were repeatedly referred to as "poles" (meaning axis poles). Coryat's poem ended: "Long may you live in joy and health, O Poles!"(see Nichols 1823, Vol 1: 231-36).[4] Hearing his illustrious guardian called a "pole" in front of an audience of dignitaries must have struck the sixteen-year-old Oxford as singularly amusing, not least because the word "pole" (which much offended the Polonians) was also a slang term for "prick" (Williams 1994, Vol 2: 1069).[5]

Oxford was a precocious learner. His tutor, Lawrence Nowell, wrote to Cecil: "I clearly see that my work for the Earl of Oxford cannot be much longer required" (Landsdowne 6/54, f. 135), a comment that prompted Oxford's first biographer, B. M. Ward, to remark: "That a scholar of Lawrence Nowell's attainments should speak thus of his pupil, aged 13½, argues a precocity quite out of the ordinary" (1928, 20-21). It was certainly noticed by Arthur Golding, who wrote to Oxford in the following year: "I haue had experience therof myself, howe earnest a desire your honor hath naturally graffed in you, to read, peruse, and communicate with others, as well the Histories of auncient tyme, and thynges done long ago, as also of the present estate of thinges in oure dayes, and that not withoute a certayn pregnancie of witte and rypenesse of vnderstandyng" (1564, iiiv).

Neither Golding nor Nowell would have been surprised when Oxford became the youngest man of his generation to be honored by both universities. One of the first nominated fellows of Trinity College, the distinguished Cambridge scholar, John Brooke, noted that the honour bestowed upon him by Cambridge University was awarded "by right" of his "excellent virtue and rare learning" (1577, Aiii). Scholar and actor Thomas Twynne — who, with his brother Lawrence, provided source material respectively for Shakespeare's *Titus Andronicus* and *Pericles* — noted the "singular delight" with which Oxford read "books of geography, histories and other good learning" (dedication to *Breviary of Britain*, 1572). So intense was his love of learning that another famous

4 George Coryat's Latin lines were delivered at New College Oxford (2 Sept 1566); the poem was first published by his son, Thomas, in *Coriates Crudities* (1611).

5 For this reason Poles preferred to be called "Polonians" rather than "Poles"; see Baluk-Ulewiczowa in Gibinska & Romanowska (2016, 35-44); see also Waugh, *DKS*, (October 2016, 9-13).

scholar, Thomas Underdowne, had to warn him against the temptation to be "too much addicted that way" (1569). Underdowne's translation of Heliodorus's *Aethiopika,* dedicated to Oxford in 1569, is cited as an important source for Shakespeare by Crewe, who noted how "traces of the *Aethiopika* persist in William Shakespeare's *Twelfth Night* (1623) and *Cymbeline* (1623), and in *The Winter's Tale* (1623)" (2009, 603).[6]

While no evidence survives that Stratford-Shakspere owned a single book, volumes known to have belonged to Oxford are recognised sources of influence on Shakespeare. An expense account of 1570 proves that he bought himself volumes in Italian and French. Shakespeare based several of his plays (*Hamlet* and *Othello* among others) on Italian and French works that had not yet been translated into English. The same account shows Oxford buying Chaucer's works (the source for *Troilus & Cressida* and *Two Noble Kinsmen*), a volume of Plutarch (upon which Shakespeare drew for *Julius Caesar, Coriolanus* and *Merchant of Venice*) and a Geneva Bible (Ward 33), of which Oxford's copy, preserved at the Folger Library in Washington, contains annotations of no fewer than 199 Biblical passages, all of which are used in Shakespeare (Stritmatter 2001, 305).

Oxford's devotion to books and learning drew many playwrights and scholars to him. Robert Greene extolled him as "a worthie favorer and fosterer of learning" to whom "scholars flock" (dedicatory letter to *Gwydonius*, 1584) and playwright George Chapman, as "of spirit passing great", who "writ sweetly or of learned subjects" (*Bussy d'Ambois*, c. 1610); George Buc, the man in charge of licensing all plays for the stage, described him as a "magnificent and very learned" nobleman (1609). Oxford's lifelong enthusiasm for poetry, language, astrology, history, military science, medicine, Classical literature, theatre and music (all subjects of which the playwright "Shakespeare" was supremely knowledgeable) are well documented. John Soothern wrote of Oxford:

> For who marketh better then he,
> The seuen turning flames of the Skie:
> Or hath read more of the antique.
> Hath greater knowledge in the tongues:
> Or vnderstandes sooner the sounds,
> Of the learner to loue Musique (*Pandora* 1584).

Composer John Farmer lauded Oxford's skill in music, noting that he had "overgone most of them that make it a profession" (1599).

6 For Shakespeare's allusion to the story of Theagenes and Chariclea from Heliodorus' *Ethiopica* (first noted by Theobald), see Furness (*Twelfe Night*, 1901, 287; n.123).

Gabriel Harvey, reported that among "Gallants" at court in 1580, "this English Poet" was considered a "fellow peerless in England ... not the like discourser for Tongue, and head to be found out" (1580, 36), and Queen Elizabeth, writing "*ex animo*" ("from her heart") described Oxford as possessed of an "outstanding mind... innately endowed with manners, virtue and learning" (1575).[7] Allied to this "outstanding mind" was a limitless generosity. Oxford's "exceeding bountie" as Angel Day described it in 1586 was remembered after his death by Gervase Markham who recalled: "It were infinite to speake of his infinite expence, the infinite number of his attendants, or the infinite house he kept to feede all people", the "bountie which Religion and Learning daily took from him" are as "trumpets so loude that all eares know them" (1624, 16-17). But the trumpets heralding Oxford's generosity were never his own. Indeed he was remarkable for his self-effacement, following Christ's example to give generously but in secret. Many of the underlined verses in his Geneva Bible attest to the importance he placed on charity and self-effacement, including from Matt. 6: "when thou givest thine almes, thou shall not make a trumpet to blowen before thee".[8]

An "infinite Maecenas", as Thomas Nashe described him, is necessarily headed for financial ruin and, typical of many poets and men of intellect, Oxford had no head for figures. Like the eponymous nobleman of Shakespeare's *Timon* he was generous to a fault and found himself squeezed by parasites quick to exploit his *largesse*. As Henry Lok recorded in a letter to Lord Burghley (6 Nov 1590), Oxford was brought to ruin by the "over many greedy horse-leeches which had sucked too ravenously on his sweet liberality" (Nelson 2003, 326-7). In 1584 William Warner, in possibly the earliest allusion to Shakespeare's *Timon*, wrote "let the Athenian misanthropos, or Man-hater bite on the Stage" — a reminder of Shakespeare's Timon who memorably snaps: "I am Misanthropos and hate mankind." Orthodox scholars tend to place *Timon* among the "late", "problem" plays (1606-7), but more recent studies have shown that it cannot postdate 1602 (Billington 1998, 351-52; Detobel 2004; Anderson 2006, 184, 207-34; Showerman 2009,

7 Quotation extracted from two letters of introduction written in Latin on the same day (24 January 1575) by Queen Elizabeth to foreign monarchs. In one, to the Holy Roman Emperor, Maximilian II, she writes: *Is eo ingenio moribus virtute doctrina est praeditus* ("He is innately endowed with manners, virtue and learning"); in the other: "*cui propter praestantes animi virtutis ex animo non vulgariter favemus*" ("We commend him not in the usual way, but from the heart, on account of his outstanding mind and virtue").

8 For further examples from Oxford's bible, see Stritmatter (2001, 27-30).

207-34; Steinburg 2013, 280-95). If Warner's 1584 allusion relates to this play, then Timon's cry "Let my lands be sold" precisely reflects the desperation that Oxford felt between 1580 and 1585 when he (like Timon) was besieged by creditors, flatterers and scroungers, and for want of cash, forced to sell thirty-two of his estates to cover debts.

It is not known how much of Oxford's patrimony was squandered on theatrical entertainments for the Queen. In 1601 he reminded Robert Cecil of his "youth, time and fortune spent in her Court" (AMS Hatfield MSS, Cal. XI.27; see Chiljan 1998, 64). The historian Edmund Bohun described him as a courtier "drawn into great expenses, Chargeable Feasts, Balls and Interludes and an excessive Gallantry" (1693, 82). In 1579 he presented a lavish comedy at Greenwich described in a letter by Mauvissiere, the French Ambassador, as "*une belle comedie qui se conclust par un marriage*" (in Woudhuysen 1981, 309-10), the French word "*comedie*" here meaning "a Play or Enterlude that begins in dissention, or sorrow, and ends in agreement or merriment" (Cotgrave 1611). This particular comedy involved a spectacular shipwreck. Anthony Mundy, remembered the scene in which "a brave and comely ship brought in before her Majesty wherein were certain of her noble Lords, and this ship was made with a gallant devise that in her presence it ran upon a rock & was despoiled. This credit was the bravest devise that I ever saw, and worthy of innumerable commendations" (Mundy 1580, 35). Mauvissiere described how Oxford had concealed himself within the ship and, after its destruction, danced his way from the wreck into the audience, where he presented a splendid jewel to the Queen. The name of this "beautiful comedy" of 1579 is unfortunately lost, but its shipwreck and final scene of happy marriage brings Shakespeare's *Twelfth Night* to mind, as does a handwritten manuscript note by Abraham Fleming (one of Oxford's secretaries) listing "a pleasant conceit of *Vere*, Earl of Oxford, discontented at the Rising of a mean Gentleman in the *English* Court, *circa* 1580" (Peck 1732, 50).[9] Is this the lampooning of Christopher Hatton as Malvolio in *Twelfth Night*? Could both records refer to a 1579 version of this comedy? If so, could Oxford have acted the part of Sebastian? It was, after all, in that same year that poet Fulke Greville sneeringly referred to Oxford as a "passionate actor" (1651, 77).[10] Some months later a courtier recalled Oxford helping him rehearse some lines: "he desired me to repeat the wordes, which after some study, calling them to rememberence … with his helpe, rehearsed

9 Peck proposed to publish this work, but failed and the MS is now lost.

10 Apropos Oxford's remonstrance in a quarrel with Philip Sidney over tennis in the spring of 1579.

them to him" (Arundel, LIB-2.1.5/24 in Nelson 2003, 209). The verse was pure mischief, a prophesy concerning Queen Elizabeth and was designed, no doubt, to "catch the conscience of the Queen" just as Shakespeare's prophetic prince, Hamlet, rehearsed the actors at the court of Elsinore: "Speak the speech, I pray you, as I pronounced it to you, trippingly on the tongue" in verses designed to "catch the conscience of the king" (II.ii).

In his *Seculum Proditori* a poet known as "Davies of Hereford" described his past acquaintance with a man of high birth; "too worthy", he wrote, to have been an actor, but one who had nevertheless played the part of a king "in game" at court (1616, F^6). According to Davies this unnamed man had "said to himself" that in acting the king he had experienced "a taste of raigne with power to leave" and so gotten "for noght, what kings do buy so dear". In his well-known verse, "My Mind to Me a Kingdom is", Oxford had expressed precisely the same sentiment, stating to himself that he could experience the pleasures of being king in his mind without need or desire to suffer the burdens to which a real king is heir. In another poem by the same "Davies of Hereford" the playwright "Shake-speare" is described with his "raigning wit" as one who had riskily "played some kingly parts in sport" before the court, suggesting precisely the same high-born fellow whom he described as having played a king "in game" in *Seculum Proditori*. The former poem was entitled "*To our English Terence, Mr. Will. Shake-speare*" — comparing "Shake-speare" to the African slave, Terence, who, according to Suetonius, had pretended the authorship of plays that were actually written by concealed poet and Roman nobleman, Quintus Fabius Labeo. Carolyn Morris provides extensive evidence that Joseph Hall's attack on a hidden high-born poet named "Labeo" in *Satyres* (1597-8) was a loosely veiled attack on Oxford (2016, 33-82). In these verses Hall accuses "Labeo" of writing running a studio of writers and shifting his fame to "another's name". John Marston, in the following year, while "scourging magnificos" (*magnifico* - "a great noble person; any person of high rank or position", *OED*) revealed the poet "Labeo" to be none other than William Shakespeare (*ibid*).[11]

Not all were so puritanical as Marston and Hall. In 1589 the anonymous author of *Arte of English Poesie* had declared that "for

11 In *Venus & Adonis* (1593) Shakespeare complains of the fair Adonis that he is "obdurate, flintie, hard as steele ... Nay more than flint, for stone at raine relenteth". John Marston, in 'The Author in Praise of his Precedent Poem' (1599), remarks of the poet and magnifico "Labeo": "So *Labeo* did complaine his loue was stone, Obdurate, flinty, so relentlesse none". In his 6th Satire Marston explains that writing *Pigmalion* his fist was guided by his genius "to scourge Magnificos".

such doings as I have seen" Oxford's "Comedies and Enterludes … deserve the highest prize" and nine years later Francis Meres placed him first on a list of 17 contemporary English playwrights named as "best for Comedy". It is hardly surprising that he should have excelled at comedy for he was considered among the funniest men of his age, with a talent for fantastical story-telling that threw his companions into fits of uncontrollable laughter. Charles Arundel recorded how he "glories greatly" in the telling of a story, "diversely hath he told it, and when he enters into it, he can hardly out, which hath made such sport as often have I been driven to rise from his table laughing. So hath my Lord Charles Howard and the rest" (1581).[12]

For over two decades Oxford was involved with Court and public theatre. In the 1580s he supported, in addition to his own bands of acrobats and musicians, several acting companies including Oxford's Men, Oxford's Boys, the Queen's Majesties Players, the Children of Windsor, Paul's Boys and the Children of the Chapel Royal (see Chambers 1923, Vol. 4: 497), making him, for a while, the single most important patron of theatre among the English nobility. In 1583 he acquired the lease on England's first public indoor theatre, later transferring it to his secretary, the playwright John Lyly and Rocco Bonetti, a fencing master, despised by Oxford, whose preposterous fencing terms are said to be ridiculed in *Romeo and Juliet*.[13] In the 1590s his players elected as their favourite performing space the yard of the Boar's Head Tavern adjacent to Oxford's home and "Great Garden" east of Aldgate. This public theatre shares its name and reputation for rowdiness with the infamous "Boar's Head Tavern" in Shakespeare's *Henry IV* plays, in which Falstaff and his men mount an ambush on messengers bringing money for the exchequer along the road from Rochester to Gravesend on 20 May, an event that precisely mirrors an ambush by Oxford's men on Burghley's servants bringing money for the exchequer along the same stretch of road between Rochester and Gravesend on 20 May 1573 (see Whittemore 2016).

In his mid-twenties Oxford wrote, "I have appointed for myself to serve my turne beyonde the seas.... In consideration whereof I am content to resign my interest and estate in Combe" (Nelson 102)[14] and

12 Charles Arundel allegations against Oxford (1581) SP 12/151/45, ff. 100-2.

13 "MER: Ah! The immortal passado! The punto reverse! The hay! / BEN: The what? / MER: The pox of such antick, lisping, affecting fantasticoes! These new tuners of accents!" (*Romeo and Juliet*, I.iv).

14 Hatfield MS CP, ii, 58 (159/113-14), f. 114; endorsed "Master of the Roolls, Erl of Oxfordes answer to the articles".

thus, like Jaques in Shakespeare's *As You Like It,* who "sold his lands to see other men's" (IV.i), Oxford sold his to see foreign countries too. From Padua (November 1575), he wrote to his father-in-law urging him to underwrite a loan of 500 crowns. Burghley agreed, setting up lines of credit through the banking firm of Baptista Spinola. Is it mere coincidence that Shakespeare's *Taming of the Shrew,* set in Padua, portrays a wheeler-dealer, who is rich in crowns, called Baptista Minola, who demands that Lucentio's marriage bond be underwritten by the young man's father? While Stratfordians are content to assume that "Shakespeare was thinking of London" when he composed this play, Richard Roe shows how specific details in that comedy — the proximity of merchants' houses to a lodging house, a university and a port within the parish of St Luke's — can only apply to 16th century Padua, and not to London, where there was no church of St Luke's until 1733 and no university until 1826 (Roe 2011).[15]

As a scene from Shakespeare's *Henry V* masterfully presents the comedy of an Englishman trying to speak French at the French court, so Oxford spoke fluent French, Latin and Italian and had first-hand experience of speaking all three languages in foreign courts. In Italy he based himself in Venice, where two of Shakespeare's plays are set. Armed with personal letters of introduction from Queen Elizabeth to the ducal heads of Italian city states, he is known to have visited Florence, Milan, Padua, Bologna, Genoa, Siena and Sicily and is assumed to have entered several cities in between. Shakespeare, who derives plots from untranslated Italian sources, set 106 dramatic scenes in Italy, making references to many of the places that lay on Oxford's trail, including 52 specific references to Venice, 25 to Milan, 23 to Florence, and 22 to Padua. In his comprehensive study of Shakespearean allusions to Italy, Richard Roe leaves no doubt that Shakespeare's precise details of Italian places, names, paintings, buildings, routes, rivers, manners, customs, habits and language, demonstrate that the playwright had first-hand knowledge of Italy.[16]

In a scene that cannot be attributed to any known source of the Hamlet story, the eponymous prince is "set naked" upon the shore having been attacked and stripped of his clothes by pirates in the English Channel, just as Oxford was attacked, robbed and stripped naked by

---

15 "England is never out of sight … Shakespeare was thinking of London when he composed the play" (Hötteman 2010, 211-12); for rebuttals see Waugh, in J. Shahan & A. Waugh, eds., (2013, 78).

16 Those arguing for Shakespeare's first-hand knowledge of Italy before the Oxfordian challenge include Brown (1838, 100); Knight, ed., (1839, 433), and Elze (1874, 315).

pirates in the English Channel on his return journey to England in 1576. As one of his companions, Nathaniel Baxter, recalled: "Naked we landed out of Italy, enthralled by pirates, men of no regard; horror and death assailed nobility" (1606).

While Oxford was abroad a false friend informed him that the baby (a daughter), born to his wife in his absence, was not his. In rage he spurned her upon his return, only to regret his behaviour when he learned of her innocence. Is it mere coincidence that Shakespeare chose to write *Othello* about a foreigner in Venice who destroyed his wife when informed by a false friend of her infidelity, only to regret his actions on discovering her innocence? Is it mere coincidence that Shakespeare also set for the stage the story of *Cymbeline* about a young nobleman, who (like Oxford) is married to the daughter of the most powerful man in Britain, who (like Oxford) leaves England for a tour of Italy where he hears of his wife's infidelities, who returns (like Oxford) in unforgiving mood to repudiate her and his father-in-law, only to seek their forgiveness later on? And is it mere coincidence that Shakespeare wrote in *The Winter's Tale* (II.iii) of a scheme to bring the queen's newborn daughter before the furious king (who denied his paternity) in the hope that the king might "soften at the sight o' the child", just as the Duchess of Suffolk (in a letter to Lord Burghley on 15 Dec 1577 (BL MS Landsowne 25, ff 56-58) concerning one whose paternity Oxford denied) schemed to "bring in the child as though it were some other child of my friend's, and we shall see how nature will work in him to like it, and tell him it is his own after?" (see Ward 1928, 154-56).

Before Oxford's departure for Italy the French ambassador to England had reported that he had "more followers and was the object of greater expectation than any other man in the realm" (Mothe-Fénelon in Cooper 1840, 361).[17] On his return he was noted for his enthusiastic, if somewhat effeminate, espousal of all things French and Italian. As the playwright, Shakespeare, displays intimate knowledge of the French and Italian peoples, their manners, customs, literature, language, their art and their laws, so Gabriel Harvey wrote of Oxford that "of French and Italian muses, the manners of many peoples, their arts and laws [he has] drunk deeply". Harvey continued his address to Oxford; "Pallas will instruct your heart and spirit as long since Apollo cultivated your mind in the arts. Your English poetry has been widely sung. Let your courtly epistle — more polished than even the writings of Castiglione himself — witness how greatly you excel in letters. I

17 [*"le comte d'Oxfort est*] *le mieulx suivy et de trop plus d'espérance que nul aultre seigneur du royaulme*".

have seen many of your Latin verses and even more of your English verses are extant" (1578, 2-7).[18]

Despite contemporary acclaim for Oxford's poetic output, little is now known of it because he, like all the courtier-poets of his generation, concealed his authorship of literary works. In the 16th Century noblemen considered poetry something to be written or enjoyed only in their "idle hours". A courtier's duty was primarily to arms, to Commonwealth and Crown; social custom prohibited him from publishing poetry or fiction under his own name. Even in manuscript, the literary courtier would sign his verse with quaint pseudonyms known as "poesies". The author of *Arte of English Poesie* (1589) writes that the nobility are "loath to be known of their skill" as poets and consequently "suffer it to be publisht without their owne names to it" (16). In this same book Oxford is ranked top among all the excellent poets of Elizabeth's court: "and in her Majesties time that now is are sprung up an other crew of Courtly makers Noble men and Gentlemen of her Majesties owne servants, who have written excellently well as it would appear if their doings could be found out and made public with the rest, of which number is first that noble Gentleman *Edward* Earle of Oxford ..." (49). Oxford's position as the pre-eminent poet of the English court, hinted as early as 1579 by Edmund Spenser in his portrait of "Cuddie", is confirmed by William Webbe in his *Discourse on English Poetrie*: "I may not omitte the deserved commendations of many honourable and noble Lordes and Gentlemen in Her Maiesties Courte, which in the rare devices of poetry, have beene and yet are most excellent skylfull; among whom the right honourable Earl of Oxford may challenge to himself the tytle of most excellent among the rest" (1586, sig. C iiiv). On a long list of poets drawn up by Henry Peacham in 1622, Oxford is placed first among those "refined wits and excellent spirits" who "in the time of our late Queene Elizabeth, which was truly a golden Age" had "honoured Poesie with their pennes and practice". The name "William Shakespeare" is noticeably absent from this list (95-6).

It is hardly surprising that a concealed poet, playwright, musician, and patron of Oxford's innate abilities and extravagant generosity should be associated, in the minds of his classically obsessed peers, with the patron god of poets and the Muses, Phoebus-Apollo. Those who liken Oxford to a modern-day Apollo include Chapman, Soothern, Lok, Lucas de Heere, Angel Day and John Lyly. Thomas Nashe explains of Oxford that he has purchased "high fame" by his pen: "being the

18 Originally in Latin.

first (in our language) I haue encountred, that repurified Poetrie from Arts pedantisme, & that instructed it to speake courtly. Our Patron, our Phoebus [Apollo], our first Orpheus or quintessence of inuention he is" (1596, M2^{v}).[19]

The admission in *Art of English Poesie* that nobles published their works without putting their owne names to them is confirmed by John Bodenham in *Bel-védere* (1600) who writes that Oxford's works are "extant among other Honourable personages writings" (sig. A^{5}), i.e. published under other men's names. Crawford identified over 200 lines in Bodenham's book that had elsewhere been published under the name "William Shakespeare" but found none that he could attribute to Oxford (1910). In Bodenham's ensuing list of "modern and extant poets that have lived together", the name William Shakspeare appears in the Apollonian centre (thirteenth of 25) of a large number of poets who can be individually linked to Oxford but who have no known connection to Stratford-Shakspere.

One of these is Thomas Nashe, who in 1592 was accused by Gabriel Harvey of "obscure lurking in basest corners". Nashe responded in a work called *Strange Newes:* "I lurke in no corners but conuerse in a house of credit as well gouerned as any Colledge, where there bee more rare quallified men, and selected good Schollers than in any Noblemans house that I knowe in England. If I had committed *such abhominable villanies, or were a base shifting companion,* it stoode not with my Lords honour to keepe me" (1592). Nashe does not name "my Lord" who "keeps" him in this remarkable household of scholars, but it is easy to identify him as the same patron whom elsewhere he identifies as "My Lord of Oxford". *Strange Newes* is dedicated to a pseudonymous patron, "Gentle M. William", who (like Oxford) is revealed to be an "infinite Maecenas to learned men", and (like Oxford) is a prolific poet who has lately run out of money, and (like Oxford) one who keeps three "maides" (his three daughters) under his roof, and whose "hospitality" has resulted in a scandal at the Archdeacons Court.

The Latin word *vere* means "truly" or "verily", and Nashe further betrays the identity of his pseudonymous dedicatee with the line:

19 Like many of Nashe's allusions to Oxford, this one does not name him, but internal evidence identifies Oxford as the only courtier famed for his poetry, who was also Nashe's patron, who served at Court, and was a knight companion in tilting tournaments with Sidney, and who lost the fortune of his youth. In this passage Nashe is responding to a living person to whom Harvey behaved condescendingly in his *Gratulationis Valdinensis* (1580), thus Detobel & Brackmann (2016, 108-9) show, by process of elimination, that Nashe can only be referring to Oxford.

"Verilie, verilie all poore Schollers acknowledge you as their patron, prouiditore and supporter".[20] When Nashe wrote of the "selected good Schollers" who acknowledge Oxford as their patron, he included poets and playwrights (1596, sig. V) such as Greene, Mundy, Lyly, Watson and Churchyard, whom he also referred to as "scholars".[21] It is from the Nashe-Harvey pamphlets that we learn (again indirectly) that the novelist, playwright and translator Robert Greene was another of Oxford's "secretaries".[22]

Why should Nashe's dedication to Oxford be anonymised? Why should Robert Greene's position within Oxford's secretariat be veiled? The answer lies in Oxford's shadowy position at the centre of a secret group of scholars, authors and poets writing and publishing learned works and propaganda pamphlets for the Crown. "I serve her Majesty and I am that I am", he wrote to Lord Burghley in an echo of Shakespeare's Sonnet 121: "I am that I am and they that level at my abuses reckon up their own". It is not known when Oxford began this service but Nelson places him at the centre of a literary propaganda group as early as 1580, when a number of his scholar-servants or "secretaries" (Abraham Fleming, Arthur Golding, Thomas Churchyard, Thomas Twynne, and Anthony Mundy) came together to write social propaganda pamphlets in the wake of the Dover Straits earthquake (223). Fleming assembled the essays into a single volume published by Henry Denham who made at least twelve books with him, including the vastly expanded second edition of Holinshed's *Chronicles*, instigated and corrected by Her Majesty's Privy Council, published under the royal imprimatur, and identified, not only as a singularly important source for Shakespeare, but as a significant contribution to "a deliberate movement to elevate the stature of England, English letters, and English language through writing and publishing maps, histories, national epics, and theoretical works on English poetry" (see Clegg 1997, 138). Another Fleming-

---

20 In old French the word *vere* means a "boar" hence Oxford's armorial crest (a boar passant) and his badge, or cognizance (a blue boar), displayed on his servants' livery. The 17 iterations of the word "boar" in *Venus & Adonis* may be an allusion to the poem's author, the 17th Earl of Oxford.

21 Nashe wrote that he was reckoned "amongst the famous Schollers of our time, as S. *Philip Sidney*, M. *VVatson*, M. *Spencer*, M. *Daniell*" in *Have with You to Saffron Waldon*, (sig. V).

22 In his dedication to *Strange Newes* — Nashe's rebuttal of Harvey's *Foure Letters* — Nashe defends Oxford against Harvey's slur of his being a "conny-catcher" (i.e., a con man). In a long tirade against Robert Greene, Harvey had written: "Lorde, what a lewde Companion was hee? What an egregious makeshift. Where should Conny-catchers have gotten such a Secretarie?" (25 D^2). Nashe is described as "sometimes secretary" to "Pierce Pennilesse" (the penniless peer, Lord Oxford) by Dekker in *News from Hell* (1606).

Denham production, Baret's four language dictionary, *Alvearie*, (1580), is cited by Koppelman & Wechsler (2014) and T.W. Baldwin (1944, 715) as a seminal source for Shakespeare. Can it be by chance alone that Mundy, Lyly, Greene, Nashe and others employed to defend the established Church (of which the Queen was "Supreme Governor") against the published onslaughts of the so-called Disciplinarians, happened also to be servants of Oxford and happened also to be poets and playwrights, cited by orthodox commentators as seminal influences on William Shakespeare?

In 1592, Nashe described a "policy of plays" as one of the "secrets of government", explaining that stage adaptations of wholesome English chronicles were "very necessary" to the moral wellbeing of a target audience of certain types — whom he identified as courtiers, lawyers, captains and soldiers (sig. F3).[23] He did not include university scholars, but they too were targets of the Privy Council's "policy of plays". The first allusion to a play *Hamlet*, dated to the summer of 1589, is contained in a lecture addressed by Nashe "To the Gentleman Students of Both Universities" in which he urges the scholars of Oxford and Cambridge to abandon the old school of Senecan translations and to embrace those "rare excersises in virtue", English chronicle plays (in Greene 1589).[24] In 1580 Oxford's theatre company was recommended to both universities by no fewer than three members of the Privy Council: the Lord Chamberlain (Sussex), the Lord Chancellor (Bromley), and the Lord Treasurer (Burghley) (in a letter from John Hatcher to Burghley on 21 June 1580, S.P. Dom., 139.26, quoted in Ward 267-68). Three years later, another core member of the Privy Council, Francis Walsingham, requested that Oxford's best actors be transferred to the newly formed Queen's Majesties Men under the management of John Lyly, who was, and remained, Oxford's secretary and director of his theatrical enterprises, including his public theatre at the Blackfriars.[25]

It would appear then that Oxford, patron and author of acclaimed poems and plays, was exerting a considerable influence on Court and public theatre, while simultaneously maintaining covert command of a government-sponsored program of learned, historical, moral and

23 Passage identified by a margent note ("The defence of Playes") from *Pierce Penilesse*.

24 Nashe writes: "if you intreate him faire in a frostie morning, he will affoord you whole *Hamlets*, I should say handfulls of tragical speaches."

25 For the relationship between Oxford's Men and the Queen's Men under Lyly see Ward (1928, 271-82); Oxford's friendship with Walsingham is referenced in a letter from Lord Henry Howard to the Queen (December 1580-January 1581), BL Cotton Titus C.6, ff 7-8.

didactic publications. Thus Harvey explained why "so many singular learned men laboured [Oxford's] commendation", for he was "the godfather of writers, the superintendent of the presse, the muster-maister of innumerable bands, the General of the feilde" (1593, 36).[26] In similar vein Oxford's in-laws, the Cecils, appear to have exerted a covert control over the public theatres used by the Chamberlain's and the King's Men. The Theatre, the Blackfriars and the Globe were all set up and managed by the Burbages, who were servants of the Cecils' long-serving right-hand man, Sir Walter Cope. Cope later became protector and benefactor of Oxford's daughter, Bridget.

In 1586, when Oxford's finances were in a parlous state, the Queen granted him an annuity of £1000 a year. Sir Francis Walsingham, the Queen's "spymaster" (Oxford's "constant and approved frend" according to Charles Howard (Nelson 200)) arranged for the money to be paid in quarterly instalments by a deed of grant which stipulated that he was to leave no account of expenditure, in wording almost identical to the formula applied to Walsingham's own secret service budget (see Ward 257). Thomas Wilson (1601) presumed Elizabeth's unprecedented generosity to have been "for his nobility's sake", but the naturally parsimonious queen set high store on Oxford's "innate learning" and "outstanding mind", did not give fortunes away for nothing at a time when the treasury was depleted due to expensive military actions against Spain. It is a curious fact that payments to the Master of Revels (the office responsible for theatrical performances at court) dropped by an average of £1048 per annum from 1587, (the year after Oxford's £1000 annuity was granted).[27] Oxford declared "I serve her Majesty", but during the last sixteen years of Elizabeth's reign, during which time she paid to him the enormous sum of £16,000, he cannot be shown to have held any important *public* position for the Crown, let alone one that would merit this colossal stipend. The government's "policy of plays" and its programme for national improvement through theatre, literature, poetry, and learning appears to have been conducted beneath the radar. Perhaps

---

26 Harvey, *Pierces supererogation*; in this passage Oxford is referred to as "Euphues" and Lyly as "Pap-hatchet".

27 Dietz (1923) records expenditures of the exchequer in just 21 years from the period 1560-1586. Payments to the Master of the Revels in these years add up to £22,560, 3s and 8d — an average of £1,074. 2 per annum in the years that have been accounted; after which Dietz records expenditures for every year from 1587 to 1602 inclusive, in which the total payments to the Master of Revels were £411. 2s and 2d (a single payment in 1594), making the average payment to the Master of the Revels in those 16 years, just £25.6 per annum.

it was to Oxford's £1000 salary that George Chapman alluded in *Tragedy of Chabot* when he wrote of "the corruption of a captain [that] may beget a gentleman-usher, and a gentleman usher may beget a lord, whose wit may beget a poet, and a poet may get a thousand pound a year" (1639, sig. H[2]). Perhaps it was to this that John Ward was alluding in 1662, when he recorded a Chinese whisper that William Shakespeare had "supplied y[e] stage with 2 plays every year, and for y[t] had an allowance so large, y[t] hee spent att y[e] rate of a 1000*l*. a year, as I have heard" (Ward in Severn 1839).

Two of Oxford's secretaries, Nashe and Greene, principal agents in the pamphlet wars, collaborated on plays together. Nashe also collaborated with Marlowe. Marlowe was arrested with Oxford's acolyte, Thomas Watson, for killing a man in a dispute over £14 owed to a tavern, the Pye Inn, Bishopsgate, "lying next the house of the Earl of Oxford" (Warner in Eccles 1934, 65). The tavern was owned by the celebrated actor Edward Alleyn and his brother, John. The Alleyns were represented by Watson's brother-in-law, Hugh Swift, one of the many lawyers known to be gracing Oxford's table at this time. Freeman locates Kyd among a circle of playwrights strongly associated with Oxford (Lyly, Watson, Peele and Achelley), while surviving letters from Kyd to Sir John Puckering show him to have collaborated with Marlowe on plays for "my Lord ... whom I have servd almost these six years, in credit until now" (in Freeman 1967, 13-21).[28] It is not possible to identify "my Lord" with certainty, but (like Oxford) he maintained an acting troupe and hired playwrights at least from 1587 and (like Oxford) was noted for his piety, and (like Oxford) was not a member of the Privy Council and held no powerful position in government. On this basis Oxford is the most likely patron to Kyd and Marlowe.[29] If Marlowe was indeed one of the many playwrights contributing to English chronicle plays under Oxford's patronage for the Crown's "secret policy of plays", evidence of his hand in the *Henry VI* plays finds a natural explanation; as does the extraordinary support given to him in 1587 by Whitgift, Burghley, Hunsdon, and other members of the Privy Council against defamers "ignorant of the affairs he went about" concerning his employment "in matters touching the benefit of this country" (PRO Privy Council Registers PC2/14/381).

Shakespeare's supposed "indebtedness" to Marlowe, Kyd, Watson,

28 Kyd's two letters to Sir John Puckering [MS Harl. 6849, ff.218-19 and MS Harl. 6848, f. 154] are transcribed in Appendix A (181-83).

29 Oxford's piety is attested by Orazio Cuoco (1577), who also confirms his liberality toward non-Anglicans, for which see Magri (2014, 199-211); Andrew Trollop (1587) writes that Oxford was "imbued with special piety"; Gervase Markham (1622) called him "*Honestas, pietas & Magnanimus*."

Lyly, Greene, Nashe and other "Cambridge wits" among Oxford's circle is richly documented. Whole phrases from their works are said to have been lifted by Shakespeare, yet the orthodox Bard was known neither to Oxford, nor to a single one of the many writers in his entourage. Was Shakespeare really in thrall to all these playwrights as the orthodox suppose, or did they work under Oxford (as assistants to a master) on the original drafts of history plays later said to be Shakespeare's?

2. Enter "Shakespeare"

In the late spring or early summer of 1593, the name "William Shakespeare" was associated for the first time with literature when it appeared beneath a dedicatory epistle to the prominent courtier, Henry Wriothesley, 3rd Earl of Southampton, then engaged to Oxford's oldest daughter, Elizabeth. The work was *Venus & Adonis*, a polished, bawdy, narrative poem, rooted both in the Latin of Ovid's *Metamorphoses* and in its English translation made by Oxford's uncle, Arthur Golding. In courtly language "Shakespeare" promised Southampton he would compose some greater work "in my idle hours"[30] said to be *Lucrece* (1594), another long poem also dedicated to Southampton, derived from the *Fasti* of Ovid, that were not translated into English until 1640. From these facts alone the literary sleuth of 1594 would have guessed that the new poet calling himself "Shakespeare" was a scholar and able Latinist, well known within court and literary circles and from these facts alone, he would have discounted Stratford-Shakspere as their author. Indeed, in a comedy performed by the students of Cambridge University (*Returne from Parnassus Part 1*, c. 1600), a wealthy patron and Shakespeare fanatic commissions an impoverished scholar to write a poem for his mistress in the style of Shakespeare. When the parody of *Venus & Adonis* is read to him, the delighted patron exclaims: "Noe more! I am one that can judge according to the proverb, *bovem ex unguibus*." Here the Shakespeare-lover has altered the well-known saying "*leonem ex unguibus aestimare*" ("to know a lion by its claws") to "*bovem ex unguibus*" ("to know an ox by its hoof"), a joke easily comprehensible to those who knew that Oxford was referred to by his contemporaries as "Ox", and

30 Detobel (2014) traces the history of the European tradition prohibiting noblemen from writing poetry except in their "idle hours", quoting early examples, e.g., German poet, Hartmann von Aue (1160-1210): "A knight who learned was / And from the books did read / When he had no better use / for his hours / also wrote poems". Thus Detobel believes Shakespeare revealed himself as a courtier in his dedication to *Venus and Adonis*.

thus the hand of Oxford has been recognised in these Shakespearean lines (IV.i.1223-24; see Macray 1886).[31]

Despite the bawdy and secular content of *Venus* the poem was licenced for publication by none other than the Archbishop of Canterbury, John Whitgift, whom Oxford's team had been assiduously defending from the Disciplinarians. Field was to become the favoured printer of Oxford's father-in-law, Lord Burghley, to whom he dedicated one of his most important publications, *The Arte of English Poesie.*

Magri provides evidence that in *Venus* Shakespeare draws from a specific copy of a painting (the "Barberini" *Venus & Adonis* by Titian) which was on display at Titian's studio in Venice when Oxford was living there in 1575 (in Malim 2004, 79-90), while Delahoyde shows that an ekphrastic description of a painting of the siege of Troy in Shakespeare's *Lucrece* appears to describe the unique details of a mural by Giulio Romano at the Palazzo Ducale in Mantua (2006, 51-66). Shakespeare praises Giulio Romano by name in *The Winter's Tale,* but orthodox scholars cannot explain how Stratford-Shakspere came into contact with this artist's work, which was only to be found painted onto the walls of the private apartments and chapels of Italian dukes.

Although at least 15 plays from the Shakespeare canon are known to have existed before 1598, there is no record of any *dramatist* called "William Shakespeare" until that year, when plays (as opposed to poems) first appeared in print under that name. Between 1593 and 1597 *all* the records pertaining to literary "Shakespeare" concern only his two published poems. Why Oxford should have chosen the pen-name "William Shakespeare" is a matter for conjecture. In 1628 the theologian Thomas Vicars suggested it was chosen as a verb-object compound of "shake" and "spear."[32] The most famous "will" ever to have shaken a spear was, of course, that of Pallas-Minerva, whose will caused the spear of Achilles to shake in his right hand, thus empowering it to slay Hector.[33] Many English Renaissance poets appealed to this patron-goddess of learning and eloquence for help in writing their

---

31 Charles Arundel (c. 1581) repeatedly referred to Oxford as "Ox" and, in one letter complained of his being confined to his chamber for four months "while Ox was grazing in the pastures" (SP 12/151/44, f. 99).

32 "*Istis annumerandos censeo, celebrem illum poetam qui a quassatione & hasta nomen habet…*" ("To these [Chaucer, Spenser, Drayton and Wither] I believe should be added that famous poet who takes a name from *shaking* and *spear*").

33 Ovid (*Metamorphoses* VII, 79) describes Achilles' "*vibrantia tela*", as opposed to "*vibrans tela*", the distinction being that his spear did its own shaking and was not shaken by the arm of Achilles (see also n. 94).

verses, and Oxford was no exception.[34] Roman dramatists held their assemblies at the Temple of Minerva on the Aventine. Gosson (1582), Stubbes (1583) and "I.G" (1615) all confirm that Pallas-Minerva, the spear-shaker, was regarded by their English contemporaries as the patron goddess of playwrights[35] and Oxford is associated with the image of Achilles (whose "heart and mind" was instructed by Pallas and whose spear was shaken by her will), in works by Harvey, Lyly, Baker and others.[36] In Shakespeare's *Lucrece* (line 1473) a seemingly irrelevant interposition of a passage about Achilles' spear guided by the invisible will of Pallas-Minerva suggests the hidden author behind the shaking spear of the poet's pen-name, while vividly recalling Harvey's 1578 description of Oxford as an Achilles reborn, inhabited by the spirits of Mars, Pallas-Minerva and Bellona: "Mars keeps thy mouth, Minerva lies hidden in thy right hand and Bellona reigns in thy body, thine eyes flash, thy will shakes spears; who would not swear that Achilles had come to life again?"[37]

That Oxford, in the 1590s, was disgraced and ostracised from the life of the court is evidenced by the uncharacteristic absence of records pertaining to him at this time and by his failure to secure a single vote in successive elections to the Companion of the Garter where once his name was popular and prominent. The title page of *Venus* (1593) hints at contemporary scandal. Juno, the goddess of fertility, is depicted in

34 Arthur Brooke in his *Romeus and Juliet*, a primary source for Shakespeare's play, wrote: "In moorning verse, a wofull chaunce / To tell I will assaye. / Helpe learned Pallas, helpe. / When none of you will scarce credit / That ere it was so bad: / Well, yet I would assay / To tell it, if I might, / But O Minerva, helpe me aye." Oxford, in his poem "Desire of Fame" (1575), wrote: "For Pallas first, whose filed flowing skill / Should guide my pen some pleasant words to write."

35 "Playes are the institution of the Diuell himselfe, and the practize of Heathen people nouzeled in ignorance: seing they took originall from Paganisme, and were dedicated to their Idol-Gods, as now also they are the house, stage and apparell to *Venus*, the musicke to *Apollo*, the penning to *Minerva* ...." I.G (1615, 58); see also Stephen Gosson (1582) and Phillip Stubbes (1583), for earlier presentiments of this point.

36 Harvey in *Gratulationis Valdiensis* (1578) writes: "*Anglia te Patrium iamque experietur Achillem...Pallas pectusque, animumque Instruet ipsatuum*" ("England shall find in you her homegrown Achilles...Pallas will instruct your heart and mind"); "I.L." (assumed to be Lyly) in *An answer to the Untruths*, London (1589), writes of Oxford (1598): "His tusked Boar 'gan foam for inward ire / While Pallas filled his breast with warlike fire".

37 From Gabriel Harvey's address to Oxford in *Gratulationes Valdinenses*: "*Mars occupat ora: Minerva in dextra latitat: Bellona in corpore regnat: Martius ardor inest; scintillant lumina; vultus tela vibrat: quis non rediuiuum iuret Achellem?*" — the controversy as to whether "*vultus*" can be translated as "will" instead of "countenance" is settled by multiple editions of Elyot's Latin-English Dictionary (1528, 1542 and 1545) where it is explained that "*vultus* of olde wryters is taken for *wylle*" (see also n. 90).

the headpiece beneath which a Latin quotation implies that the poet has chosen to set, in pure Apollonian verse, such vile matter as is marvelled at by the vulgar.[38] The sonnets of "Shake-speare", written in the first person, explain that their author is embroiled in a scandal, that his "name receives a brand" (111), he is "despised" (37), "shamed" (72) and "vile esteemed" (121), "in disgrace with fortune and men's eyes"; he has made himself "a motley to the view" (90); he feels "all alone" and beweeps his "outcast state" (29); he suffers a "bewailed guilt" (36) because of a "vulgar scandal stamped upon [his] brow" (112), and so Oxford wrote movingly of "the losse of my good name" in a poem ("Fram"d in the front of forlorne hope") which Nelson reasons "might have been connected to any of the numerous scandals in Oxford's life" (388).

Orthodox scholars accept that the contemporary printed allusions to Shakespeare are "cryptic", but have made little effort to explain why this should be the case, or to unravel their hidden meanings. Instead they are dismissed as of no biographical value.[39] But to understand Shakespeare the man, it is necessary to understand what his contemporaries wrote about him and since the majority of these allusions are set as cryptic verses, it is beholden upon the biographer to investigate their deeper meanings.

In the whole decade of the 1590s Shakespeare's name appears only five times in printed allusions. All of these instances point to Oxford as the poet behind the pseudonym, and all but one hint at a scandal. These five references, each glossed below, use typical ciphering techniques of the period — puns, allusions, symbols, acrostics, anagrams, charades and such devices as were commonly used by writers of the "Jacobethan" age to avoid censorship or prosecution for libel. Defamation of a nobleman was a treasonable offence tried by the Star Chamber, for whom "Nobility

38 "*Vilia miretur vulgus: mihi flavus Apollo / Pocular Castalia plena ministret aqua*" from Ovid, *Amores*, I, xv, 35-36.

39 In *Shakespeare Beyond Doubt* (2013), Stanley Wells boggles at the "cryptic nature" of *Groatsworth* (79), calling Skoloker's 1604 allusion to Shakespeare in "*Diaphantus*" [sic]: "a cryptic allusion" (79) and suggesting that Davies of Hereford's epigram to Shakespeare is "somewhat obscure in its allusiveness" (79). In email correspondence with the present author (13 October 2013) Wells remarks of Covell's allusion to Shakespeare (1595): "certainly the author was deliberately being cryptic, like the author of *Willobie his Avisa*. But I have no solution to the puzzles he poses"; of the inscription on Shakespeare's Stratford monument Wells writes that it "somewhat cryptically calls upon the passer-by to pay tribute to his greatness as a writer", (2003, 47-48). David Ellis, reviewing James Shapiro's *1606: The Year of Lear* (March 2016) writes: "almost all the fifty or so references to [Shakespeare] by contemporaries which E. K. Chambers collected together are, from a biographical point of view, worthless".

and men of mark" were considered "the flowers that stand about the Prince's Crown garnishing and giving a grace to it: to deface any one of them is an open injury offered to the Crown itself" (Anon 1590, sig. B²). It was therefore treasonable to publish — in print or written letter — the reasons for Oxford's infamy, to identify him as an agent of the crown, or to name him as the play-maker "Shakespeare". This explains quite simply why all the extant references to literary Shakespeare are cryptic and why they need to be read with special attention. The five printed references to literary Shakespeare of the 1590s are as follows:

a. Willobie his Avisa. *Willobie his Avisa* (1594) is a long, anonymous, tongue-in-cheek poem that contains the first printed third-party allusion to the poet "Shake-speare". Scholars have long been intrigued by this work, which narrates the attempts of six suiters to seduce the lady Avisa and which was censored, with others critical of Oxford, by Archbishop Whitgift in 1599. Toward the end of the poem appears an "old player" (referred to only as "W.S.") spouting jumbled parodies of lines from Shakespeare's *Passionate Pilgrim* and Oxford's *A Lover Rejected Complaineth*, while advising a "new actor" ("H.W.") how to seduce Avisa. The coincidence of "W.S." and "H.W." sharing a mistress, just as "William Shakespeare" and Henry Wriothesley, Earl of Southampton appear also to share a mistress in "Shake-speares Sonnets" (41 and 144) was first noticed by Collier in 1858. While the identifications of "W.S." and "H.W." as Shakespeare and Southampton have been accepted by some orthodox scholars, all remain oblivious to the inherent dangers that this poses to Stratfordianism, for attentive study reveals that "W.S.", who first appears in the 44th canto of the poem, is making not his first, but his *second* appearance in the work, under different initials. "W.S." (who admits to having already tried his luck with Avisa), is easily identifiable as the same character as Avisa's second suitor (Cantos 23-33) who appears under the initials "D.B.", a once rich, but lately impoverished, overly generous, musical, playwriting, poetical lord and patron. In his attempt to seduce Avisa "D.B." had kept up a "continued course of courtesy, with Jewles, Rings, Gold and divers gifts" (Canto 23); when he returns as "W.S." he advises the young "H.W." to "apply Avisa with Divers things, sometimes with gold sometimes with rings" (Canto 47), a conceit that was noted by Lee (1895) as constituting "identical counsel" and "in the same metre" as the advice offered to the wooer in Shakespeare's poem "When as thine eye hath chose the Dame" from *Passionate Pilgrim*. Likewise "D.B." is said to "smile while others smart" (Canto 27) while on his reappearance as "W.S." he "takes pleasure for a time to see H.W. bleed" (Canto 44). When "D.B." informs Avisa that he has portrayed her in his literary works, she responds, "O Mightie Lord, that guides the Spheare; Defend me by thy mightie will". In this, the hasty reader may perceive only an appeal to God, but those who recall how the will of Pallas went to the defence of Achilles, (who promptly exclaimed "Pallas guides my spear!") may note the association between the will of this poetical Lord ("D.B.") and the name of the poet ("Will Shake-speare") who "paints poore Lucrece rape". Allusions to Shakespeare and Oxford in both the "D.B." and "W.S." Cantos could have left *Willobie's* learned contemporary readership in no doubt that Oxford was hiding behind the initials "W.S.", which stood for "William Shake-speare."

b. William Covell. The second printed reference to "Shakespeare" the poet appears in a book called *Polimanteia* (1595). In an essay concerning the alumni of Oxford, Cambridge and the Inns of Courts the words "Sweet Shakspeare" are set as a margent note by a line containing a unique and cryptic epithet "courte-deare-verse";

eaſie in ſuch ſimplicitie) deluded by
All praiſe worthy. dearlie beloued *Delia*, and fortunatelie
Lucrecia fortunate *Cleopatra*; *Oxford* thou maiſt
Sweet Shak-ſpeare. extoll thy courte-deare-verſe happie
Eloquent Gaueſton. *Daniell*, whoſe ſweete refined muſe, in
contracted ſhape, were ſufficient a-

This epithet contains the letters of "our de Vere" in their correct word and letter order, allowing the remaining letters (t, r, e, s, c, e and a) to form a perfect anagram of "a secret". Thus the message glossed by the margent "Sweet Shak-speare" reads "our de Vere — a secret" with the words "de Vere" neatly placed beneath the italicized name of the poet's title "*Oxford*". While orthodox scholars affect to disbelieve the intentionality of this cipher, none has yet succeeded in offering any explanation as to how the margent "Sweet Shak-speare" serves to explain, elucidate or contribute anything to the line by which it has been so precisely and conspicuously affixed.

c. Richard Barnfield. The third printed reference to Shakespeare of the 1590s is provided by Richard Barnfield in a poem called "A Remembrance of some English Poets" (1598). Spenser, Daniel and Drayton are praised in separate stanzas of four lines each, while the fourth and final stanza, addressed to Shakespeare, is extended to six lines by an extra couplet:

And *Shakespeare*, thou, whose hony-flowing Vaine,
(Pleasing the World) thy Praises doth obtaine.
Whose *Venus*, and whose *Lucrece* (sweet, and chast)
Thy Name in fames immortall Booke have plac't.
  Live ever you, at least in Fame live ever:
  Well may the Bodye dye, but Fame dies never.

The surface meaning of these lines is obvious ("Shakespeare's works should live for ever") but a closer reading reveals a critical attitude to the poet. The repeated reference, "in fames" and "in Fame" (lines 4 and 5) invokes old definitions of "infame", defined as: "ill fame, infamous, an infamous person, one branded with infamy" (OED). By placing the word "ever" twice in line 5, and ending lines 5 and 6 with "ever" and "never" Barnfield invokes Oxford in a word-game that would have been easily recognisable to his contemporaries. Here the pun allows for a paraphrase of Barnfield's last two lines: "Your name be placed in the immortal leger of infamy; live E.Ver, at least live, E.Ver, by your infamy, for though you shall die, your evil repute will never be forgotten". In the final couplet Barnfield switches pronouns from "thou/thy" to "you" which, at first glance, appears to shift his address from Shakespeare to *all* of the poets previously named (Spenser, Daniel, Drayton, *and* Shakespeare); however, the double use of "in fame" establishes a connection between the addressee of the quatrain (Shakespeare — "thy/thou") and the addressee of the final couplet (E. Vere — "you"). While a pseudonymous poet ("Shakespeare") would be informally addressed as "thee/thou", a nobleman would be formally addressed by a commoner as "you".

d. Francis Meres. The fourth allusion to Shakespeare from the 1590s appears in a book called *Palladis Tamia* (1598) by theologian and numerologist, Francis Meres. In a chapter entitled "A comparative discourse of our English Poets, with the Greeke Latine and Italian Poets" Meres compares English poets with equal numbers of classical or Italian poets, beginning each paragraph with an "as" clause and proceeding to a "so" clause. Thus a typical example sets six Italian poets against six English poets: "As Italy had *Dante, Boccace, Petrarch, Tasso, Celiano* and *Ariosto*: so England had *Mathew Roydon, Thomas Atchelow, Thomas Watson, Thomas Kid, Robert Greene* & *George Peele*". When not arranging his classical and English authors symmetrically (as above), Meres adopts a pattern of "trinities" based on the holy observation with which he opens his dedication to Thomas Eliot "*Tria sunt omnia*" (Three is all): "As Greece had three Poets of great antiquity, *Orpheus, Linus* and *Musaeus*; and *Italy*, other three auncient Poets, *Livius Andronicus, Ennius* & *Plautus*: so hath England three auncient Poets, *Chaucer*, *Gower* and *Lydgate*".

On the surface Meres is simply informing his readers that England can match any other nation for poetry, but by arranging poets into structured, symmetrical or triadic patterns, he is also pursuing a deeper theological agenda that aims to silence Puritan objections to poetry as "ungodly" by proving poetry an emanation of God's will. His adherence to his method is persistent; only four of his 58 paragraphs (7, 34, 37 & 39) appear to abandon triadic or symmetrical structures and on close inspection even these anomalies are shown to be illusory. In three of them (7, 37 and 39) Meres uses a single name to represent two different persons, thus even these paragraphs are, like the others, symmetrically or triadically balanced.[40]

In the fourth anomalous paragraph (34) the names "Edward Earle of Oxforde" and "Shakespeare" are among the 17 English poets listed as "best for Comedy" and the appearance of both names on the same list has prompted some to suppose that Meres knew them to be two different people. James Shapiro writes: "Crushingly, for those who want to believe that the Earl of Oxford and Shakespeare were one and the same writer, Meres names both and distinguishes between them, including both Edward Earl of Oxford and Shakespeare in his list of the best writers of comedy" (2010, 268). Careful consideration of Meres' method and purpose, however, reveals the very opposite to be the case: that Meres was aware of Oxford's use of the pseudonym "Shakespeare" and, like other writers in the 1590s, ciphered this fact into his published work.

At first glance paragraph 34 appears to set 16 classical poets against 17 English, where the reader would expect a symmetrical balance (16:16) in conformity with his policy; but Meres is again deceiving the unwary reader, this time by employing *two* names to represent *a single* playwright. It is no accident that this 16:17 imbalance should occur in paragraph 34,

40 This discovery was first made by Detobel & Ligon (2009), in which they supposed the four anomalous paragraphs to be 7, 34, 46, and 39. However, paragraph 46 is symmetrically balanced (6:6), but its allusion to unnamed and unnumbered "translators of Senecas Tragedies" causes confusion. In private email correspondence with the present author Robert Detobel confirms that 37, not 46, is the fourth anomalous paragraph. In 37 *one* classical name, *Mymnerus Collophonius*, is used to represent *two* persons. Nineteenth century reprints of this passage (e.g., Egerton Brydges and Joseph Haslewood) inserted a comma between Mymnerus and Colophonius to indicate that they were two different authors (Mymnerius and Nicander, also known as "Colophonius"), but Meres deliberately omits the comma, thus creating the allusion of one name (*Mymnerus Collophonius*) referring to a single comic poet, known as "Mymnerius of Colophon".

for the number 34 contains two 17s and the deciphering reader is invited to ask: if *two* names refer to just *one* playwright, and if the overspill occurs on the English side with 17 names (the highest number on any list in the entire "Discourse"), is no. 17 somehow doubled in paragraph 34? In other words, is there an English poet represented by the number "17", who appears twice among the English poets under two different names? As the name "Shakespeare" is placed in the Apollonian centre of the English list (9th of 17), so the "Earle of Oxforde" is placed in the Apollonian centre of *all* of the poets in paragraph 34 (17th of 33).[41] Thus is Oxford identified as number "17" not only by virtue of his position as the 17th playwright in Paragraph 34, but also by virtue of his title, 17th Earl of Oxford. Having established Oxford as number 17 (the central poet), the reader now needs to restore the Classical / English symmetry of Meres' paragraph 34 to 16:16 by identifying and eliminating his double.

Oxford's name appears first on the English list because (according to some) Meres considered him the best of the English comic playwrights, or (according to others) because of his social rank. But, to a numerologist like Meres, "*unus non est numerus*", or, as Clapham explains in his *Bibliotecha Theologica* (1597), "One properly is no number". In Shakespeare's Sonnet 136 the poet explains his desire to disappear into nothing behind the pseudonym "Will": "My name is Will" he writes "and my will one, among a number one is reckon'd none / Then in the number let me passe untold." By treating Oxford as "none" (zero), and laying the sixteen classical poets above his name alongside the sixteen English poets below it, Stritmatter (2014) discovered that Meres had carefully paired each of the classical playwrights to an English counterpart. For example, Menander (first on the classical side) pairs with Gager (first on the English side) because Menander was the imitator of Euripides and Gager the adapter of Euripides; Lyly, who wrote a famous comedy about nymphs (*Love's Metamorphosis*) is paired with Alexis Terius (fourth) who wrote a play called *The Nymphs*; Nicostratus and Lodge (fifth) are paired because Nicostratus wrote *The Moneylender* and Lodge's most famous play, *A Looking Glass for London* (1592), is about a moneylender; Amipsas and Gascoigne (sixth) are paired because Amipsas wrote *The Adulterers* and Gascoigne caused an infamous scandal with bawdy poems about adultery in 1573, and so on and so forth. Observing this consistent

41 For the symbolic importance of numerical centrality to English Renaissance thought see Fowler (1970, 23-32). Fowler here quotes Catari (1647) on the reasons for Apollo's position in the midst of the Muses: "The central position is given to Apollo not only here but also in the universe, because he diffuses his virtue through all things — which is why he is called the heart of heaven" (24).

pattern, Stritmatter asks why Meres should have paired Shakespeare with Aristonymos (both eighth on their respective lists), for nothing is known of Aristonymos except that his name means "noble name" or "aristocratic name". Since Oxford is the only poet with an aristocratic name among the seventeen English playwrights, Meres thus exposes Shakespeare as Oxford's sought-for double. Oxford (as Shakespeare) assumes the Apollonian position at the centre of the English playwrights (9th of 17), while the apparent asymmetry of paragraph 34 (16:17) is restored to balance with 16 classical playwrights set against 16 English playwrights, one of whom (no. 17) uses two names.

e. John Weever. Meres' technique of number-doubling to link the author to his pseudonym (his "double") was also used by John Weever in *EPIGRAMMES* (1599), in the fifth and final appearance of Shakespeare's name in printed sources of the 1590s. In his Epigram 11 ("Fourth Weeke") Weever mocks a "certain writer" called "Spurius" who has composed a brazen poem about Venus (sig. E^{2b}).[42] Since Shakespeare's infamous *Venus & Adonis* (1593) had been printed in no fewer than four editions by 1599, it would have been obvious to Weever's contemporaries that "Spurius" was "William Shakespeare", and since the word "spurious" means "not really proceeding from its reputed origin, source or author" (*OED*), Weever's readers would naturally have inferred that "Spurius" had published *Venus & Adonis* under a pseudonym. The "doubling" technique is confirmed by turning from this "Spurius" epigram (11) to its double (22), in which witty verses about a poet, who has also written bawdily about Venus, reveal Spurius' double to be none other than "William Shakespeare". Epigram 22 begins: "Honie-tong'd *Shakespeare* when I saw thine issue / I swore Apollo got them and none other". This unrhymed couplet is rich in meaning, the most obvious being that Weever supposed "Apollo", not "William Shakespeare", to be the true author of Shakespeare's works. As already shown, it is Oxford who is cast as "Apollo" ("our chief") among his contemporaries and since Weever intended his epigrams to be biting topical satires, it may fitfully be assumed that he was here reposting the "secret" of his Cambridge tutor, William Covell, that "sweet Shakespeare" is the pseudonym of "our de Vere" (*ibid*, A7a).[43]

---

42 Weever, "Fourth Weeke", Epig. 11 (sig. E^{2b}): *In Spurium quendam scriptorem*: "*Apelles* did so paint *Venus* Queene, / That most supposed he had faire *Venus* seene, / But thy bald rimes of *Venus* savour so, / That I dare sweare thou dost all *Venus* know".

43 "To the generous Readers" (A7a); this entire pamphlet is reproduced in facsimile in Honigmann (1987).

Thus are all five printed allusions to the literary name Shakespeare of the 1590s all shown to be carefully conceived conundrums each, by devious means, revealing "Shakespeare" (or "Shake-speare") to be the pseudonym of the central concealed poet and playwriting patron known to his contemporaries as the "poetical Earl of Oxford" (Wood 1691, 795).

3. Exit Oxford

On 24 June 1604 Oxford died at his house at Hackney having transferred his few remaining assets to members of his family in the weeks before his death. "Shakespeare", who drew upon hundreds of published literary and scholarly sources, cannot be shown with any degree of confidence to have derived anything from any printed source published after 1604. In the seven years from 1597 to Oxford's death, no fewer than thirteen new Shakespeare titles were published or registered for publication, many with title-pages proclaiming authorial correction, revision or augmentation. But immediately following his death the Shakespearean production-line fell silent. No new Shakespeare title appeared in print for four years except for a King's Men comedy called *The London Prodigal*, falsely ascribed on its title page "By W Shakespeare" in 1605. As J. T. Looney noted, there was "nothing more published with any appearance of proper authorization for nearly 20 years" (1975, 357).

The anonymous author of a 1605 pamphlet (*Voiage into Rushia*) described recent murders at the Russian court of Boris Godunov as "a first but no second to any *Hamlet*", naming playwrights who might have adapted this real-life Russian tragedy for the stage — Sidney, Jonson, Fulke Greville, and du Bartas. Despite his knowledge of *Hamlet* the author does not mention Shakespeare by name, but continues: "I am with the late *English* quick-spirited, cleare-sighted *Ovid*: It is to be feared Dreaming" (K & K2^{v}).[44] Here the author appears to be referring to Oxford, whom Harvey had publicly described as "this English Poet" who is "winged like to Mercury" (i.e., "quick-spirited"), "eyed like to Argus" (i.e., "clear-sighted") and "nos'd like to Naso" (i.e., resembling "Ovid"). Oxford was reported by historian Thomas Coxeter (1689-1747) to have been a translator of Ovid and was nephew and patron to Shakespeare's favourite translator of Ovid, Arthur Golding. Stratford-Shakspere did not die until 1616 and could not have qualified as "late" in 1605, yet Francis Meres (1598) describes Shakespeare as possessed

44 See also Cole (May 2014)

of the "sweete wittie soule of Ovid" and when the author and *Hamlet* fan explains that this "late English Ovid" had written that "it is to be feared dreaming" he is surely referring to Hamlet's famous "to-be-or-not-to-be" speech:

> To die, to sleep -
> To sleep - perchance to dream: ay, there's the rub,
> For in that sleep of death what dreams may come
> When we have shuffled off this mortal coil,
> Must give us pause (III.i).

Moments before delivering this great monologue, Hamlet is seen "poring uppon a booke" (Q1), which scholars since 1839 (see Douce 1839, 238; Hunter 1845, 243) have identified as *Cardanus Comforte,* whose English editions of 1573 and 1576 were not only dedicated to Oxford but also expressly "*published by commaundement of the right honourable the Earle of Oxenford*", who knew the work in Italian and, in his own words, had "long desired" to have it published in English to "comfort the afflicted, confirme the doubtful, encourage the cowarde, and lift up the base minded man" (1573). Of all contemporary books *Cardanus Comforte* was most assuredly "Oxford's book". In 1934 Stratfordian scholar Hardin Craig concluded: "without exaggeration that *Cardanus' Comforte* is pre-eminently "Hamlet's book," since the philosophy of Hamlet agrees to a remarkable degree with that of Cardan" (1934, 18).

The provenance of the sole surviving Elizabethan manuscript (c. 1585-95) of any acknowledged "Shakespearean" work can be traced to the ownership of a cousin of Oxford's, Anne Cornwallis, whose father acquired Oxford's mansion, Fisher's Folly, in the early 1590s. Bound as *Poems of Vere Earl of Oxford & Co*, this unascribed transcription of Poem XVIII from Shakespeare's *Passionate Pilgrim* is held in the Folger Shakespeare Library in Washington, D.C.[45] The sale of Oxford's last home, King's Place, Hackney in 1608 by his down-scaling widow is cited by some Oxfordians as a possible reason why several Shakespeare works appeared for the first time in print four years after Oxford's death. *King Lear,* for instance, was published in a quarto edition as "by William Shak-

45 Once the "Cornwallis-Lysons MS", now catalogued as "Leaves from a poetical miscellany of Anne Campbell, Countess of Argyll" (Folger V.a.89), an anthology of poems from the 1570s and 1580s, bound as "MSS Poems by Vere Earl of Oxford & Co", inscribed "Anne Cornwaleys her booke"; Halliwell-Phillipps dated it 1585-90 but the presence of one poem, "When as thine eye hath chose the dame", printed in *Passionate Pilgrime* under Shakespeare's name (1599), confounds the orthodox scholar and the Folger Library consequently dates it "c. 1600".

speare" in 1608. Based on ancient chronicles, this play tells of a widower who ostracises himself by alienating his ancient patrimony to his three daughters, precisely mirroring Oxford's alienation of the 500-year-old seat of the Vere family (Castle Hedingham in Essex) to his three daughters after the death of his first wife in 1588. Scholars accept that this poor quarto was not overseen by the author while recent attempts by James Shapiro to assign the composition of *Lear* to 1606 are comprehensively undone in the critical anthology, *Contested Year: Errors, Omissions and Unsupported Statements in James Shapiro's "1606 Year of Lear"* (Anderson, Waugh & McNeil 2016).

In 1609 a quarto edition of *Troilus & Cressida* was published as "written by William Shakespeare". Following Clark, some Oxfordians suppose this work to have originated in the lost play *Agememnon & Ulysse* performed by Oxford's boys at Court in 1584, to which comic interludes about Pandarus and the two lovers were added in the 1590s (1931, 449-55). A record in the Stationers' Register shows that *Troilus* (or some version of it) had been publicly performed by the Chamberlain's Men sometime before February 1603; prior to this, the play appears to have been "stayed" by "grand possessors", but a manuscript copy evidently escaped the censors. A prefatory epistle published in one of the 1609 quartos that states the play has never been performed in public, may therefore be confidently dated to sometime *before* documentation of a public performance in the Stationers' Register for 1603. The epistle is addressed to the "Eternal reader" and bears the title "A Never Writer, to an Ever Reader. News" ("an E.Vere writer to an E.Vere reader"?), suggesting that Oxford wrote it himself (c. 1595-1602), and addressed it to future readers whom, he hoped, might encounter the play in print after the censors' ban was lifted. Also in 1609 appeared for the first time in print a book entitled SHAKE-SPEARES SONNETS. The orthography of "Shake-speare" (with the name hyphenated on the title page and running header throughout the book) and the dedication to "OVR EVER-LIVING POET" has led many to suppose that the name was a pseudonym of a poet who (like Oxford) was deceased at the time of publication.

One of Oxford's official duties as hereditary High Chamberlain of England was to attend to the security and comfort of the Queen on her visits to Westminster Hall. Even today the Chamberlain of England greets and escorts the Queen into the Hall at openings of Parliament. In Oxford's day Elizabeth alighted from her boat on the Thames, and it was his function as High Chamberlain to escort her to the Hall under an elaborate canopy carried on poles by men of honour and high dignity. When Shake-speare writes (Sonnet 125) "Were it ought to me I bore the canopy / With my extern and outward honouring", authorship enquiry points away from Stratford-Shakspere (who would never have been permitted to carry the Queen's canopy) and toward Oxford, who was uniquely responsible for the bearing of the canopy on these occasions. Not only does the "Shake-speare" of the sonnets write as a learned, sophisticated 40-year-old nobleman, but he describes himself three times as "lame" (Sonnets 37 & 89), just as Oxford deplores his own lameness three times in letters to Burghley and Cecil. Moore shows that the three epithets that Shakespeare applies to himself in Sonnet 37 ("poor", "lame", and "despised") all reflect the documentary record for Oxford at a time when Stratford-Shakspere was prospering with no hint of poverty, lameness or scandal (2009, 234-39).

Stratfordian scholar, Alastair Fowler, demonstrates how Shake-speare's 154 sonnet sequence is structured geometrically and numerically as an equilateral triangle based on the number 17 — a number of considerable significance to Oxford (2004, 183-90). In many of these poems Shake-speare bewails his tainted reputation, expressing his belief that his name will be obliterated from the record, so that only his work will live on: "If you read this line, remember not the hand that writ it" (71); "In me each part will be forgotten … your monument shall be my gentle verse" (81); "My name be buried where my body is and live no more to shame nor me nor you" (72); "After my death … forget me quite" (72); "no longer mourn me when I am dead … do not so much as my poor name rehearse" (71); "I once gone to all the world must die" (81); "I'll live in this poor rhyme … and thou in this shall find thy monument" (107); "not marble, nor the gilded monuments of princes, shall outlive this powerful rhyme" (55).

Following Thorpe's edition of the Sonnets in 1609, no new work by Shakespeare appeared in print for 13 years — a long silence that was eventually broken by printer Thomas Walkley, who in 1622 printed *Othello* in the same year as he professed himself a dutiful servant of the Vere family, dedicating another of his books to three of Oxford's grandchildren and praising his "virtuous" daughter, Elizabeth.

Oxford was buried in the church of St Augustine, Hackney. In her will his widow, Elizabeth (*née* Trentham), expressed her desire for her body to be placed "as neare unto the bodie of my said late deare and noble lorde and husband as maye bee.... Onelie I will that there be in the said Church erected for us a tombe fitting our degree." An uncarved and uninscribed tomb of grey marble, said to be that of the Earl of Oxford, was destroyed when the church was demolished in the 1790s, but its image has survived. Sometime after March 1616 William Basse, who, according to Sidney Lee, may have been secretary to Oxford's son-in-law, Lord Norreys (1900, 1293)[46], wrote a poem campaigning for Shakespeare to be removed from his "uncarved marble" tomb and placed in Westminster Abbey next to the remains of Beaumont, Chaucer, and Spenser. But, wrote Basse, if social "precedence", even in death, prohibits his burial next to these commoners, then he must continue to occupy his own tomb as "Lord", not as "tenant", of his grave. There is no sign that Oxford's uncarved marble tomb at Hackney was ever upgraded with his name, titles or achievements of honour carved upon it, but there is evidence that he was quietly reinterred in Westminster Abbey as his first cousin, Percival Golding recorded (c. 1619): "Of him [Oxford] I will only speak what all mens voices confirme: He was a man in minde and body absolutely accomplished with honourable endowments. He died at his house at Hackney in the monthe of Junne Anno 1604 and lieth buryed at Westminster" (College of Arms archive, Vincent MS 445).[47] Extensive evidence for Oxford's reinternment in Poets' Corner on the exact spot above which the monument to Shakespeare was erected in 1740 is given in my own paper "Hidden Truths" (2017, 14-46).

Oxford's identity as "Shakespeare" was not forgotten in the years that followed his death; nor was his ignominy. He was omitted from Robert Naunton's extensive survey of Queen Elizabeth's court favourites (*Fragmenta Regalia*, 1643) even though Naunton's daughter married Oxford's grandson. Within four months of his death, his youngest daughter, Susan, was engaged to Philip Herbert (one of the dedicatees of the Shakespeare *Folio* of 1623). Their nuptials were lavish and the Court was entertained with performances of eight different Shakespearean plays, seemingly in the playwright's honour. Stratford-Shakspere did not attend.

A book of cryptic emblems and anagrams, devised by the Shakespeare fan, Henry Peacham, and published in 1612 as *Minerva*

46 Lee writes: "from the references made in Basse's poems to Francis, Lord Norreys, it has been inferred that the poet was at one time also attached to his household at Rycote, Oxfordshire".

47 Christine Reynolds, Librarian at Westminster Abbey, informs the present author that records of bodies removed from other places to be reburied at Westminster Abbey were not entered into the Abbey registers.

Britanna ("British Minerva") depicts, on its title page, the hand of a concealed author emerging from behind an Elizabethan theatre curtain (see below):

Above left: Original title-page with the hand of a concealed playwright writing mente videbor *('With the mind I will be seen'); Above right: a manipulated image, with central section turned upside-down), shows a concealed author, robed and sitting upon an earl's coronet, with the letters rearranged to spell* tibi nom. de Vere *('your name is de Vere'), thus identifying 'Minerva Britanna', the British 'will that shakes a spear' (Will Shake-Speare) as the concealed playwright, the Earl of Oxford.*

The hand has just written the Latin words MENTE.VIDEBOR ("with the mind I shall be seen"). The "I" of this phrase puns with the letter *i* — thus inviting the reader to engage his mind to find the hidden letter *i*. There is, of course, the strong semblance of an *i* in the quill nib and the dot it is drawing, giving the message "MENTE.VIDEBORI", a nonsense in Latin, but as Turner Clark (1937) discovered, a perfect anagram of "TIBI NOM. DE VERE" ("To you the name de Vere" or "Your name is de Vere"). Thus, the British Minerva, the British patron of playwrights and the concealed will that shakes the spear, is revealed by the mind's *i* to be Edward de Vere, Earl of Oxford. On the scroll around the poet's wreath is written "VIVITUR INGENIO

CAETERA MORTIS ERUNT" ("Genius survives when all else is claimed by Death"), a message repeatedly endorsed by "Shake-speare" in his sonnets, reminding the reader that Oxford's works will survive even when his name is forgotten.

The prefatory pages of Shakespeare's *Folio* (1623) may have provided the evidential starting point for modern Stratfordianism, but over time they have proved a negative asset to the cause. Ben Jonson, who appears to have assembled the *Folio* under the patronage of Lord Pembroke and with the possible assistance of Oxford's cousin, Francis Bacon, creates a mire of ambiguity around everything that is written about Shakespeare, providing the learned reader with a multitude of clues to the true identity of the author. The Heminges-Condell letters (shown to be the work of Ben Jonson by George Steevens in 1770) may allude to Stratford-Shakspere's play-broking, but reveal nothing about his authorship. In the epigram "To the Reader", set as a caption to Droeshout's famous engraving of an egg-headed, left-handed, sartorially-challenged clown, Jonson embeds the message "Ver had his wit, Ver writ his Booke", unlocked by a key suggested by the title and subscribed initials "B.I." (Armstrong quoted in Horne (1972-73, 13).[48] In the ensuing encomium, "To my beloved THE AUTHOR Mr WILIAM SHAKESPEARE", Jonson spends sixteen lines explaining why the letters of "THE AUTHOR" are printed in a font twice the size of those used for "Mr WILLIAM SHAKESPEARE", or (more precisely) why he will not praise the author's *name* — for those of "silliest ignorance", he writes, will mistake an echo for a true sound; those of "blind affection" will only grope in darkness for the truth, while those of "craftie malice" will "pretend" to praise, but "thinke to ruine, where it seem'd to raise". Having dispensed with his reasons for refusing to praise Shakespeare's name, Jonson begins his encomium "to my beloved THE AUTHOR" on line 17 (the symbolic number for the 17th Earl of Oxford): "I, therefore will begin. Soule of the Age! The applause! delight! the wonder of our Stage! My *Shakespeare*, rise." Jonson continues praising *his* "Shakespeare" as the "sweet Swan of Avon", using "Avon" (the name of at least seven rivers in England) to pun on "Avon", the original name of Hampton Court. Jonson is telling his readers that this "gentle" (i.e., noble) dramatist was a courtier-poet, whose works were written to be performed before the King and

48 The message is retrieved by counting the metrical feet 11:9:11:9, suggested by the 11 letter title "To the reader" and the initials "B.I" at bottom, which stand for the 9-letter name "Ben Ionson."

Queen at Hampton Court (see Waugh 2014, 97-103).[49] Jonson further describes his "Shakespeare" as one who "outshone" his contemporary peers, naming Kyd, Lyly and Marlowe, three playwrights and likely servants of Oxford in the 1580s, none of whom wrote a single play *after* 1593, when the name "Shakespeare" made its first appearance on the literary scene.[50]

Jonson describes *his* Shakespeare as a persistent reviser or editor of his own work, one who "sweated" to "strike the second heat upon the Muses anvile", whose "filed lines" would "shake a lance" at the "eyes of ignorance". The last decade of Oxford's life was spent in relative poverty and exclusion from Court. He was bereft of servants. Nashe, Lyly, Mundy, and Churchyard had moved to other patrons. Marlowe, Watson, Kyd and Greene were all deceased by 1594. Oxford appears to have spent the last decade of his life in anchorite isolation at his house in Hackney revising and rewriting the plays that he and his band of scholars and playwriting associates had assembled for Court and public performance from the late 1570s to the early 1590s. Shakespeare's plays appeared in more revised printed states than those of any other contemporary playwright and in the last six years of Oxford's life new Shakespeare quartos appeared with notices upon their title pages explaining that they were "newly augmented", "newly corrected", "newly ammended", "amended", "enlarged" by their author.[51] No new Shakespeare play appeared in print after Oxford's death advertised in this way, suggesting either that the author had stopped correcting his own plays, or that he had died in 1604.

Other authors did however continue to edit and revise the Shakespearean canon after Oxford's death. Stylistic analysis may be correct in identifying the Jacobean hands of Middleton, Fletcher and others in plays like *Macbeth*, *Timon of Athens*, *Henry VIII* and others, since the updating and revising of old court plays was common-place for each new production. Thomas Heywood (c. 1607) records that "court plays have been yearly rehearsed, perfected and corrected

49 For "Avon" as a name for Hampton Court noted by Leland, Camden, Weever and others, see Waugh, (2014, 97-103).

50 "For, if I thought my iudgement were of yeeres, / I should commit thee surely with thy peeres, / And tell, how farre thou didst our *Lily* out-shine, / Or sporting *Kid*, or *Marlowes* mighty line." Ben Jonson, "To the Memory of my beloved THE AUTHOR" Mr William Shakespeare", F1 (1623), lines 27-30.

51 Quarto editions which advertised new revisions, often by the author, include. *Henry IV* part I (Q2, 1599); *Loves Labors Lost* (1598); *Hamlet* (Q2, 1604), *Romeo and Juliet* (Q2, 1599) and *Richard III* (Q3, 1602).

before they come to the public view of the prince and the nobility" (1612, sig E1^{v}). Despite posthumous corrections found in a small minority of Shakespeare's plays, the individual voice that resonates through most of the canon remains that of a lofty courtier-poet, an exile, writing in pursuit of an Ovidian ideal, one who has intimate knowledge of the court but writes of it from the perspective of a respectful but critical outsider, one who repents his life through his works and one, who in true Ovidian spirit, ultimately erases his own identity as he metamorphoses into his art. From his earliest years Oxford had sought "neither external wealth nor the praise of poetry" (Coryat 1905, 395-96) and like Shake-speare, he appears to have accepted that his name would be "buried where my body is."

Stratfordianism did not begin in 1623 with the publication of the Shakespeare *Folio*. Records from 1623-50 indicate that Jonson's ambiguous nods and winks created no Stratfordian mind-set. The Stratfordian movement evolved gradually as the Jonsonian joke that the Puritans had failed to get slowly and deleteriously morphed from open secret among the learned classes, to pleasant myth and finally to accepted history in the second half of the 17th century. The first unequivocally Stratfordian commentary first appeared in 1680s and 1690s. Writers like Fuller, Langbaine and Winstanley drew their conclusions from literal readings of the prefatory pages of the four Shakespeare folios, ignoring their predecessor, Endymion Porter, who had accused Jonson and Randolph (respective editors of Shakespeare's First and of the Second *Folios*) of contriving to "rape" Shakespeare's fame (Bradley & Adams 1922, 189),[52] and ignoring a whole generation of post-1623 commentators who had continued to employ ingenious devices to share among their learned contemporaries the fact that "Shakespeare" was the pseudonym of the 17th Earl of Oxford. These include William Davenant, who in 1637, warned poets that their eyes would be "mocked" if they looked to Stratford-upon-Avon "in remembrance of Master William Shakespeare." In a verse that shares Oxford's known pleasure in identifying his own name in words like "e*ver*", "fe*ver*", "qui*ver*", "deli*ver*", etc, D'Avenant hid "our Vere" in the thrice-named "River" that he challenged his readers to "look if they could spie", while audaciously ridiculing the shallow poetry of Fulke Greville, Lord Brooke, whose home at Warwick Castle was situated upon the banks of the Warwickshire Avon, a few miles from Stratford:

52 "Even Avon's swan could not escape / These letter-tyrant elves; / They on his fame contrived a rape / To raise their pedant selves"; Endymion Porter, "Upon Ben Jonson, and his Zany, Tom Randolph" (c. 1628); reprinted in Bradley & Adams, eds., (1922, 189).

Beware (delighted Poets!) when you sing
To welcome Nature in the early Spring;
Your num'rous Feet not tread
The Banks of Avon [...]

The piteous River wept it selfe away
Long since (Alas!) to such a swift decay;
That reach the Map; and looke
If you a River there can spie;
And for a River your mock'd Eie,
Will finde a shallow Brooke (1638, 37-38).

Jonson's friend, the playwright Richard Brome, left a description of Shakespeare as "that English Earle, that lov'd a Play and a Player so well" in his play *Antipodes* (1638), while John Warren (1640) stated that the "learned" or those of "true judgment" would be astonished to discover that the glory for "lofty" Shakespeare's "high-tun'd straine" had been taken up by a "twice-lived" and "Virbius-like" impostor. Virbius, a name derived from the Latin *vir* (man) and *bis* ("twice", "double" or "twofold") puns *vir* on Oxford's name (Vere) to suggest "twice", "double" or "two-fold" Vere, making clear the fact that Warren, like so many of his contemporaries, knew that Stratford-Shakspere, who had written nothing, was reaping the posthumous glory:

What, lofty *Shakespeare*, art again reviv'd?
And *Virbius*-like now show'st thy self twise liv'd,
'Tis love that thus to thee is shown,
The labours his, the glory still thine owne (1640).

Back in mid-1590s, as the name "William Shakespeare" first appears on the literary scene, the documentary record for Oxford as a famous poet curiously evaporates and by the 19th century his literary fame was all but forgotten. John Plumer Ward (1827) wrote of him "who in the days of Elizabeth united in his single person the character of her greatest noble, knight and poet" (1827, 88), but Alexander Grosart, who published eighteen of Oxford's poems in 1872, remarked that "an unlifted shadow somehow lies across his memory" (1872, 359). W. J. Courthorpe, Oxford Professor of Poetry, praised the "wit", "terse ingenuity", and "remarkable concinnity of style" of Oxford's verses in 1897 and Sidney Lee (1899) acknowledged the high esteem in which his poetry was held by his contemporaries, opining that he "wrote verses of much lyric beauty". But all of these commentators were writing before the publication of *"Shakespeare" Identified* (1920). Since then it has become fashionable among Stratfordians to sneer at the small number of youthful poems (half of which are song lyrics composed by the age of 16) that are extant under Oxford's name. Lewis (1944, 267) typically finds them "for the most part undistinguished and verbose"; Kathman (2012, 259) deplores their "plodding alliteration and shaky versification", while Nelson (158-59) considers them "atrocious" and "numbingly repetitive" with a consistent and pervasive "egocentric, cry-baby attitude". None of these commentators refers to the remarkable similarity of style and idea that exists between Shakespeare's and Oxford's verses as illustrated by Oxfordian scholars Sobran, Wainwright and Goldstein. Indeed so alike are Shakespeare and Oxford in pastoral mood that a seventy-two-line canto, assembled from four to eight line gobbets of each poet by Louis Benezet, has proved impossible to disentangle by even the most able of literary sleuths (1937).[53] The leading pre-1920 Stratfordian scholar, Sir Sidney Lee, could not help but notice how Oxford and Shakespeare wrote verses "in a kindred key" (1920, 227).

While the documentary record proves that Oxford was revered by his contemporaries as a first-rate playwright and scholar who operated at the hidden heart of English literary and theatrical life, modern orthodoxy insists that the only complete canon of thirty-six first-rate plays to have survived from this period — one that is intimately concerned with kings, courts, the nobility, dynastic squabbling, Italy, language, scholarship and so on, be assigned to Stratford-Shakspere, a figure who made no claim to be a playwright or scholar, who has no educational record and who is entirely absent from the rich literary record of his lifetime. "These facts alone," wrote J. T. Looney, "each in its own way so amazingly strange and wholly unique, being contemporary and complementary, would justify, without further proof, a very strong belief that the Shakespeare plays are the lost plays of the Earl of Oxford" (197).

53 Known as the "Benezet Test", first printed in Benezet, (1937); reprinted in Whalen (1994, 143-45).

Chapter 4

My Shakespeare: Christopher Marlowe

Ros Barber

All the evidence that supports the case for Marlowe — as with all other candidates — is circumstantial. I make the case for Marlowe not because I am certain he wrote the works, but because I consider him the best candidate for the vacancy, given the curious absence of evidence for the man from Stratford. The case for Christopher Marlowe as the chief author of the works known as Shakespeare's is strong in one very vital regard. Marlowe is the *only* authorship candidate whose skills in dramatic composition, blank verse, and lyric poetry evidence the genius-level writer required to create the Shakespeare canon. And the greatest obstacle for Marlowe's authorship of the Shakespeare canon — his apparent death in 1593 before most of the plays were written — is, paradoxically, a strength.

The best reason to hide his identity

Marlowe had the best reason of any authorship candidate to hide his identity. What was at stake for Marlowe was not a loss of dignity, but his life. By the early 1590s, Marlowe was not just the most accomplished author of his generation; he was an "intelligencer", working to undermine plots against the Queen's life. He began this work while he was still a student at Cambridge University. In 1587, the Queen's Privy Council, represented by five of the most powerful men in the country, wrote to Cambridge to urge that university to grant his MA, despite a report "that Christopher Morley was determined to have gone beyond the seas to [the Jesuit college at] Rheims", where plots against the queen's life were hatched. Their Lordships — including John Whitgift the Archbishop of Canterbury, Christopher Hatton the Lord Chancellor, Henry Carey the Lord Chamberlain and the Lord Treasurer William Cecil — reported "that in all his actions he had behaved himself orderly and discreetly whereby he had done her Majesty good service, & deserved to be rewarded for his faithful dealing." They stressed that "it was not her Majesty's pleasure that any one employed as he had been in matters touching the benefit of his Country should be defamed by those that are ignorant in the affairs he went about."[1]

Nevertheless, six years later, Marlowe's work as an intelligence agent began to catch up with him; he was again being defamed, and more dangerously. An informer said that "one Marlowe is able to show more sound reasons for Atheism than any divine in England is able to give to prove divinitie & that Marloe told him that he hath read the Atheist lecture to Sir Walter Raliegh & others."[2] A Catholic double agent, Richard Baines, wrote out a comprehensive list "Containing the opinion of one Christopher Marly Concerning his Damnable Judgment of Religion, and scorn of gods word";[3] the list mirrors Baines's own published confession when he was tortured by the Catholic priests he had been spying on (Kendall 2003, 40).

The accusations of heresy and atheism levelled against Marlowe at this time were more than enough to have him imprisoned, tortured, and executed. And there were further moves to have Marlowe removed from the game. On May 5th, a document known as the Dutch Church Libel was posted on the wall of a Huguenot church, stirring up hatred against protestant refugees. This poem in iambic pentameter looks like a deliberate attempt to implicate Marlowe in the recent unrest against foreigners, referencing his plays *The Massacre at Paris* and *The Jew of Malta*, and being signed "Tamberlaine". Marlowe's former room-mate, Thomas Kyd was arrested, and papers seized — "vile heretical conceits" — which Kyd, under torture, "affirmeth that he had from Marlowe". On May 18th 1593, the Privy Council issued a warrant for Marlowe to be apprehended; on 20th May Marlowe presented himself

1 PRO Privy Council Registers PC2/14/381. This and other items relating to Marlowe in government documents are transcribed in Kuriyama, (2002, 202-3). I have modernised the spelling of this and certain other documents for clarity.

2 BL Harley MS 6848 f.190r,v.

3 BL Harley MS 6848 ff 185-86.

"for his indemnity therein" and was released on his own recognisance, "commanded to give his daily attendance on their Lordships until he shall be licensed to the contrary."

The official record of Marlowe's apparent death ten days later is widely considered a cover-up, independent of any authorship claim.[4] If the "convenient" timing of it were not suspect enough, the only recorded witnesses to his death were three professional liars. Two were current or former intelligence agents and one of these (plus the supposed murderer) had links with Marlowe's friend and patron (and first cousin once removed of the head of the Secret Service), Thomas Walsingham. Marlowe is said to have been stabbed through the eye in an argument over the "reckoning" (the bill) after an all-day meeting at Eleanor Bull's house in Deptford. Marlowe's biographer Charles Nicholl determined that Mrs Bull's house was not a "tavern". Eleanor Bull had strong court connections: she was "cousin" to Blanche Parry, Chief Gentlewoman of the Privy Chamber, Elizabeth's most trusted attendant. She was related to the Lord Treasurer, William Cecil (Nicholl 2002, 42).

This has led to some scholars believing that Marlowe was assassinated. Yet it has been repeatedly demonstrated that those put forward as the instigators of Marlowe's murder had no reason to murder him (Hammer 1996). In any case, were an assassination required, why not simply stab him in a dark alley? It is a fact that Lord Burghley, at loggerheads with Whitgift and losing ground to him in terms of Privy Council influence (Sheils 2004), failed to prevent the execution of puritan John Penry at the Archbishop's behest, the day before Marlowe met with Robert Poley, Ingram Frizer and Nicholas Skeres at Deptford (Cross 2004). As Kuriyama points out, the men present with Marlowe at widow Bull's house, though known to be expert liars, were not assassins (2002, 139). The supposed murderer, Ingram Frizer, was a loyal servant of Marlowe's friend and patron Thomas Walsingham. Swiftly pardoned for the killing, Frizer was doing business for Walsingham the very next day, and continued in the service of Thomas Walsingham to the end of his life, being rewarded by James I with a series of leases in reversion of crown lands (Bakeless 1942, I: 170). Nevertheless, we are left with questions concerning government involvement at the highest level. Why was a copy of the Baines note sent to the Queen? Why was the heading and content of the note altered in the copy she was given?

4 A fuller exploration of the evidence around Marlowe's death can be read in Farey's "Marlowe's Sudden and Fearful End".

The reader should consider what they might do in similar circumstances. Faced with his probable torture and execution but in a privileged position due to his Privy Council and secret service connections, Marlowe had the means, motive and opportunity to escape. As Roy Kendall points out "deaths in the murky word of espionage can often be 'blinds' for disappearances, and vice versa" (2003, 149). We know it was common for government agents to operate on the continent under assumed names (Kendall 106).[5] In an era before photographs and modern methods of travel, faking a death to execute an exile was a manageable proposition. Deptford, near the mouth of the Thames, was a perfect place to disappear from. Why might Marlowe, facing probable torture and execution, have an eight hour meeting with these particular men in this particular place? If you needed to stage a disappearance, this would be the perfect combination of location and personnel. Faking one's death to avoid actual death is not an unreasonable action: most of us would choose a fake death (and exile) over real death if it seemed the only viable means of survival. That one is supposed to be dead, and risks real death if discovered, is a far stronger motivation for concealing oneself behind a "front" than the shame of writing for the public stage.

Government involvement in Marlowe's apparent death includes the location being owned by a cousin of the Queen's most trusted attendant, the Queen's unusually rapid pardon of the supposed murderer, and the Queen's coroner William Danby conducting the inquest. The most likely substitute body, that of John Penry — transported to a spot two miles away to be executed without warning the day before, and never located — would have likely been in the control of Danby (Farey 2005).[6]

How would the jury be duped by a substitute body? They are very unlikely to know what Marlowe looked like, as he was not local to the area. The jury of yeoman would have had no reason not to believe the three witnesses who identified the body as Marlowe's, since the witnesses were all gentlemen, and thus their social superiors. In any case, the supposedly fatal wound, a stabbing through the eye, would be sufficient not to make anyone look too closely at the face. As Shakespeare's Duke Vincentio says when carrying out just such a body substitution trick in *Measure for Measure*, "Death's a great disguiser, and you may add to it".

There is evidence to support the idea that Marlowe's faked death was a Privy Council compromise. The Baines Note, containing the

5 Anthony Standen, for example, used the names Monsieur De Faye, Andree Sandal, Saintman, and Pompeio Pelegrini.

6 John Penry's body as a substitute for Marlowe's was first suggested in More (1997).

fatal accusations against Marlowe, was edited. It makes sense that the final version marked as "sent to her H[ighness]" has been stripped of the more salacious accusations, leaving only the statements pertaining to Marlowe's statements about religion.[7] But what might be the reason to change the title, with its reference to Marlowe's "sudden and violent death", to the more equivocal "sudden and fearful end of his life"? For someone wary of lying on an official document, this phrase is the perfect get-out: the "death" has gone, and the violence too (for there is no violence in a faked death); yet truthfully Marlowe's life as he knew had indeed come to an "end", and no question he would have found this end both "sudden and fearful". The hand that made these changes has been identified as Lord Keeper Puckering's (Nicholl 2002, 323). This supports the idea of Marlowe's arranged demise as a Privy Council compromise between those who wanted him kept alive as a valuable asset (William Cecil and his allies) and those who wanted him dead as an example to atheists (Archbishop Whitgift, Puckering and their allies).

It is sometimes argued that Marlowe cannot be Shakespeare because they existed (and wrote) at the same time: in the orthodox narrative, Shakespeare is in London by the late 1580s or early 1590s, when the first plays now known as Shakespeare's — the early *Henry VI* plays for example — were being staged. But the *Henry VI* plays have a long history of being attributed in whole or in part to Marlowe, and none of those early plays were attributed to Shakespeare in the Stratford man's lifetime. If we go by unequivocal documentary evidence alone, William Shakespeare the author was "born" shortly after Marlowe's death.[8] The first recorded appearance of the name "William Shakespeare" in connection with any creative work is on the dedication of the long narrative poem *Venus and Adonis*. Marlowe's apparent death occurred on 30th May, and less than two weeks later *Venus and Adonis* was on the bookstalls. In other words, the extant documentary evidence points to perfect timing: exit Christopher Marlowe, enter William Shakespeare.

Breadth of social experience and education

Marlowe's birthplace, Canterbury, was a city of considerable importance: the seat of the Church of England, and a place connected to the wider

7 BL Harley MS 6853 ff.307-8.

8 Robert Greene's "upstart Crow" of 1592, despite the epithet "Shake-scene", and though widely believed to be Shakespeare, is much more likely to be the actor Edward Alleyn. See Pinksen (2009).

world through its position on the Southern extension of Watling Street, connecting London to the main port at Dover. It had a population of 5000, around 2000 of whom were Huguenot refugees. As a key stopping place between London and Dover, Canterbury saw "a steady stream of diplomats, soldiers, merchants and messengers going to and from France" (Riggs 2004, 30).

Christopher Marlowe was born in 1564, the same year as the man we know as William Shakespeare. Like his Stratford counterpart, Marlowe's father was a leather-worker: where John Shakespeare clad hands, John Marlowe shod feet. Shakespeare's lower class characters are not stock characters. They are well-observed in a way that suggests considerable direct experience: Launcelot Gobbo in the *Merchant of Venice* for example, or the witty cobbler in the opening scene of *Julius Caesar.* Marlowe, too, used such characters for comic relief: the magic-abusing servants of *Doctor Faustus*; the soldiers in *A Massacre At Paris* trying to work out the best way to dispose of a corpse. Marlowe was elevated from these humble beginnings through a first-class education. A scholarship to the prestigious Kings' School gave him the required skills to win another scholarship to Corpus Christi College, Cambridge. At the King's School, students were required, even at play, to "never use any language but Latin and Greek"; they were required to compose speeches and verses in Classical Latin. The Parker scholarship which took him to Cambridge required that "the best and aptest scholars" should be able to sight read music, and sing ("at first sight to solf and sing plainsong"), and ideally "make a verse".

Marlowe studied for six years at Cambridge, the University whose slang and other specific references were first identified in the plays by Boas (1923). His MA gave him the status of "generosus" (gentleman), and entering the Queen's service as an intelligence agent, Marlowe mixed with the full gamut of society. He told Sir Robert Sidney (the Countess of Pembroke's brother) he was "very well known" to Lord Strange (the future 5th Earl of Derby) and the 9th Earl of Northumberland, known as the "Wizard Earl" for his interest in chemistry. He was also connected to Sir Walter Raleigh, to whom he was said to have "read the atheist lecture", and to Thomas Hariot, the astronomer who worked for both Raleigh and the Earl of Northumberland; he moved in circles dedicated to the advancement of human knowledge. Yet despite mixing with scientists, courtiers, and noblemen, and undertaking duties that may well have taken him to foreign courts, he remained familiar with the yeoman class sensibilities strongly depicted in the Shakespeare canon.

Whoever wrote the canon had similar social breadth to Marlowe: he not only knew the ways of courtiers and nobleman, but of tavern keepers and cobblers.

Genius-level writing

Since we are considering which flesh and blood human was actually capable of becoming the most revered English dramatist and poet of all time, the importance of demonstrable literary genius should not be underestimated. If other candidates are capable of writing genius-level plays and poems, we have limited or no supporting evidence.[9] There are no extant plays for main candidates besides Marlowe. Where poems attributed to these other candidates have survived, they do not exhibit the qualities of Shakespeare's, begging the question of why anyone would set their name to inferior works while publishing or distributing superior ones under a pseudonym. Marlowe, on the other hand, has the profile and track record appropriate to a writer of genius. His first hit for the public stage, *Tamburlaine*, was first performed in 1587 when he was twenty-three. Its success spawned so many inferior imitators that some forty years later Ben Jonson would complain in his commonplace book, *Discoveries*, of "the Tamerlanes and Tamerchams of the late Age, which had nothing in them but scenical strutting and furious vociferation to warrant them to the ignorant gapers." Marlowe's *Doctor Faustus* was popular from the 1590s to the closing of the theatres in 1642. His Ovidian epyllion *Hero and Leander* was widely admired; he translated Ovid's *Elegies*. The writer known as Shakespeare was similarly inspired by Ovid (Bate 1993).

Marlowe's dramatic style is in every way the forerunner of the style which would become Shakespeare's. Marlowe was the first person to write really successful plays in blank verse (the style which the author known as Shakespeare perfected). He was the progenitor of three other important dramatic features which "Shakespeare" developed: the English history play (*Edward II*),[10] the internal-state soliloquy, as opposed to the expositional or character-introducing soliloquy (in *Doctor Faustus*), and the sequel (*Tamburlaine Part 2*). Throughout the Shakespeare canon, the author paraphrases or references Marlowe repeatedly, which might

9 Allowing that one rules out, as one must, the circular argument that their skill is evident in the works of Shakespeare.

10 It may be argued that the *Henry VI* plays came before *Edward II* (dates are uncertain), but we now have growing stylistic evidence that Marlowe wrote the originals of these plays too.

be identified as what Bakeless calls "Marlowe's habitual self-repetition" (1942, II: 227). In the traditional telling, the shared stylistic features of Marlowe and Shakespeare, and the repeated references, amount to a very strong "influence".

Robert Logan speaks of "the firmness with which Marlowe's influence rooted itself in Shakespeare and developed, for it continued to thrive for 18 years after Marlowe's death, roughly from 1593-1611, the remainder of Shakespeare's career" (2007, 8). Peter Ackroyd says "Marlowe was the contemporary writer that most exercised him. . . . He haunts Shakespeare's expression, like a figure standing by his shoulder" (2005, 140). Stephen Greenblatt says of the influence of Marlowe's *Tamburlaine* on Shakespeare that "from its effect upon his early work, it appears to have had upon him an intense, visceral, indeed life-transforming impact" (2004, 189). Russ McDonald calls Marlowe "one of Shakespeare's most influential teachers," claiming "that Shakespeare's plays would have been very different from what they are — and may not have been at all — were it not for the Marlovian example" (2004, 67). Harold Bloom declares Marlowe "London's dominant dramatist from 1587 to 1593" and states that "Marlowe, himself a wild original, was Shakespeare's starting point, curiously difficult for the young Shakespeare to exorcise completely" (2002, 10).

There may have been a good reason why it was "curiously difficult" for Shakespeare to exorcise Marlowe completely: one can hardly "exorcise" oneself. It is interesting how many orthodox scholars recognise the unusual persistence of this "influence" by expressing Marlowe's "presence" in the canon through metaphors where Marlowe's spiritual form possesses or inhabits Shakespeare. Jonathan Bate expresses it particularly strongly: "Shakespeare, I suggest, only became Shakespeare because of the death of Marlowe. And he remained peculiarly haunted by that death" (1997, 105). If the two writers are in fact one person, this ghostly mystery is solved. The soul of a writer may mature and gain experience, but it cannot be dislodged. Thinking of Marlowe as *ur*-Shakespeare explains a great deal about the relationship of the two canons. As Patrick Cheney says, what "Marlowe had begun ... Shakespeare would complete" (2008, 25). Reading Sonnet 76 in this light allows us the interpretation that Shakespeare knew very well that his Marlovian roots were showing:

> Why write I still all one, ever the same,
> And keep invention in a noted weed,
> That every word doth almost tell my name,
> Showing their birth and where they did proceed?

Working in the nitty gritty of textual analysis, scholars have long found it difficult to distinguish Marlowe from Shakespeare. Until the 1920s it was common for scholars to give all or part of the early Shakespeare plays (*Henry VI, Titus Andronicus, Taming of the Shrew*) to Marlowe. Recently, computational stylistics has led to Marlowe being given an official co-authorship credit for all three of the *Henry VI* plays. But those who imagine this rules out Marlowe as a candidate because the tests "prove" that Marlowe and Shakespeare have discernibly different styles have not understood how Marlowe and Shakespeare marker words (and patterns of words) are derived in these tests, nor how the tests ignore the possibility of the evolution of a writer's individual style over time.[11] Nor how, even when measures are chosen specifically as a means of separating the two canons, there are often occasions (as with Act 4 of *2 Henry VI*) where they cannot be distinguished (Segarra *et al* 2016). When evolving stylistic markers are measured in individual plays — whether it is feminine endings and enjambment, or the relative use of certain words — the results consistently show a smooth and evolving continuum between the Marlowe and Shakespeare canons as the "Marlowe signal" of the early works diminishes and the "Shakespeare signal" of later works increases (Merriam and Matthews 1994).[12] Where a stylistic marker doesn't change much over time — as seems to be the case with word length frequency, measured by Mendenhall in 1901 — Marlowe's style is an exact match for Shakespeare's (Farey 2000, Appendix IV).

Those who say that Marlowe cannot have written the Shakespeare canon because he could not write comedy are ignoring the comic scenes the printer Richard Jones admits to cutting from *Tamburlaine,* those that survive in *Doctor Faustus* and *A Massacre At Paris*, the bawdy humour of *Hero and Leander*, and the fact that *The Jew of Malta* is most effectively played as a farce. Those who say that Marlowe cannot have written the Shakespeare canon because he did not write strong women are ignoring his Dido, Hero, and Isabella. Obviously there are significant differences between the skills displayed in *Tamburlaine* (c.1587) and *Othello* (c.1604). But these can be explained by maturity and practice: the output of a

11 They also overlook the persistent issue of inadequate sample sizes; Burrows and Craig (2016) used 2000-word segments when Maciej Eder, independently testing their methods, described the results for segments under 3000 words as "simply disastrous" (2015). The Word Adjacency Networks methodology favoured by Segarra *et al.* (2016) not only significantly conflicts with the results of other methodologies on the same plays, but uses scene-size samples; as low as 105 words.

12 See also Appendix V and VI of Farey, "A Deception in Deptford".

fledging writer aged 23 will clearly be different from the output of the same writer at 40. Marlovian theory would explain why, as Logan notes, Marlowe's influence was so "firmly rooted". The self may mature and gain experience, but cannot actually be dislodged. Unlike any other authorship candidate (including the man from Stratford), Marlowe is demonstrably and generously equipped to write the Shakespeare canon.

Direct evidence for Marlowe

Did anyone at the time notice the strong similarity between Shakespeare's writing and Marlowe's? There are strong reasons to believe that Gabriel Harvey did.[13] Harvey was living with a bookseller in St. Paul's in the first seven months of 1593. Harvey was in a position to be very knowledgeable about Marlowe. He had been a don at Cambridge when Marlowe was a student there. He had attended Christ's College in Cambridge at exactly the same time as Richard Baines, the man whose "Note" that year lead to Marlowe's arrest. Harvey's brother Richard was the rector of the church at Chislehurst, where Marlowe's patron Thomas Walsingham lived, and where Marlowe was arrested. Harvey was also engaged in a war of words with Marlowe's close friend, Thomas Nashe.

On April 27th, Harvey wrote of his suspicions regarding a certain pamphlet which had been registered anonymously. *Venus and Adonis* was registered anonymously on April 18th. In the letter published in *Pierces Supererogation,* Harvey says "I could here dismaske such a rich mummer... as would vndoubtedly make this Pamflet the vendiblest booke in London, and the Register one of the famousest Autors in England" (1884, II: 312). But Harvey will not "dismask" this "mummer",[14] being "none of those, that utter all their learning at once" and being also concerned that "the close man" might have "some secret frendes, or respectiue acquaintance; that in regarde of his calling, or some priuate consideration, would be loth to haue his coate blased, or his satchell ransacked." Harvey's awareness of the man's "calling" and associated "secret friends" — friends who would not appreciate Harvey blowing his cover — resonates with our understanding of Marlowe as a government

13 A fuller exploration of the Harvey-Nashe quarrel in reference to *Venus and Adonis* can be found in Barber (2009).

14 Since a "braggard with motts" is unlikely to be a "mumbler" (*OED* 1), "Mummer" must mean the only other definition of the word at this time (*OED* 2a): "a person who acts in a mummer's play". (The definition "actor" did not arise until the 18th century). Mummers traditionally wore masks; Merriam-Webster gives the definition "one who goes merrymaking in disguise".

intelligence agent. That the work was to be published by Richard Field, Lord Burghley's printer, may have suggested to Harvey that the move was officially sanctioned by Marlowe's government employer.

Launching into a description of a "braggard with motts", Harvey mocks the author for trying to "arm himself with a brave Posie"— a motto. *Venus and Adonis* was prefaced with two lines of Latin poetry from Ovid, which in its original context lead on to a couplet predicting a triumph over death: "Then thogh death rackes my bones in funerall fire, / Ile liue, and as he puls me downe, mount higher." Harvey says "the Troian Horse ... was not such an Asse, to aduaunce himselfe with any such prowde Imprese". Dissimulation is in anyway pointless, says Harvey, since "The Tree is knowen by the fruite; and needeth no other Posie" (308). In other words, he recognises the style of this (at this point) anonymous pamphlet. Hinting at the Ovidian nature of this anonymous pamplet, he calls the author "Ovid's lover", saying "Ouids loouer must not attempt, but where he will conquer", adding "Foretel not, what thou intendest to atcheiue, lesse peraduenture being frustrate, thou be laughed to scorne, and made a notable flowtingstocke" (309). Immediately after allusions to "priuy Counsell" and "Secretary" he states "There be more queint experiments in an Vniuersitie, then many a politique head would imagine" (310), and this reminds him of the former Dean, one Doctor Perne, of whom he said earlier in the text "[i] t was in him, to giue instructions vnto Ouid, for the repenning of his Metamorphoses anew" (300). *Venus and Adonis* is widely accepted as a "repenning" of Book X of Ovid's *Metamorphoses.*

Harvey's knowledge appears to go deeper than his suspicion that *Venus and Adonis* is one of those "quaint" Cambridge experiments encouraged by Doctor Perne. He considers the author an "Asse... especially for defeating one without cause ... [that] ... might possibly haue it in him, to requite him aliue, and dead" (313). "Alive, and dead" is pertinent to our theory, but who is this person who thought the author defeated "without cause" who might "requite" him so? If the author is Marlowe, there are good reasons to suspect this is Harvey's college friend Richard Baines (Barber 2009, 99). And two pages later, after a typically Harveyian detour about Doctor Perne — a religious "turncoat" whom he says might have been Baines's "catechist for religion", Harvey confirms this identification by saying "Braue Mindes, and Ventrous Harts, thanke him for this inualuable Note, that could teach you to atcheiue more with the little finger of Pollicy, then you can possibly compasse with the mighty arme of Prowesse" (315). And then refers to the contents of the Baines

Note, saying "he that disclosed the same [i.e. Baines], is perhaps to leaue an immortall Testimoniall of his [i.e Marlowe's] Indian Discoouery". The first item on the list of Marlowe's "damnable opinions" known as the Baines Note is "That the Indians and many Authors of Antiquitei have assuredly written of aboue 16 thowsande years agone, wher Adam is proued to haue leyved within 6 thowsande years".

Harvey appears to know about the Baines Note, and its contents, on the 27th April. Of the Note's consequences, he says "Was not he shrewdly encountred, that was prestigiously besieged, and inuisibly vndermined with that weapon of weapons? What other supply could haue seconded, or rescued him, but Death." The mention of Marlowe's rescue by "Death" is a month premature. But Harvey is conscious that the fatal accusations of atheism contained in the Baines Note have coincided with the anonymous registration of a narrative poem in Marlovian style. He has roundly mocked the Ovidian motto fronting the work, undoubtedly aware of the couplet that follows it, which predicts a triumph over death. "Foretel not" he says in that passage, "what thou intendest to atcheiue, lesse peraduenture being frustrate, thou be laughed to scorne, and made a notable flowtingstocke" (309). He has seen the Trojan Horse arrive outside the gates. He understands what comes next. Though registered anonymously, it seems likely that *Venus and Adonis* already includes the dedication; Harvey signs off with a conspicuous (and italicized) echo of the "idle hours" in the *Venus* dedication: "I writ onely at idle howers, that I dedicate onely to *Idle Howers*" (1884, V2: 330).

After *Venus and Adonis* was published, Gabriel Harvey published a poem called "Gorgon, or the wonderfull yeare". Scholars of Elizabethan literature find it notoriously obscure. But most agree it contains allusions to Marlowe.[15] What Nashe calls Harvey's "goggle-eyde sonnet of *Gorgon*" gives its fullest and most coherent reading when interpreted as a reaction to Marlowe's *Venus and Adonis* appearing under the Shakespeare name on the book stalls of St. Paul's. St. Paul's (as "Powles") is referenced six times in Harvey's poem. Harvey is "goggle-eyed" at something he calls "The mightiest miracle of Ninety Three". This is not as is sometimes suggested Marlowe's death, a predictable and inevitable event. But the word "miracle" would certainly be fitting for Marlowe's apparent resurrection.

15 Hale Moore summarises the scholarly reactions to Gorgon up to 1926, and offers an exploration of the Marlowe allusions (1926). Gorgon's reference to Marlowe are noted by Bakeless (1942, I, 126, 43). The Feaseys note Gorgon's allusions to Marlowe and their similarities to a section of Harvey's *Pierces Superorogation* (1949).

If the poem is Harvey's reaction to the sudden appearance of a new poetic genius at exactly the point a previous one (with very similar writing style) was eclipsed — for contrary to the orthodox narrative, there's no evidence that the name William Shakespeare was known in any literary or theatrical circles before the appearance of *Venus and Adonis* — then the title "Gorgon" works on two levels. Firstly, Marlowe compared Tamburlaine to "Gorgon, prince of Hell" in *Tamburlaine Part I* (IV.i.18) and "Tamburlaine" is Harvey's name for Marlowe in this poem. Secondly, if Harvey believes that "Shakespeare" is a pseudonym for Marlowe, then "Gorgon" alludes to Pallas Athena, the spear-shaking goddess of wisdom whose aegis (protective shield), bore the Gorgon's head.

Harvey does not say that Marlowe is alive, but he does not seem sure that he is dead. "Is that Gargantua minde / Conquerd ...?" he asks in the first of a flurry of questions about the "mind triumph'd on Kent", and later "Is it a dreame? Or is the Highest minde, / That ever haunted Powles … Bereaft of … breath…?" Marlowe's death is framed only as a question. "*Weepe Powles,*" says Harvey early on in the poem, "*thy* Tamberlaine *voutsafes to dye*". "Vouchsafe" suggests an element of collusion, on Marlowe's part, in his own death: that he consents, or chooses, to die. At the end of the poem, Harvey compares Marlowe to "the ugly bugg who *scorned* to die" [my emphasis]. Thus he has both chosen to die, and refused to die. The couplet of the closing *L'envoy* describes him only as "down", or fallen.

Harvey describes Marlowe as one whose "mind triumph'd on Kent". Kent was Marlowe's birthplace, but this is not enough to make sense of "triumphed". If Marlowe escaped prosecution (through apparent death), then he had triumphed over John Whitgift, Archbishop of Canterbury, who would not only have been the Privy Council member pressing for his death, but had licensed the anonymous *Venus & Adonis* to be published. Deptford, the location of that triumph, was also at that time in the county of Kent. That Harvey is writing about *Venus and Adonis* is strengthened by:

> *I mus'd awhile: and having mus'd awhile,*
> *Jesu, (quoth I) is that* Gargantua minde
> *Conquerd* […]?
> *Vowed he not to Powles* A Second bile?

For "Shakespeare" did indeed vow to produce a "second bile" in the dedication of *Venus and Adonis* where he promised Southampton to "take advantage of all idle hours, till I have honoured you with some graver labour".[16]

Thomas Nashe, in response, calls Harvey "Gabriel Graue-digger" and referencing Tamburlaine says, "Ile hamper him like a iade as he is for this geare, & ride him with a snaffle vp & down the whole realme" (1958, II: 180). "[P]oore deceased Kit Marlow" is one of the "quiet senseless carcasses" that Harvey has "vilely dealt with". As you would expect, Nashe maintains that his friend is dead. But his "full answer" to the "sinful doctor" corroborates our reading of "Gorgon" as a reaction to *Venus and Adonis*. In *Haue vvith you to Saffron-vvalden. Or, Gabriell Harueys hunt is vp* (1596) Nashe insults the poem (III, 133) and calls him "a precious apothegmatical Pedant, who will finde matter inough to dilate a whole daye of the first inuention of Fy, fa, fum, I smell the bloud of an Englishman" (III, 36-37). "First invention" echoes the dedication of *Venus and Adonis* and the unwritten next lines of the nursery rhyme are: "Be he alive or be he dead? I'll grind his bones to make my bread". Thus Nashe communicates to Harvey that he has understood "Gorgon" as a potentially life- threatening "hunt" — perhaps the hunt alluded to on the title page. Nashe mentions the transformation and metamorphosis of names in relation to Kent, and throws the conflation of Marlowe and Tamburlaine back on Harvey by calling him "Scythian Gabriell". In another relevant section, Nashe writes that putting "*that fairest body of* Venus *in Print … with a witness*" obviates the need for a virginity test (i.e. a test to show that the book really was the "first heir" of the author's "invention").

Harvey published nothing further on the matter. The following year, Nashe went on the run from the authorities for his hand in writing the play *The Isle of Dogs*. Two years later, the Bishops' Ban decreed "That all NASSHes bookes and Doctor HARVYes bookes be taken wheresouer they maye be found and that none of theire bookes bee euer printed hereafter"; this was a public conversation the authorities wanted banned and burned.

Other contemporary documents demonstrate apparent confusions between the Marlowe and Shakespeare canons.

William Covell, who attended Cambridge at the same time as Marlowe, appears to have confused Shakespeare and Marlowe in his *Polimanteia* (1595). In a section celebrating the graduates of England's two universities, a printed marginal note reads:

16 It is worth considering that "graver" here may also be a pun, along the lines of Mercutio's "Ask for me tomorrow, and you shall find me a grave man" in *Romeo and Juliet* (3.1.65).

All praise
worthy. Lucrecia
Sweet **Shak-**
speare.
Eloquent
Gaveston.
Wanton
Adonis.
Watsons
heyre.

Why include a reference to "Eloquent Gaveston" between Shakespeare's two poems *The Rape of Lucrece* and *Venus and Adonis*? Orthodox scholars Katherine Duncan-Jones and H. R. Woudhuysen think this an erroneous reference to Michael Drayton's *Piers Gaveston* (2007, 5). But another explanation is that Covell was thinking of the "eloquent Gaveston" that opens and dominates Marlowe's *Edward II*. It is, after all, Marlowe (not Drayton) who is best described as "Watson's heir"; Marlowe was nine years younger than his friend Thomas Watson, and something of his protégé. Perhaps Covell, who was a year behind Marlowe at Cambridge, also thought he noticed the verse style of his fellow alumnus and made the leap.

In the Stationers' Register in January 1600, another conflation of Marlowe and Shakespeare is evident. Marlowe's translations of Ovid's *Amores*, the source of the *Venus & Adonis* epigram, had been published bound together with John Davies's *Epigrammes*, and was listed on the Bishops' Ban of 1599 as *Davyes Epigrams, with marlowes Elegyes*. Seven months later, Eleazar Edgar registered "*A book called Amours by J.D. with certen oyr [other] sonnettes by WS*". J. D. was how Sir John Davies identified himself when his epigrams were bound with Marlowe's translations of *Amores*, and *Amours* strongly suggests this is the *Amores* of the original unlicensed publication. The only element that differs is the substitution of the initials "WS" for those previously given as "CM". Given the fame of the name by this time, it is likely that in 1599 "William Shakespeare" would be the first name that a reader would identify as the author when faced with the initials "WS". This entry in the Stationers' Register, then, may be read as the only documented attempt to exchange "Christopher Marlowe" for "William Shakespeare" on a publication.

At a similar time, the author of the manuscript work, *The Newe Metamorphosis,* wrote about Marlowe in the present and future tense. As Lyon proved conclusively through the author's mention of salient autobiographical details, the author of this text is Gervase Markham (1919). Evidence for Markham's personal connection to Marlowe has recently been established (Barber 2016). In *The Newe Metamorphosis,* Markham refers to "kynde Kit Marlowe". This tribute is rarely quoted in its full form, because the full form is problematic to orthodox scholars. Markham, writing in 1600 or later, refers, in the present and then future tense, to Marlowe completing the narrative of Hero (from his half-finished *Hero and Leander*):

> kynde Kit Marlowe, if death not prevent-him,
> shall write her story, love such art hath lent-him

One might explain away all these texts as errors, but it seems a profound coincidence that they are all making "errors" about exactly the same author. Under the Marlovian narrative, Harvey's inscrutable poem is no longer perplexing, Nashe's references are no longer mysterious, and confusions of identity or tense connected to Marlowe's works are no longer errors: all of this data stops being anomalous.

Marlowe in the Sonnets

Marlowe's narrative maps powerfully onto Shakespeare's sonnets. Paul Edmondson & Stanley Wells, considering the argument that the sonnets were simply a writing exercise, conclude that "though Shakespeare's sonnets, like all his work, unquestionably reflect his reading, and though not all of them are intimate in tone, it is not unreasonable to look in them for reflections of his personal experience" (2004, 21).

Read from the perspective of the Marlovian narrative, the group of poems sometimes referred to as the sonnets of separation become sonnets of exile. Their allusions to travel (27:2, 34:2), a journey undertaken with heavy heart (50:1), a physical separation, sundry losses (34:10) and things lacked (31:2) down to the shape of familiar birds and flowers (113:6) — "th'expense of many of a vanished sight"(30:8) — can now be read as allusions to Marlowe's long journey on horseback across Europe to a final destination in foreign climes (in the case of the Marlovian narrative, Northern Italy). Sonnet 50, "How heavy do I journey on my way", can be taken as expressing an exile's reluctance to continue on a journey in which "my grief lies onwards and my joy behind". The "large lengths of miles" (44:10) are referred to as an "injurious distance" (44:2), the poet as being in "limits far remote" (44:4). But the friend is constantly in his thoughts: "thyself away, art present still with me" (47:10). Sonnet 45 can be read as describing an exchange of letters: the joy of receiving one swiftly followed by despair when the reply is sent and the wait for a new missive begins:

> oppressed with melancholy,
> Until life's composition be recurred
> By those swift messengers returned from thee
> Who even but now come back again assured
> Of thy fair health, recounting it to me.
> This told, I joy; but then no longer glad,
> I send them back again and straight grow sad (45:8-14).

The "suborned informer" (bribed false witness, or hired spy) in Sonnet 125, which some commentators have read as a cryptic reference to a real individual, is hard to explain under the orthodox narrative. Katherine Duncan-Jones believes it refers to "Time" whom she calls "the explicit addressee of sonnets 123-5", despite the fact that only the first of those sonnets explicitly addresses Time (1997, 363). Adopting a Marlovian narrative gives us the biographical basis for a literal reading, and we may assume it is Richard Baines that Marlowe is addressing when he writes

> Hence, thou suborned informer, a true soul
> When most impeached, stands least in thy control
> (125:13-14).

A similar difference in approach can be taken to the line in sonnet 62 where the poet describes himself as being "Beated and chopped with tanned antiquity". Duncan-Jones' gloss on this line suggests that "since Shakespeare's father was a whittawer, who prepared leather for gloves, Shakespeare may well have believed his own skin to have undergone this process", but in the light of the Marlovian narrative, the line can be read as the poet becoming literally weather-beaten as he travels towards Italy. Under this reading, "whatsoever star that guides my moving" (26:9) could be taken as Fate not simply determining the course of a particular life, but a physical journey as well. "[T]his separation" (39:7) leads to "absence" (39:9), to the two friends being "twain" (36:1, 39:13), a situation the poet appears in various sonnets to rationalise ("For thy sweet love remembered such wealth brings" (29:13), for example), or try to come to terms with as in "let us divided live" (39:5).

Sonnet 29 immediately following two "journey" sonnets, can be read as explicitly referring to Marlowe's state of exile:

When in disgrace with fortune and men's eyes
I all alone beweep my outcast state,
And trouble deaf heaven with my bootless cries,
And look upon myself, and curse my fate… (29:1-4)

This poet and playwright of acknowledged genius, is

The prey of worms, my body being dead,
The coward conquest of a wretch's knife (74:10-11).

Why any other possible author would refer to themselves as being stabbed is not clear. Under this narrative, Richard Baines, whose note to the Privy Council suggested "all men in christianitei ought to endevor that the mouth of so dangerous a member may be stopped" has effectively prevailed. Marlowe will not write as Marlowe again. And yet he fears even his writing style might give away his anonymity, since he continues to write "still all one, ever the same… That every word almost doth tell my name" (76:5, 7).

With the name of Marlowe effectively dead, the exiled poet lives only through his writing, and — vicariously — through his friend:

You are my all-the-world, and I must strive
To know my shames and praises from your tongue;
None else to me, nor I to none, alive (112:5-7).

The orthodox reading takes this as metaphorical; the Marlovian reading makes it literal. But where a reading may be either metaphorical or literal, the Marlovian reading is not always the literal one. An example is Sonnet 48.

How careful was I, when I took my way,
Each trifle under truest bars to thrust,
That to my use it might unused stay
From hands of falsehood, in sure wards of trust;
But thou, to whom my jewels trifles are,
Most worthy comfort, now my greatest grief,
Though best of dearest, and mine only care,
Art left the prey of every vulgar thief (48:1-8).

Duncan-Jones's gloss for line 5 says "To a wealthy young nobleman, the valuables of a professional playwright would no doubt seem trifling." But reading the sonnets as letters home from exile, sent to a loved one, the "trifles" entrusted to the friend — the poet's jewels — are the sonnets themselves, and the friend has been inadvisably sharing them. This would chime both with Francis Meres's 1598 mention of Shakespeare's "sugred sonnets" being shared amongst his friends, and the publication of two of the sonnets in Jaggard's *Passionate Pilgrim* in 1599. The poet is concerned that it is the friend who will be put in danger:

> And even thence thou wilt be stol'n, I fear;
> For truth proves thievish for a prize so dear (48:13-14).

Far from being a sonnet referring to "the security of his earthly possessions" (Duncan-Jones 1997, 206), sonnet 48 can now be read as a warning to a friend who is literally giving too much away.

When reading the sonnets as a narrative of exile, it is possible to detect a note of despair verging at times on the suicidal (32:1; 66:1). Mining recent personal experience for his metaphor, the poet in the Marlovian narrative begins Sonnet 74:

> But be contented when that fell arrest
> Without all bail shall carry me away (74:1-2).

His lost name plagues him in these moribund contemplations, and is linked with a concern to protect his friend, who cannot be discovered to be associated with him:

> When I, perhaps, compounded am with clay,
> Do not so much as my poor name rehearse [...]
> Lest the wise world should look into your moan,
> And mock you with me after I am gone (71:10-14).

The name that should not be rehearsed comes up again in the following sonnet:

> My name be buried where my body is,
> And live no more to shame nor me, nor you (72:11-12).

The nature of the shame is elusive in the orthodox narrative, but in the Marlovian one we have a clear cause. Sonnet 111, which "has been frequently read as an allusion to Shakespeare's public profession as an actor-dramatist" by orthodox scholars, bears a stronger reading when it relates to Marlowe, whose posthumous reputation was destroyed by those such as Beard:

> Thence comes it that my name receives a brand,
> And almost thence my nature is subdued
> To what it works in, like the dyer's hand;
> Pity me, then, and wish I were renewed (111:5-8).

The "brand" on the Marlowe name has lasted over 400 years; Marlowe's reputation is still so sullied that many could not countenance him as the author of the Shakespeare works even if there were proof he survived. As a result of his "harmful deeds" as government agent, his nature is "subdued / To what it works in" — to words. Writing is his only way of communicating with the world from which he is exiled.

But writing is also his strength, and from a position of exile he not only gains perspective but a greater depth of thought: "Ruin hath taught me thus to ruminate" (64:11). The celebration of writing as both powerful and redemptive is a theme to which the sonnets repeatedly return:

> … unless this miracle have might:
> That in black ink my love may still shine bright (65:13-14).

Yet time to "ruminate" brings the poet to negative thought as much as to positive, and twice the poet echoes the Latin inscription on the putative Corpus Christi portrait of Marlowe: "consumed with that which it was nourished by" (73:12) and "the worst was this: my love was my decay" (80:14).[17] He also continues to be bothered by the slurs on his reputation, at times so bitterly that he begins sonnet 121 "'Tis better to be vile than vile esteemed", and ends it "All men are bad, and in their badness reign." The badness of the world is associated explicitly with slander in Sonnet 150:

> Now this ill-wresting world is grown so bad,
> Mad slanderers by mad ears believed be (150:11-12).

Sonnet 66 now becomes a much more personal diatribe than the

17 The Latin inscription on the 1585 Corpus Christi portrait is *QUOD ME NUTRIT ME DESTRUIT*; what nourishes me destroys me.

orthodox narrative allows, with several of the lines appearing to apply directly to the exiled poet's situation:

> ...And right perfection wrongfully disgraced,
> And strength by limping sway disabled,
> And art made tongue-tied by authority,
> And folly, doctor-like, controlling skill... (66:7-10).

In the Marlovian narrative, William Shakespeare is the frontman for the poet's work, and under this reading, "gilded honour shamefully misplaced" could be taken as an allusion to Shakespeare's being mistaken as the author.

The limping mentioned here is a repeated metaphor that has, with the exception of René Weis (2007), been largely overlooked by orthodox Shakespearean scholars; elsewhere, the poet refers to himself as being "made lame by fortune's dearest spite" (37:3).[18] Fortune's spite appears again in sonnet 90:

> Then hate me when thou wilt, if even now,
> Now while the world is bent my deeds to cross.
> Join with spite of fortune, make me bow (90:1-3).

The speaker considers himself deeply unlucky and feels the world has turned against him, misinterpreting his deeds. This, an aspect of the sonnets that has often perplexed those reading from the orthodox perspective, fits perfectly with the Marlovian one.

Other long-standing interpretive problems dissolve on adopting Marlovian authorship theory. The "paradoxical claim that [*Shake-speare's Sonnets*] will be remembered for its subject-matter (the fair youth), not for its author" which is "taken to its furthest extremes" in Sonnet 81 (Duncan-Jones 1997, 272), ceases to be any kind of paradox when we adopt the Marlovian narrative. Though the name "Shakespeare" became very well known, the author behind the name recognised he would not be credited. The two sonnets that pun on the word, and the name, "Will", can be read as the poet's attempt to fully inhabit his pseudonym so that he feels less disempowered and over-looked: "Think all but one, and me in that one Will" (135:14), and

> Make but my name thy love, and love that still;
> And then thou lov'st me, for my name is Will (136:13-14).

18 Weis, reading the image literally, has concluded that Shakespeare was physically lame.

The rival poet referred to in sonnet 86, who cannot be unequivocally identified in the orthodox narrative, can be confidently identified as George Chapman in the Marlovian one. Previous scholars, starting with William Minto in 1874, have suggested Chapman as the Rival Poet (Acheson 1903; Minto 1874, 222; Robertson 1926), but since no direct link could be found between Chapman and Shakespeare, the presumed author of the sonnets, no consensus could be reached. Chapman, however, had a clear relationship not only to Marlowe but to Marlowe's patron and friend Thomas Walsingham. In 1598 Chapman revised, extended and had published Marlowe's unfinished *Hero & Leander*, contributing more lines than Marlowe had written, altering the poem's structure, and dedicating it to Thomas Walsingham's wife, Audrey. Having one's poetic creation taken over would be cause for jealousy enough without the added complication that Chapman appears to have become Marlowe's friend and patron's new favourite. Chapman claimed to have been visited by the spirit of Homer whilst translating his *Seauen bookes of the Iliades of Homere,* published, like *Hero and Leander*, in 1598 (Chapman 1941, 174.II: 76-77). His identity seems certain when we imagine it is the "dead" Marlowe who asks

> Was it his spirit, by spirits taught to write
> Above a mortal pitch, that struck me dead? (86:5-6)

Under this narrative the identification of the rival poet as George Chapman is unproblematic because we have a proven biographical parallel with the situation described in the sonnets. Walsingham patronised and formed close relationships with both Marlowe and Chapman. Viewed through this biographical frame, at least fifteen sonnets (78 to 92), and possibly more, are addressed directly to Walsingham ("both your poets", Sonnet 83). When reading the sonnets, there are numerous important interpretative decisions that are wholly dependent on the assumed biography of the author behind the works.

Editors have revised the punctuation of 81:6 such that it reads "Though I, once gone, to all the world must die", but the Quarto version "I (once gone)" would work better for the Marlovian narrative, adding to the more obvious meaning (which the revised punctuation makes emphatic) a pun on Marlowe, thought dead, being already "once gone". Another editorial amendment illustrates even more strongly how one possible narrative might be concealed by the adoption of another. The final couplet of Sonnet 112 reads, in the Quarto:

> You are so strongly in my purpose bred
> That all the world besides me thinkes y'are dead (112:13-14).

This is frequently emended to "That all the world, besides, methinks, are dead" but as Duncan-Jones comments, "none of the proposed emendations … yields easier sense" than to read "y'are" as "you are" (1997, 334). Since the traditional narrative does not allow easy understanding of this couplet, her paraphrase is nevertheless torturous: "(because I have excluded the rest of the world from my consciousness) I believe that to everyone except me you are dead — you have existence only for me." The Marlovian narrative, however, allows the couplet to be understood very plainly, if we read it as addressed to Thomas Walsingham, whose regular attendance at court ceased after Marlowe's apparent death. Under this narrative, the couplet's meaning is: "All the world besides you thinks *I'm* dead. And you're so protective of my secret that you have also dropped from view."

The Marlovian narrative can account for many of the apparent inconsistencies in the sonnets. For example, it gives a rationale for the poet claiming to have been silenced ("As victors of my silence cannot boast" 86:11) when he is clearly still writing. It can also elucidate the precise nature of the addressee's offence in sonnets 33-36. In the orthodox narrative, there appears to be some confusion about the "stain" (33:14) "shame" (34:9) and "disgrace" (33:8, 34:8) which, via the poet's apparent forgiveness in sonnet 35, become "those blots that do with me remain", so that by sonnet 36, the "shame" is now associated with the poet (36:10). Edmondson & Wells note the direct diction employed "in what seems like a lover's quarrel" and Duncan-Jones, trying to find clarity of meaning in the orthodox narrative, suggests "[t] he young man has wronged his friend; in making excuses for him the poet colludes with him and shares his fault" (334).

Read from the perspective of Marlowe in exile, a richer story emerges. Here is Sonnet 34 in full.

> Why didst thou promise such a beauteous day
> And make me travail forth without my cloak,
> To let base clouds o'ertake me in my way,
> Hiding thy bravery in their rotten smoke?
> Tis not enough that through the cloud thou break,
> To dry the rain on my storm-beaten face,
> For no man well of such a salve can speak

That heals the wound and cures not the disgrace;
Nor can thy shame give physic to my grief;
Though thou repent, yet I have still the loss;
Th'offender's sorrow lends but weak relief
To him that bears the strong offence's cross.
Ah, but those tears are pearl which thy love sheds,
And they are rich, and ransom all ill deeds.

In the Marlovian scenario, the friend was instrumental in Marlowe's planned escape, but did not foresee the consequences: the damage to Marlowe's reputation after his apparent death in a knife-fight. The "rotten smoke" could be an allusion to the unflattering rumours and slanders that are now circulating. The friend is sorry, but Marlowe — and his name — must bear "the strong offence's cross." The Marlovian narrative clearly identifies the "separable spite" which leads the poet to conclude, two sonnets later:

I may not evermore acknowledge thee,
Lest my bewailed guilt should do thee shame,
Nor thou with public kindness honour me,
Unless thou take that honour from thy name:
But do not do so… (36:9-13).

If we allow ourselves to imagine that these are private sonnets by Christopher Marlowe, written in exile under a pseudonym that allowed him to communicate with his friend whilst remaining hidden from those who would have him killed — poems successfully attributed for four hundred years to the businessman who agreed to play his front man — we can conclude that the poet's friend and patron heeded those instructions.

Marlowe in the Plays

A writer's work should never be read as thinly veiled autobiography. We should not be looking for an author with three daughters because Lear has three daughters. But there are arguments for connecting the life and the work when for example, a significant and inexplicable change has been made to the source material. Such is the case for Juliet: sixteen years old in the source, Arthur Brooke's poem *The Tragical History of Romeus and Juliet*, but in *Romeo and Juliet*, she is thirteen when she dies.

Marlowe's prematurely married sister Jane died in childbirth at that age. But even more pertinent than biographical parallels, the *themes* to which a writer regularly returns will tend to be those of personal significance.

The Marlowe story fits Shakespeare's obsessive themes. Shakespeare is obsessed, for example, with resurrecting characters believed to be dead. Thirty-three characters across eight Shakespeare plays are wrongly thought to be dead. Seven of these deaths are deliberately faked: Juliet (*Romeo & Juliet*), Hero (*Much Ado About Nothing*), Helena (*All's Well Tha End's Well*) and Hermione (*The Winter's Tale*); plus Falstaff (*1 Henry IV*), Claudio (*Measure for Measure*), and Innogen (*Cymbeline*), who all fake their deaths to avoid being actually killed. While pretending to be dead, Innogen becomes "Fidele" who is also mistakenly thought to be dead for a time. Some of these false deaths are in the sources Shakespeare has chosen to develop but many of them are additions. The "problem" plays and the late plays, in particular, are riddled with them. Under the Marlovian narrative, this obsession with resurrection can be seen as a sort of wish fulfilment, or indeed a plea.

Deaths are often faked because of slander, false accusation, and loss of reputation: precisely the problems that beset Marlowe. Marlowe's reputation was so sullied by his enemies that even now, four hundred years later, some people consider him too degenerate a character to have written Shakespeare's works. Little wonder, then, that he would obsess over slander and "the bubble reputation". From the main plot of *Othello*, through the subplot of *King Lear* involving Edgar and Edmond to the main plots of *Cymbeline* and *Much Ado About Nothing*, an honourable character is falsely slandered and consequently killed, or forced into some form of exile. In the tragedies they remain dead or exiled; in the comedies they are restored to their lives.

"The note of banishment, banishment from the heart, banishment from the home sounds uninterruptedly from *The Two Gentlemen of Verona* onward till Prospero breaks his staff, buries it certain fathoms in the earth and drowns his book" says Stephen Daedalus in James Joyce's *Ulysses* (1980, 180). "Banishment is both the action which defines the canon and the reason for its existence" writes orthodox scholar Jane Kingsley-Smith in her ground-breaking study *Shakespeare's Drama of Exile* (2003, 1). "Again and again," she continues "he writes a scene of banishment, reworking the details of earlier plays, redirecting the emphasis from loss of language to loss of nation, from loss of the beloved to loss of self" (8). Embedded in the orthodox paradigm, she locates no plausible or substantive reason as to what might propel the author to write plays in which "the audience is consistently asked to imagine itself banished" (29).

A similar understanding of Shakespeare's works as a canon of exile has been reached by Stephen Greenblatt, whom James Shapiro has called "the best reader of Shakespeare in America today" (in Howard 2010). Shapiro is deeply critical of Greenblatt's New Historicist approach, which he perceives as dangerously opening the door to a similar approach by non-Stratfordians, and one can see why. Greenblatt could be mistaken for advancing a Marlovian argument when he writes:

> Again and again in his plays, an unforeseen catastrophe … suddenly turns what had seemed like happy progress, prosperity, smooth sailing into disaster, terror, and loss. The loss is obviously and immediately material, but it is also, and more crushingly, a loss of identity. To wind up on an unknown shore, without one's friends, habitual associates, familiar network — this catastrophe is often epitomized by the deliberate alteration or disappearance of the name and, with it, the alteration or disappearance of social status (2004, 85).

Regarding Prospero, he writes, "why, if [Shakespeare] is implicated in the figure of his magician hero, might he feel compelled to plead for indulgence, as if he were asking to be pardoned for a crime he had committed?" (376-7). From a Marlovian perspective, it is as though Greenblatt and Kingsley-Smith have seen through the works to the real author, but are unable to understand what they have seen. And let's consider Prospero: a wiser and older — and exiled — version of Marlowe's Doctor Faustus. The comparison is explicitly made by the author himself: both "Prospero" and "Faustus" come from Latin words meaning "fortunate". One character signalled the end of Marlowe's career, as Marlowe's conflation with his protagonist led to accusations of atheism against him; the other signalled the end of Shakespeare's. Faustus declares he will burn his books; Prospero that he will drown his. It is as though with water, and compassion, Prospero douses the fire and passion of his youthful counterpart:

> As you from crimes would pardoned be,
> Let your indulgence set me free.[19]

19 *The Tempest* was performed before King James on 1st November 1611. Might this speech have been primarily addressed to him?

Chapter 4

Summary

Marlowe was a gifted blank verse dramatist, penner of history plays, and Ovid-influenced poet whose works are stylistically on a continuum with Shakespeare's; the only candidate of whom this is true. As someone facing execution as a result of his work to protect the queen's life, whose life would have depended on his concealment, he had the best reason of all the candidates to hide his identity. His circumstances from lowly birth through exceptional education to gentleman, and through royal service to the friendship of noblemen and courtiers, offer the right mix of experience required for a writer of Shakespeare's social breadth. Timing supports Marlowe as author: the name William Shakespeare appears in the literary record for the first time just two weeks after Marlowe's apparent demise in an incident so mysterious that the majority of scholars who have examined the evidence believe the inquest was some kind of cover up. To read the sonnets as Marlowe's is to resolve numerous problems of tone and interpretation that exist under the orthodox narrative, including the identity of the Rival Poet. Recurrent themes throughout the plays — particularly those of slander, loss of name and reputation, exile, resurrection, and mistaken and doubled identities — fit well with what would have been Marlowe's post-exile obsessions. Contemporaneous evidence supports the idea that some writers of the time — including one very much in touch with the Elizabethan literary scene — recognised Shakespeare's style as Marlowe's. If true, it explains both why the canons are so similar and inter-related, and why they deviate in subject matter and preferred imagery. The effect of losing one life and identity would be profound. Suffering can prove a unique source of wisdom: of broader perspective, and a deeper understanding of the human condition. As former poet laureate, Ted Hughes, expressed it: "The way to really develop as a writer is to make yourself a political outcast, so that you have to live in secret. This is how Marlowe developed into Shakespeare" (2007, 120). Perhaps it is time we listened to Prospero's valedictory words, pardoned this exiled conjuror, and set him free.

Chapter 5

Our Shakespeare: Henry Neville 1562-1615

John Casson, William D. Rubinstein and David Ewald

Henry Neville was born c1562-4, a descendant of the famous Nevilles of medieval England and was educated at Merton College, Oxford. Between 1578-82 Neville accompanied his tutor, Henry Savile, on a tour of Europe. Neville was elected a Member of Parliament in 1584 and served as an M.P. for the rest of his life (except 1601-3). In 1599 he became Ambassador to France. Returning to England in 1600, he became involved in the Essex rebellion and in 1601 was imprisoned in the Tower of London for treason, alongside the Earl of Southampton. Freed by James I in 1603, he spent the rest of his life unsuccessfully seeking high office and became what would now be termed a leader of the opposition in Parliament. His main residence was Billingbear near Windsor. He died in July 1615.

For any authorship candidate to be convincing he/she needs to be supported by a wide range of multi-facetted evidence, which must be consistent with what is already known of the works of Shakespeare. Evidence for Neville's authorship is provided by his:

1. Life experience which offers a precise match for the development and content of the plays;

2. Social network which places him in the nexus of people whom the Bard knew, some of them providing evidence of his involvement in theatre;

3. Education and knowledge of the subjects and locations of Shakespeare's plays and sources, as evidenced by his annotated books;

4. Manuscripts and note-books containing material relevant to the Shakespeare plays;

5. Vocabulary in his letters and the internal evidence of the plays and poems;

6. Reasons for secrecy. Contemporary writers made covert references to Neville as a poet.

We now review these different classes of evidence and then look briefly at two plays: *Richard III* and *The Merry Wives of Windsor*. We offer new evidence as well as summarising previously published information.

1. Life experience, life/work fit

For an authorship candidate to be credible his dates should be consistent with the accepted dating of Shakespeare's works, all of which are generally believed to have been written between the late 1580s and 1613. Neville's life span of 1562-1615 meets this criterion. Indeed, it is significant that after *The Two Noble Kinsmen*, co-written with Fletcher in 1613, Shakespeare did not write anything else. This fit between the life and works is further evidenced by many aspects of Neville's life that match the Bard's writings. For example, one of his favourite sources of imagery was falconry and it is known that Neville's father was a keen falconer. He was also master of the royal hounds, a forester and a courtier, all of which explains Shakespeare's familiar use of these as sources of imagery. Other examples of Neville's life experience matching the special interests of the Bard include the following: he had an iron foundry where he manufactured and exported cannon; he travelled by sea; he served as an ambassador and on Parliamentary committees on illegitimacy, falconry and hunting; his own political ambitions were frustrated; he was a land owner, forester and farmer; he married his sons and daughters happily; he played the lute; he suffered from gout.

In 1583, Neville travelled to Scotland with Walsingham and the Earl of Essex, furnishing him with experience of Scotland and the Scots, which Shakespeare displays in *Edward III*, *Henry V* and *Macbeth*. The same year Walsingham set up the Queen's Men who performed establishment propaganda plays including the early versions of *King*

John, *Henry V* (which contained the seeds of *Henry IV*), *Richard III* and *King Leir*, all of which Shakespeare later re-wrote. As sheriff of Berkshire from 1595 and deputy lieutenant from 1596, Neville was responsible for recruiting soldiers, as is Falstaff in *2 Henry IV*. In 1597, he sat on Parliamentary Committees dealing with the "irksome and outmodish recruitment of soldiers", which we see in 3.2. of *2 Henry IV* (James 2008, 340). The two parts of *Henry IV* were written between 1596-8 and so Neville's experience was contemporary with Shakespeare's writing. Additionally, being both a J.P. and an M.P. from the age of 21/22, Neville knew the law and law-making. He was involved in legal cases all his adult life, giving him the legal knowledge that scholars have found deeply embedded in Shakespeare's writing. Neville made lists of "interrogatories" (legal questions) and these are still extant in the Berkshire archives (document: D/EN/L2/1/1). The word "interrogatories" is in several Shakespeare plays from *King John* (3.1.147) to *Cymbeline* (5.4.393).[1] Shakespeare's plays show a clear evolutionary trajectory, first set out by Edward Dowden (1875). Early in his career, Shakespeare wrote mainly Italianate comedies and history plays. There was a major break in Shakespeare's writing from 1600/1, after which he wrote the great tragedies and the problem plays. He then turned to romances and ended his career writing three plays with John Fletcher. A biography of the actual author must be able to explain this development and Neville's own life consistently explains much about the chronology of Shakespeare's plays. Neville spent two years in the Tower with the Earl of Southampton (to whom Shakespeare had dedicated his two longest poems). They were both stripped of their titles, with Southampton being known as "Mr. Henry Wriothesley" until he was released. Towards the end of their imprisonment Southampton composed his version of an *Encomium of Richard III* and dedicated it to Neville (see below). This experience of imprisonment traumatised Neville, who went overnight from a rising court favourite to a convicted traitor. His response, we suggest, was to re-work *Hamlet* in 1601, write the bitterly cynical *Troilus and Cressida* in 1602 and *Othello* in 1602/3, all of which can be seen as reflecting on his experience of the Essex rebellion (Casson & Rubinstein 2016).

Neville's imprisonment explains those sonnets which speak of their

1 The singular shortened form "inter'gatory" is in *The Merchant of Venice* (5.1.300) and the plural, "inter'gatories" in *All's Well That Ends Well* (4.3.184); the word does not occur in the original version of *The Troublesome Raigne of John* so was added when Shakespeare revised the play. The earliest date of this revision is held to be 1596 which is the year George Peele died and the same year *The Merchant of Venice* was written.

author having received "a brand", "a stain", being "in disgrace" and "I all alone beweep my outcast state" (29, 33, 35, 109, 111). In sonnet 35, Neville seems to forgive Wriothesley (pronounced Rosely: "roses have thorns") whose testimony at his own trial led to Neville's conviction. *Shake-speares Sonnets* was entered for publication on the Stationers' Register on 20 May 1609. There has been much speculation about why it was published at that particular time, whether the often cryptic sonnets are autobiographical, whether they were published with the author's approval and what was meant by the mysterious dedication:

TO.THE.ONLIE.BEGETTER.OF.
THESE.INSVING.SONNETS.
Mr.W.H.

Positing Neville as the author enables us to answer some of these questions. In our view, *Shake-speares Sonnets* was published in May 1609 to coincide with the granting of the Charter of the second London Virginia Company (on 23 May 1609). The dedication "wisheth the well-wishing adventurer in setting forth", and at the time an adventurer was an investor (the word recurs in our current vocabulary in "venture capital"). We agree with most other scholars that Mr. W. H. was a disguised reference to Henry Wriothesley who, with Neville, was an investor in the Company. The publication, we suggest, marked the marriage of Neville's eldest son, Henry, to Elizabeth, the daughter of Sir John Smythe (Casson & Rubinstein 200).

There is a connection between *Shake-speares Sonnets* and *The Tempest* (dated to 1610-11). Neville may have hoped that the Company would restore his diminished financial fortunes. In a letter dated 18 August 1609 Thomas Smythe (brother of John and Treasurer of the Virginia Company) thanked Neville for a delivery of timber for shipbuilding and promised payment.[2] In June 1609, nine ships had set out to settle Virginia under the Company's auspices and one of these, the *Sea-Venture*, on her maiden voyage, was wrecked at Bermuda. After a year on the island, the survivors managed to build two boats, sail to Jamestown, Virginia, and were able to send an account to London. This was the "Strachey letter", written by William Strachey (1572-1621). Dated 15

2 The letter states that the timber was for ships of the East India Company, of which Thomas was the governor. Thomas ends by sending his regards to Neville's son and new wife (his niece). The letter is in the Berkshire Record Office archive: D/EN/F6/1. Shakespeare used the word "timber" (and "timbered") from c1600 onwards, first in *As You Like It*. The usage in *Othello*, c1602, refers to a ship: "His bark is stoutly timbered" (2.1.48).

July 1610, it was addressed to "an excellent Lady" in England, who was, we suggest, Sarah, wife of Sir Thomas Smythe (the aunt of Neville's daughter-in-law). It reached London in September 1610. Circulation of the Strachey letter was restricted, by an oath of secrecy, to members of the Company's Council and it was not published until 1625 (see Clarke 2011, 13-27). The importance of the Strachey letter lies in the fact that it is almost universally accepted as one of the main sources for *The Tempest.* Neville was a member of the Council of the Company. He would have had the opportunity to read the letter and could therefore have used it in a play that reflected the wreck of his own hopes, past political betrayals, the importance of his daughter's marriages and the approaching end of his own career.

Just before he was released from the Tower in March 1603, Neville wrote a list of things to do, titled "Remembrances", that included "stocking my grounds and providing ewes that will twinne", followed by reference to his "lambs of the year".[3] Before this time Shakespeare had already mentioned ewes and lambs in *The Merchant of Venice* (4.1.74); in *Much Ado About Nothing* (3.3.68); in *As You Like It* (3.2.72). The only time the Bard referred to "twinned lambs" is after Neville made this note: in *The Winter's Tale* (c 1610-11) Polixenes says that he and Leontes "were as twinn'd lambs" (1.2.66). In 1610, two daughters were born to Neville, Anne and Elizabeth. If these girls were twins this might explain the reference to "twinn'd lambs". The play celebrates a daughter's wedding and Neville celebrated the marriages of two daughters that same year.[4]

2. a) Social network

Neville knew Henry Wriothesley, 3rd Earl of Southampton, Shakespeare's patron. He had met Wriothesley when the latter was a boy and they spent two years in prison together after the Essex rebellion. Hamlet calls Horatio, "O Damon dear" (3.2.275). Since the Greek legend of Damon and Pythias tells of two friends, both of whom were imprisoned and under threat of execution, and were later pardoned, this reference in *Hamlet* resembles Neville and Southampton's situation in 1601-3. Southampton supported Neville's candidacy to be

3 This document, D/EN/F45/1-2, is at the Berkshire Records Office. The word "remembrances" entered Shakespeare's vocabulary from *Hamlet* (3.1.93) onwards. The word is singular in the first quarto of 1603 but becomes plural in the 1604 second quarto. Neville's use predates the plural form appearing in the longer, second version of *Hamlet.*

4 Mary, who married Edward Lewknor, and Frances, who married Richard Worsley, in May 1610.

Secretary of State and was identified as Neville's "champion" by John Chamberlain in 1612 (McClure 1939, 387). In 1613 Henry Howard, Earl of Northampton, acknowledged the close friendship between Neville and Wriothesley, describing Neville as Southampton's "Dear Damon" (James & Rubinstein 2005, 246).

Neville knew many others who were significant for Shakespeare. Amongst these was the poet Philip Sidney, who influenced the Bard and whom Neville would have met as a boy because their fathers were close friends. Neville travelled around Europe with Robert, Philip's brother, and the two stayed in touch throughout their lives. Philip praised Neville in a letter to his brother. Neville's home at Mayfield was just 15 miles from the Sidneys' house at Penshurst Place so between 1582 and 1585, when Philip went to fight in the Netherlands, it is possible that Neville visited them. Neville met Charles de Goutaut, the Duke of Biron, upon whom Berowne in *Love's Labours' Lost* is based. He referred to Marshall Biron in a letter dated 24 April 1600 and he may have previously encountered Biron in France during his travels of 1578-82. Sir Henry Killigrew, his father-in-law, met Biron in 1591 when fighting in France under Essex. Biron came to England in 1598 as French ambassador, the same year Neville was chosen as English ambassador to France and the year *Love's Labours' Lost* was first printed. Neville also knew Antonio Perez, a model for Don Armado in the same play and met Count Orsino who visited London at the time of *Twelfth Night*. Neville met the ambassador to Barbary, el-Ouahed ben Messaoud, a possible model for Othello. An annotation in Neville's copy of *Leicester's Commonwealth* is evidence he knew Dr. John Dee, the mathematician who, it has been suggested was the model for Prospero (Worsley MSS 47: Casson & Rubinstein 222). He also knew Thomas Overbury, whose imprisonment underlies *The Two Noble Kinsmen* (*ibid* 234). Neville knew William, 3rd Earl of Pembroke, to whom the *First Folio* was dedicated. Pembroke was his political ally to become Secretary of State from 1610 and there are letters recording their meetings in 1613. Pembroke purchased the ward-ship of Neville's grandson after his father's death in 1629 (*ibid* 37). Neville's father-in-law was one of the editors of the 1587 edition of Holinshed's *Chronicles* which is the source used by Shakespeare for many of his plays. Neville knew Ralph Newbury, (1535-1608) the printer of Holinshed. In 1603, Newbery purchased the manor of Wolfines in White Waltham from Neville. While still in prison Neville reminded himself to "write to Mr.

Newbery",[5] as he needed to raise money to pay the heavy fine imposed on him. Finally, both are buried at Waltham St. Lawrence.

There is clear evidence of connections between Neville and two of Shakespeare's publishers: Thomas Thorpe and William Jaggerd. Southampton's *Encomium of Richard III*, which he dedicated to Neville, was eventually printed in a collection of *Essays of Certain Paradoxes* in 1616 by Thomas Thorpe, who had published *Shake-speares Sonnets* in 1609. The date of publication of the *Encomium*, 1616, is one year after Neville died. A copy of this edition is to be found in the Neville library at Audley End House. The printed version is based on Southampton's version, including virtually all the additions he made to the text. It does not have the dedication to Neville which is in the manuscript however (see Bradbeer & Casson 2015, 199). The fact that the version printed by Thorpe is that given by Southampton to Neville is evidence of a connection between Neville and Thorpe because this unique manuscript must have been the source. A copy of Thomas Milles' *A Catalogue of Honor* which was annotated by Neville between 1610-12 (he referred to Prince Henry being alive and he died in 1612) is also in the library at Audley End. This book was printed by William Jaggard, who was the printer of *The Passionate Pilgrim* (the first volume to include Shakespeare sonnets) and both the *False* and *First Folio* of Shakespeare's plays. Neville's copy of *A Catalogue of Honor* seems to have been a proof copy (the picture of James I was printed upside down). Neville was carefully correcting the text and suggesting cuts. Some of his suggestions were indeed picked up by the editor because there are printed slips of these corrections pasted into another copy of *A Catalogue of Honor* to be found in the British Library. This then is evidence of a possible relationship between Neville and Jaggard in 1610-12. Finally, Neville was connected to the most important people in the land. He knew Francis Walsingham, Robert Devereux, Earl of Essex and Elizabeth I. He was related to Robert Cecil and Francis Bacon.

2. b) Interest in and connections with theatre

Neville's annotated books show he was interested in theatre. He made brief annotations on Plautus' Latin play *The Menaechmi*, which was a source for *The Comedy of Errors*. Scholars have noted that this play was not available in translation in Shakespeare's time so he must have read it in Latin. Neville made notes on classical theatres; on ancient Greek

5 This note, dated 3 February 1602 (old style calendar; so it was actually written in 1603), is at Berkshire Record Office: D/EN/F45/1-2.

playwrights; he owned books of plays by Italian and Spanish playwrights; on the Northumberland Manuscript he noted Thomas Nashe's banned play *The Isle of Dogs* and copied out speeches for court entertainments; he used theatrical metaphors in his letters;[6] he was a member of the Mermaid club with Ben Jonson, Francis Beaumont, John Fletcher, William Strachey (whose letter was a source for *The Tempest*) and Hugh Holland (who wrote a commendatory poem for the *First Folio*). Jonson wrote an ode addressed to Neville while he was still alive. When the *First Folio* appeared in 1623 Jonson is believed to have written much of the introductory material and been the main editor of the collection. At the time Jonson was employed at Gresham College. In testimony given in a Chancery case on 20 October 1623 he is described as "*Beniamin Johnson* of Gresham Colledge in London gent. aged 50. yeares and vpwards".[7] Jonson lectured on rhetoric at Gresham College at the time he was working on the *First Folio.* Gresham College had been founded in 1597, under the will of Neville's great uncle, Sir Thomas Gresham. Neville's father had been the chief mourner at Gresham's funeral. The Neville family was in a position to use its influence to obtain the post for Jonson so that he could edit the plays of William Shakespeare. In 1599 John Chamber addressed a Latin poem to Neville and included the words, "Too little is your excellence seen by the common people of the Earth, were it not for the kindly company of the Muses who sing through you, granting you various arts: the refined Thalia, (Muse of Comedy) giving you the eloquence to pour forth what you Will" (Casson & Rubinstein 119). The word "Will" in Chamber's poem ("Velles" in Latin) is capitalised, unlike any other word in the poem that is not the beginning of a line or a proper name, suggesting that Chamber was aware of Neville's pseudonym. By 1599, when Chamber's work was published, Shakespeare had written most of his famous comedies (although none of his greatest tragedies) and this poem suggests that some of Neville's friends were aware of his career as a playwright. The same year Neville wrote a short comic poem which he signed (*ibid* 115). George Carleton was Neville's vicar in Mayfield from 1589. He eventually became bishop of Chichester and married Neville's widow, Anne, in 1619. In 1603 Carleton wrote a Latin poem in which he hinted that Neville was a poet and possibly writing tragedies for the stage. In 1603 Shakespeare's *Hamlet* was published and he had written *Othello.* In the dedication of *Heroici Characteres* Carleton encouraged Neville with,

6 Reflecting on Henry IV's actions in France in 1600 Neville wrote that they were "like to prove the first act of the tragedy …" (Duncan 1974, 126 and Sawyer 1725: Vol 1, 183).

7 Ian Donaldson: *Life of Ben Jonson* from <http://universitypublishingonline.org/cambridge/benjonson/k/essays/jonsons_life_essay/10/> accessed 11/10/2016.

"Who would deny that these should not be further exalted on stage in Tragedy?" (Bradbeer & Casson 176). Both Chamber and Carleton were suggesting that Neville, blessed by the Muses, was a poet.

Shakespeare's co-authors included George Peele, Christopher Marlowe, Thomas Nashe, Thomas Middleton, George Wilkins and John Fletcher. We have some indirect evidence that Neville knew them or had some connection with them. Peele and Middleton both went to Oxford; Peele was there when Neville was at Merton. Peele wrote fondly of his time hunting in Windsor and of the garter ceremony. Neville lived near Windsor and was responsible, with his father, for hunting in the Windsor forest and attended the garter ceremony (see below). Neville listed Nashe on the Northumberland Manuscript. Both Marlowe and Neville knew Francis Walsingham: Neville went on a diplomatic mission to Scotland with him and Marlowe worked as one of his spies. Middleton has been identified as the author of *A Yorkshire Tragedy* and the play includes hints of Neville (Casson 2009, 191-202). It also has connections with Wilkins' *The Miseries of Enforced Marriage* which includes a character called Faulconbridge (a Neville family name). Before Fletcher joined Shakespeare to co-write the last three plays, Beaumont and Fletcher gave Neville the manuscript of their play *A King and No King*. It was published by Thomas Walkley with a dedication to Neville in 1619. Walkley published the first quarto of *Othello* in 1622 with a note saying the writer was dead.

3. Education and knowledge of the subjects and locations of Shakespeare's plays and access to sources

Henry Neville was fully qualified to have written the works of Shakespeare. He could read Latin, Greek, French, Spanish and Italian. His Oxford tutor, Henry Savile, was a leading Greek scholar, mathematician and astronomer. Neville owned books on astronomy and was acknowledged by John Chamber as an astronomer (Casson & Rubinstein, 62, 118). During their 1578-1582 tour of Europe, Neville travelled with Savile to Paris, then to Strasbourg (where Robert Sidney joined them) and on into Germany. One of Savile's aims was to meet European astronomers, principal amongst whom was Tycho Brahe. Tycho's observatory was, from 1576, on an island within sight of Elsinore and he made observations of a super nova in 1572 which is believed to be the star mentioned in *Hamlet* (1.1.39; Falk 2014, 51, 148). Tycho studied at Wittenberg University where Hamlet had been for his education. Johannes Praetorius, professor of astronomy at Wittenberg in 1571 and, from 1576, professor of mathematics at Altdorf (where Savile and Neville met him) wrote a study of comets in 1578. Savile, who also studied comets, corresponded with him from 1581 (Gingerich & Westman 1988, 14). Wittenberg lies between Denmark and Prague where Savile and Neville met the astronomer Tadeáš Hájek, a colleague of Tycho's. In 1581 they were in Wroclaw (Breslau) Poland, where they met Paul Wittich, an astronomer who had been a student at Wittenberg and had visited Tycho in August-November 1580. Savile made notes on Wittich's thoughts after that visit (Goulding 1995, 161). Interestingly, Poland is referred to three times in *Hamlet.* In 1590, Tycho sent copies of his portrait to Savile's brother Thomas which included references to his ancestors "Rosenkrans" and "Gvldestere". Another astronomer who observed Tycho's supernova was Thomas Digges (1546-1595). He knew John Chamber and Henry Savile as they worked together on a government commission about whether to adopt the Gregorian calendar. Digges' mother-in-law was Ursula Neville, daughter of Neville's great uncle, George 5th Baron Bergavenny (who appears as Abergavenny in *Henry VIII*). Leonard Digges, his son, contributed verses to the *First Folio.* Leonard's brother, Dudley, was an M. P. and investor in the second London Virginia Company. Anne St. Leger, their mother, later married Thomas Russell, overseer of William Shakspere of Stratford's will. Russell's half-brother, Henry Berkley, married Neville's daughter Elizabeth in 1608 (James & Rubinstein xviii).

Savile and Neville visited many places in Italy where Shakespeare's Italian plays are set. When in Padua in 1581, Savile worked with Giovan Vicenzo Pinelli on ancient Greek texts including Dionysius of Halicarnassus (Woofson 1998, 269), a large annotated volume of which is amongst Neville's books in the Audley End Library.[8] Savile received a letter from Alvise Lullini, dated 20 April 1582, from Venice, saying he was searching for various works including those of "the Halicarnassian". Lullini concluded with, "My salutations to Mr. Neville". The histories of Dionysius of Halicarnassus are a possible source for *Coriolanus* and one of Neville's annotations refers to Ancus Martius who is mentioned in the play (see below). The Arden edition of *Coriolanus* considers the Roman Histories of Dionysius of Halicarnassus, Dio Cassius and Appian as ultimate sources but dismisses the possibility Shakespeare consulted them because they were not available in translation in his time

8 The library was transferred from Billingbear, where Neville lived, to Audley End sometime in the late 19th or early 20th century, saving it from the disastrous fire of 1924.

(Brockbank 1994, 32). Neville owned copies of all three: his Dio Cassius is in the library at Merton College, the other two are at Audley End. Savile visited Rome in 1581 and Neville may well have accompanied him. They travelled through Florence, Arthur Throckmorton noting Savile's arrival there in his diary. Neville's library contains books published in Florence in 1580 and 1581 which suggests that he may have bought them in that city. Shakespeare's knowledge of Florence has been demonstrated by Richard Roe in *The Shakespeare Guide to Italy* (2011).

Neville's annotated books contain many references to words, images and stories we find in Shakespeare's poems and plays. We suggest that many of these were made when Neville was a student and so predate the writing of the plays. The annotations show him accumulating the knowledge that informed Shakespeare's writing. One example is the annotation "*veni, vidi, vici*", Caesar's famous boast on his conquest of Britain.

Appian's Roman History: page 135 in the Dionysius of Halicarnassus section (Private Collection)

This occurs in *Love's Labour's Lost* when Boyet reads Armado's letter: "*Veni, vedi, vici* … he came, saw and overcame" (4.1.70). It is remembered again in *Cymbeline* when the Queen translates it as "Came, and saw, and overcame" (3.1.25). This might be dismissed as a commonplace known to any Latin educated schoolboy but there are many other annotations that recur in the plays and poems. Three annotations about Tarquin show that Neville was aware of this tyrant before Shakespeare wrote *The Rape of Lucrece*. The first annotation is "L. Tarquinius", which stands for Lucius Tarquinius.

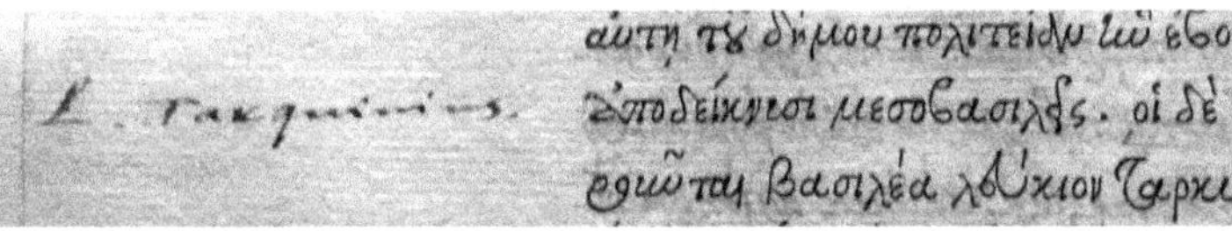

L. Tarquinius, Dionysius of Halicarnassus: page 136 (Private collection)

Another annotation clarifies that Tarquinius was also called Superbus: the Proud.

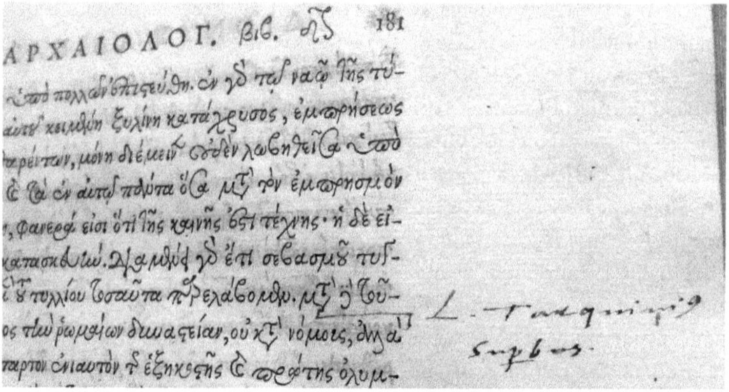

L. Tarquinius Sup_bus., Dionysius of Halicarnassus: page 181 (Private collection)

This is how Tarquin is named in the Argument at the start of *The Rape of Lucrece*: "Lucius Tarquinius, for his excessive pride surnamed Superbus …". In another annotation Neville noted that "here Ancus Martius and Tarquinius Collatinus are missed out". Collatinus was Lucrece's husband.

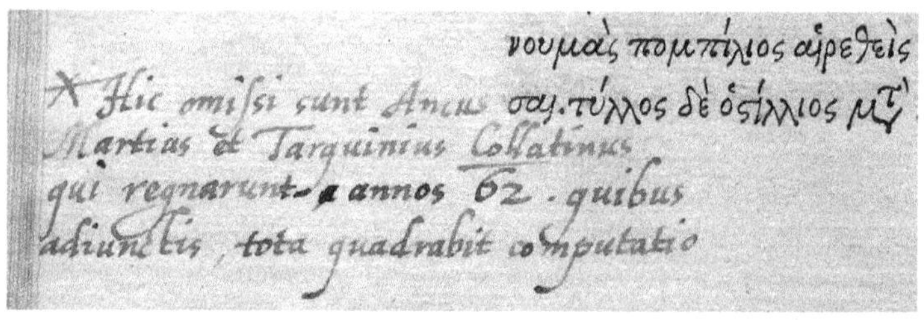

Hic omissi sunt Ancus Martius et Tarquinius Collatinus, Dionysius of Halicarnassus: page 45 (Private collection)

Ancus Martius was the name of the fourth king of Rome. His successor was Lucius Tarquinius Priscus who was father or grandfather of Lucius Tarquinius Superbus, the rapist of Lucrece and the last king of Rome. Coriolanus was contemporary with Tarquinius Superbus and this is referred to in the play (2.2.94). Shakespeare repeatedly referred to Tarquin in other works: *Titus Andronicus*, *Julius Caesar*, *Macbeth*, *Coriolanus* and *Cymbeline*. With Neville identified as the Bard we can begin to understand why this story of rape recurred. In *Leicester's Commonwealth* there is an implicit reference to the aftermath of the rape of Lucrece. In complaining about Leicester's intolerable sexual appetite "upon men's wives" the writers refer back to historic examples of how previous times have punished such behaviour: "offences … were extremely punished in princes themselves, and that not only in the person delinquent alone, but also by extirpation of the whole family for his sake, as appeareth in the example of the Tarquinians among the Romans" (Peck, 87/61). In his manuscript of *Leicester's Commonwealth*, Neville copied out a marginal note, "the exterpacõn of the Tarquinians" (Worsley MSS 47, 14; Casson 2010, 195).

The underlying political meaning of *The Rape of Lucrece* is revealed in the final section of Shakespeare's opening argument: "with one consent they all vowed to root out the whole hated family of the Tarquins; and bearing the dead body to Rome, Brutus acquainted the people with the doer and manner of the vile deed, with a bitter invective against the tyranny of the king: wherewith the people were so moved, that with one consent and a general acclamation the Tarquins were all exiled, and the state government changed from kings to consuls." This last sentence hints at a political, even anti-monarchy, stance and uses the same image of the extirpation/rooting out of "the whole family". The issue of electing kings is touched on in *Titus Andronicus*, *1 Henry VI*, *Julius Caesar* and *Pericles*. As a member of Parliament Neville may have expected to play a role in the choice of the next monarch. He could also have known about the sexual abuse of Anne Neville by Edward IV one hundred years earlier. In *3 Henry VI* Warwick confronts Edward with his offences including, "th'abuse done my niece" (3.3.188). The identity of this woman is not certain, but Shakespeare would have read about this in Hall or Holinshed, who both mention it. Bulwer-Lytton (1891, xvi) was able to show that the most likely victim of the king's rapacity was Warwick's daughter, Anne, who was then a teenager, as no niece was present at that time and so reference to a niece may have been an attempt to screen the identity of the actual victim. Shakespeare later shows us Anne being seduced by Richard III, Edward's brother and thus perhaps regarded as guilty by association. The major political consequence of this rape was that Richard Neville revolted against Edward IV and dethroned him (albeit temporarily and at the eventual cost of his own life). Shakespeare is thus recalling a family tragedy behind the story of the rape of Lucrece, both having political consequences that affect the succession to the throne. Richard Neville, Earl of Warwick, was a first cousin of Neville's great grandfather (James 2008, 352).

Further evidence that Neville's interests in Roman history matched those of Shakespeare's is an annotation in a volume of Appian stating that Antony fled to his house after the assassination of Julius Caesar

"Antoni(u)s domû(m) fugit", Appian, page 250, (Private Collection)

In North's *Plutarch*, a major source of Shakespeare's play, it states Antony "cast a slaves gowne upon him, and hid him selfe", and with Lepidus, "fled into other mens houses, and forsook their own" (Daniell 1998, 369, 330). Neither of these details is in the play which follows the Appian annotation:

> Cassius: Where is Antony?
> Trebonius:Fled to his house amazed.
> (3.1.96)

There are numerous annotations that show Neville was familiar with the story of the assassination of Julius Caesar long before Shakespeare wrote the play, three annotations highlighting Antony's eulogy after Caesar's death and his will (Casson & Rubinstein 101). There are also many annotations on Antony and Cleopatra. Such classical learning is clearly recalled by the Bard when Octavius describes the dead Cleopatra: "she looks like sleep, as she would catch another Antony in her strong toil of grace" (5.2.340). The Cambridge edition of the play explains that "a toil" is a net or snare (Bevington 2013, 268). One of Neville's annotations translated reads, "The death of Antony in Cleopatra's net".

Mors Antonii in sinu Cleopatræ: Appian: page 305 in the Dionysius section, (Private Collection)

The word "*sinus*" is Latin for a fishing net. This is dramatised on stage when Cleopatra and her women lift Antony into her monument with ropes.

Love's Labour's Lost has been dated to 1594-5. Whilst no source has ever been discovered for the plot, a number of works have been identified as influencing the play. Several of these books are in the

Neville library at Audley End. These include a 1560 annotated copy of Castiglione's *Book of the Courtier*, a 1551 edition of Terence's Latin play *Eunuchus* in which one character is the braggart Thraso (the word "thrasonical" appears in *Love's Labour's Lost* (5.1.12)); a 1558 edition of the *Adagia* of Erasmus and the word "honorificabilitudinitatibus" used by Costard in the play (5.1.40) is to be found on page 662. A version of this word, "honorificabiletudine" appears on the Northumberland Manuscript, which has Neville's surname at the top and Shakespeare's at the bottom and dates from 1596-7, before *Love's Labour's Lost* was first published in 1598. This edition of *Adagia* has annotations which suggest it may have been a source for Shakespeare including one which translates a Latin proverb as "old wives fables, winter tales" (see Casson & Rubinstein 68) for a complete list of works in Neville's library that are possible sources for *Love's Labour's Lost*).

Of the many specialist subjects the Bard was familiar with one less noticed is lapidary: knowledge of the supposed healing power of precious stones. An example is the beneficial effect on poor eyesight of gazing at an emerald to be found in *The Lover's Complaint*: "The deep-green emerald, in whose fresh regard weak sights their sickly radiance do amend" (lines 213-4).[9] This poem was published at the end of *Shake-speares Sonnets* in 1609. Dudley Carleton, who had been suffering from a painful kidney stone, wrote to Ralph Winwood on 7 April 1609, saying that he was "put in Comfort by Sir *Henry Nevill* and Sir *Thomas Bodley* who are both as you know good Lapidaries" (Sawyer 1727: Vol 3, 7). In the library at Audley End there is an edition of *Della Summa de Secreti Universali in Ogni Materia* by Timotheo Rossello, of herbal remedies which include recipes that use ground pearl. It was published in Venice in 1580, the year before Neville visited the city. The name "Nevill" is written in one annotation on page 47: this was the spelling Neville used in signing extant letters in 1601, 1602 and 1613. On pages 83-4 Rossello offered a remedy for the stone (*la pietra*) which Neville annotated. In a letter dated 28 December 1600, Neville wrote that he had suffered "a shrewd Fit of the Stone" (Sawyer 1725: Vol 1, 286). Shakespeare did refer to kidney stones two years later when Thersites lists "loads of gravel i'th' back" (5.1.18) in *Troilus and Cressida*. Hansen (1977, 211) gave examples of Shakespeare's references to the healing

9 In a letter to Winwood, dated 11 March 1605 (1606) Neville alluded to a possible eye problem: "And thus Sir, having almost spent my Eyes, which were bad before I will end somewhat abruptly, … HENRY NEVILLE" (Sawyer 1725: Vol 2). The idea that gazing on an emerald was beneficial to the eyes goes back to Theophrastus, a pupil of Aristotle in 300 BC (Kunz 1916, 21).

power of stones starting with Duke Senior in *As You Like It*, who talks of the "precious jewel" believed to be found in a toad's head and to be an antidote to poison. Hansen listed the *Colloquia* of Erasmus as a source for this belief. The *Colloquia* is also a recognised source for *Love's Labour's Lost*. There is a 1591 edition of the *Colloquia* at Audley End.

The books at Audley End contain handwritten marginal notes and underlining's that pertain to: *The Comedy of Errors; Taming of The Shrew; Venus and Adonis; Titus Andronicus; The Rape of Lucrece; Love's Labour's Lost; Much Ado About Nothing; Julius Caesar; Henry V; Hamlet; Macbeth; Coriolanus; Antony and Cleopatra; Pericles; Cymbeline; Twelfth Night* and *The Winter's Tale*. Other unmarked books in the Neville library are sources for *The Two Gentlemen of Verona, A Midsummer Night's Dream* and *As You Like It*. For all the plays not listed above we have been able to show there are Neville connections. For example Neville had visited Venice, Florence and Vienna which are the locations of *The Merchant of Venice*, *Othello*, *All's Well That Ends Well* and *Measure for Measure*. James & Rubinstein (51) offered evidence that the Hall's *Chronicles* discovered by Keen and Lubbock in 1940 was annotated by Neville and Casson's study confirmed this (Casson 2010, 73-94). Neville's grandmother, Eleanor Windsor, was the sister of Anne Windsor Corbet, whose husband Roger's sister, another Anne, was the mother of Richard Newport who had signed his name in the volume. Newport was therefore related to Neville. Hall's *Chronicles* is an acknowledged source for Shakespeare's history plays and in this volume and in his copy of *Leicester's Commonwealth*, Neville made specific notes about the Salique Law (that barred the succession of a woman) which Shakespeare referred to in *Edward III* and *Henry V* (Bradbeer & Casson 79).

4. Manuscripts and notebooks contain material relevant to the Shakespeare plays

Neville left four notebooks/manuscripts that are relevant to Shakespeare authorship: *Leicester's Commonwealth* c1585 (Worsley MSS 47 in Lincoln Archives); the Northumberland Manuscript c1597 (at Alnwick Castle); his diplomatic notebook 1599-1600 (in the National Archives at Kew); the Tower Notebook 1602-3 (Worsley MSS 40 in Lincoln Archives). *Leicester's Commonwealth* and the Tower Notebook with their relevant annotations have been shown to be sources for the history plays (James & Rubinstein; Casson 2010; Bradbeer & Casson). The Northumberland Manuscript is perhaps the single most important document linking

Neville with William Shakespeare. It dates from before that name appeared on any play. It also contains the earliest manuscript quotation from *The Rape of Lucrece* and refers to both *Richard II* and *Richard III*. All these manuscripts and Neville's extant letters offer the opportunity to compare Neville's handwriting with Hand D of the manuscript of *Sir Thomas More* (see Casson & Rubinstein 152).

5. Vocabulary in his letters and the internal evidence of the plays and poems

The Shakespeare history plays have a pro-Neville bias, showing the Bard continually referred to matters that interested Neville himself. Many minor characters have Neville connections (Bradbeer & Casson). New examples continue to emerge, for example Poins is a fictional friend of Prince Hal in *1 & 2 Henry IV*, which were written 1596-8. The name is spelt "Pointz" in the *First Folio*. In 1595, Neville's stepmother Elizabeth (née Bacon) married Sir William Peryman and became stepmother to Jane who married Thomas Poyntz. He died in 1597. After this Poins does not appear again on stage (although he is mentioned in *The Merry Wives of Windsor:* 3.2.66). Neville used the same rare vocabulary in his letters as the Bard used in the plays. *Hapax legomena* are words that occur only once in a writer's works. They have been used by scholars to determine authorship. In his letters Neville used many words that occur only once in Shakespeare's oeuvre (at a rate of approximately one every hundred words). Given that we have no Neville letters dated earlier than 1599 it is remarkable how many of these *hapaxes* date from the same year or were earlier than Shakespeare's usage. There are numerous examples of this rare vocabulary in previous books on Neville (Casson & Rubinstein 95, 106, 245).

6. Secrecy, cryptic clues and references to Neville as a poet

Any credible authorship claim must be able to suggest why the real author used a pseudonym. Although the identity of the real author was intended to be a secret, it is possible that some contemporaries knew the truth and left us hints. Neville was son of a courtier who was a signatory of Henry VIII's will and close to Elizabeth I. His father-in-law was an ambassador and diplomat. Neville himself was described as "discrete" by John Davies in his poem *Microcosmos*. He was involved in secret diplomacy and used codes in his letters. Men in his position did not want to be identified as playwrights. Co-authorship may have been a way of disguising any one writer's identity but we contend there was one central intelligence and this was Neville, sometimes co-writing and imitating others' styles. *Imitatio* was a practiced skill of Renaissance writers and this word occurs on the Northumberland Manuscript. Like all secrets this one leaked, the Northumberland Manuscript being the earliest such leak, the dedication to *Shake-speares Sonnets* being another (James 2008; Leyland & Goding 2015).[10] In 1615 Beaumont wrote a letter-poem to Ben Jonson in which he stated, "And from all Learning keep these lines as clear as Shakespeare's best are, which our heirs shall hear preachers apt to their auditors to show how far sometimes a mortal man may go by dim light of Nature…" (Chambers 1966: Vol. 2). Why "preachers" would be "apt" to tell their "auditors" about Shakespeare's lack of education is unclear. Biographical information about playwrights in Elizabethan/ Jacobean England was extremely rare, with public interest in the biography of literary figures emerging only much later. The first published biography of William Shakespeare did not appear until 1709. Beaumont's lines are cryptic and suggest that there would be a deliberate effort to emphasise Shakespeare's untutored background. These lines are followed immediately by: "as free as he, whose text was, god made all that is, I mean to speak: what do you think of his state, who hath now the last that he would make in white and orange tawny on his back at Windsor?" These cryptic lines may be a reference to Neville's funeral near Windsor in July 1615. Chambers commenting on this poem, pointed out that English ambassadors to France wore a uniform of white and orange tawny (1966, Vol. 2: 224). Presumably Neville was laid out in this livery, representing the highest office he held in his lifetime. The coupling of a mysterious reference to Shakespeare having written by the "dim light of nature" with an apparently unrelated reference to Neville's funeral may be evidence of

---

10 The dedication to the 1609 edition of *Shake-speares Sonnets* is odd. The text consists of 144 letters, with a full stop after every word, laid out over twelve lines. This led Brenda James to put it first into a 12x12 grid. Further exploration of different grids led to her finding the name "Henry Neville". Until James found this unexpected name no one had ever suggested Neville might be Shakespeare. By a different method, Leyland and Goding discovered the statement, "Mr. Sir Henry Neville he is your sonnets poet" as they deciphered the dedication. Moreover, they found an extensive and predictable pattern in which words in the dedication can be paired meaningfully with specific sonnets. They also found similar encryption was used by Neville in diplomatic correspondence.

an agreement in Neville's lifetime, presumably with his prior consent, to pass off Shakespeare from Stratford as the author and to depict him as a 'natural' genius, lacking formal education.

The next year, in 1616, William Browne's *Britannia's Pastorals* (book 2) was published with a cryptic section referring to Shakespeare without naming him (other poets are named). Browne was under the patronage of the Herbert family who were supporters of Neville, his son and grandson. A number of cryptic references seem to point to Neville as the nameless poet. Browne wrote, "Th'applause of common people never yet pursued this swain" (Cole 2014, 20). This recalls John Chamber's 1600 poem dedicated to Neville which stated, "Too little is your excellence seen by the common people" (Casson & Rubinstein 118). Browne suggested this poet was deeply wronged yet that his merit mounted so high that it challenged the stars "though low his passage be", the latter phrase suggesting he had been wrongly denigrated and had suppressed his identity (Cole 27). This matches Neville's life experience. James Whitlock, writing at the time of his death stated that Neville "was as ignobly and unworthily handled as ever gentleman was …" (Duncan 1974, 275). Chamber had earlier suggested to Neville that, "Joyfully you go to the stars, where your many faceted qualities make you immortal and admit you amongst the gods before your time" (see Casson & Rubinstein 118). Browne's poem also suggests that this poet would be regarded as a god. This unnamed yet Shakespearean poet's attitude to fame recalls Ben Jonson's epigram 109 to Neville. The date of this publication, within a year of Neville's death, suggests that it may have been as close to a eulogy for Neville as Browne felt he could go.

The first person to suggest in print that "Shake-speare" was a pseudonym was Thomas Vicars, Neville's son-in-law. After some years at Oxford, Vicars entered the household of George Carleton, Bishop of Chichester. Carleton married Neville's widow, Anne. Vicars married her daughter, Anne Neville. So Vicars knew Neville's wife, his close friend, Carleton, and daughter, and he may have been let into the family secret. In 1628, the year Carleton died, Vicars published the third edition of his book on Rhetoric. In this he added to the Latin text where he had named several English poets and referred to Shakespeare indirectly: "to these I believe should be added the famous poet who takes his name from shaking and spear" (Schurink 2006, 73). This phrase suggests knowledge that the name Shake-speare was a pseudonym (Casson & Rubinstein 41).

To complete this section, let us briefly consider the various relatives of Neville who had close associations with the theatre or with writing. Neville's grandfather, Edward, was involved in court masques and dramatic entertainments. He was known to improvise verses. He impersonated Henry VIII in a masque and hoodwinked Wolsey. This incident is staged in Shakespeare's play *Henry VIII* but with the true story altered to remove Edward and replace him with the king (Bradbeer & Casson 126). Neville's father was involved in court entertainments and the establishment of the first Blackfriars theatre. Neville's uncle owned a theatre company, Lord Abergavenny's Men. Neville's grandson, Henry Neville (1620-94) was a writer. Especially interesting is his *Isle of Pines*, a satirical work of 1668. It is a story, reminiscent of *The Tempest*, in which George Pines and four women are marooned on an island. Spiced up with sexual license, the book is a utopia that goes sour, offering reflections on culture, governance, religion and politics. He also wrote other satirical works on the nature of government. Casson discovered a handwritten sonnet in the end pages of a book of Spanish plays in Audley End library, the 1607 edition of *Las Comedias del Famoso Poeta Lope de Vega Carpio*, which he has identified as by this Henry Neville (Casson 2017). The sexual imagery in the sonnet echoes Shakespeare's sonnets. Born in 1619, just four years after his grandfather's death, Henry may not have known the secret of the Shakespeare authorship although there were close relatives alive who almost certainly would have known: his father Henry (died 1629), his grandmother Anne Neville (née Killigrew, died 1630), George Carleton (who had married Anne and died 1628), Anne's cousin Robert Killigrew (died 1633) and Thomas Vicars (Anne's son-in-law, died in 1638). Robert was a trustee of Neville's lands, an MP and like Neville, an investor in the second London Virginia Company. He owned a copy of Shakespeare's second sonnet which is now in the British Library. Robert's son Henry Killigrew was father of the poet Anne Killigrew (1660-1685). Another of Robert's sons, Thomas (1612-1683), was an actor, playwright and theatre manager. In 1669 a royal warrant gave the King's players, the company established by Thomas Killigrew and Sir William Davenant, the exclusive right to perform twenty of Shakespeare's plays. Thomas built the Drury Lane Theatre in London. Thus Neville's daughter and grandson were poets and Anne Neville's descendants were poets and playwrights. Now we will briefly consider two plays and the evidence they offer for Neville's authorship.

1. Richard III

The earliest document we have by Neville is his copy of *Leicester's Commonwealth* (c 1584-5), in which he made a marginal annotation: "Rich: Duke of Gloucester an vsurper" (Worsley MSS 47: 57; Casson 2010, 223). Before the second quarto (1598) was published with the name William Shake-speare on the title page it was listed as by William Shakespeare on the front cover of the Northumberland Manuscript folder (dated 1596-7). As this was owned by Neville (Burgoyne xvi) and contained other manuscripts we can presume that at some time the folder contained a manuscript of the play. Neville was thus the only known owner of this manuscript (indeed of any Shakespeare manuscript) before it was published. In *Richard III* Hastings laments the "momentary grace of mortal men" (3.4.96) in a speech that draws directly on Horace's Odes I.5. Neville's copy of this poem in his volume of the Odes is annotated, showing that he had studied it.

When Neville was in the Tower he did historical research and made a specific note of "d. Glouster in *nominee Rex*" in his 1602 notebook. His fellow prisoner the Earl of Southampton dedicated a manuscript of *The Encomium of Richard III* to him in 1603. We suggest that Southampton was trying to convince Neville that the evil reputation of this King whom, he wrote, had been made "infamous in pamphletts and playes", was unjustified. The evident explanation is that Southampton knew that Neville was the author of the popular stage depiction of Richard as a monster. Neville continued to have a negative view. He mentioned Richard III in a 1607 speech he made in Parliament. In 1611-12, correcting his copy of *A Catalogue of Honor*, he deleted "tooke vpon him" and inserted the word "vsurped" to describe Richard's kingship. In *Henry VIII* Shakespeare wrote of "Th'usurper *Richard*" (1.2.197). This play, dated 1612-13, would have been written just after Neville's annotation in *A Catalogue of Honor.*

There are twenty members of the Neville family either on stage or mentioned in *Richard III*. Shakespeare seems to have endeavoured to protect the reputation of two women members of the Neville family. Despite the character assassination of Richard III, his mother and wife, who were Cicely Neville and Anne Neville respectively, are not criticised and their behaviour is honourable. Many other facets of the play point to Neville's authorship (see Bradbeer & Casson, chapter 7). New research has illuminated another hidden Neville connection. While aiming to destroy rival claimants to the throne Richard reveals his plans for his brother Clarence's daughter whom "meanly have I match'd in marriage" (4.3.37). This is not historically true: Henry VII arranged for Margaret (whose mother was Isabel Neville) to marry his cousin Richard Pole. Thomas More, whose history of Richard III was an important source for the play, does not mention this marriage. Shakespeare's other sources, Hall and Holinshed, correctly show that the woman Richard "meanly matched" was Cecily Plantagenet, daughter of Edward IV, whom he married to Ralph Scrope, a junior member of Richard's household.[11] Hall used the words, "the marriage of a mean esquire". When Henry VII later annulled this marriage, Ralph married Eleanor Windsor who, after his death, married Edward Neville, becoming Neville's grandmother. This is an example of Shakespeare's sleight of hand in removing a possible reference to Neville's grandparents, just as his grandfather Edward was discreetly omitted from *Henry VIII*.

2. The Merry Wives of Windsor

We have previously made *The Merry Wives of Windsor* a test case for the authorship (Casson & Rubinstein, chapter 6). Neville's house at Billingbear was a dozen miles from Windsor through the forest of which Neville and his father were custodians. The play shows a detailed knowledge of the local geography of Windsor and Berkshire where Neville served as M.P. and held other offices. In our previous study we showed how a mysterious joke about three Germans stealing horses in 4.3. and 4.5. becomes clearer when we posit Neville as the author. The joke refers to Frederick I, Duke of Württemburg, who had visited Windsor in August 1592 and had hunted deer in the royal forest. At that time Neville's father was the steward of Mote Park, Windsor. Frederick was elected to the Order of the Garter in 1597. His surname, Mompelgard, is reversed in "Cozen-Garmombles" in the first quarto of 1602 (4.5.73); this was changed to "Cozen-Jermans" (Germans) in the *First Folio*. The first quarto refers to "a Germaine Duke". Neville

11 Ralph Scrope was a descendant of Stephen Scrope (who is in *Richard II*). Stephen Scrope's brother was Archbishop Richard Scrope (in *1 & 2 Henry IV*). Stephen Scrope's son was Henry Scrope who is arrested for treason in *Henry V*: this treason is noted in the annotated Hall's *Chronicle* which we have shown above has connections with Eleanor Windsor (Keen and Lubbock 1954, 139). *Richard III* was written while Neville's father was still alive whereas *Richard II, 2 Henry IV* and *Henry V* were written after his decease. It is possible that Neville aimed not to embarrass his father while he was alive, from the staging of Cecily's inglorious marriage to his mother's first husband, Ralph Scrope. *Venus and Adonis* was published under the name William Shakespeare in 1593, after Neville's father had died in January that year.

travelled through Germany during his European tour. In a diplomatic letter dated 9 May 1600 Neville wrote about meeting the "Ambassador of Wirttenberg" (Sawyer: Vol 1, 183). In 1595, Mompelgard's ambassador, Hans Jacob Breuning Von Buchenbach, came on a mission to enquire about the Duke's expectation of being made a Knight of the Garter (*The Antiquary* 1903). Neville, having been appointed sheriff of Berkshire that year was the courtier chosen to accompany this ambassador and his three German companions, Hormoldt, Rittell, and Krebss, by river and coach from London. The ambassador's own account attests to Neville's presence; "When we came to the Court we were conducted by M. De Nivell into the Presence Chamber where the Knights of the Garter had assembled and were waiting to accompany Her Majesty" (Rye 1903, 109). He wrote that Neville "never left our side during the whole of the subsequent proceedings" and described the garter ceremony. This is the earliest account of Neville as a courtier. Many scholars have suggested that Shakespeare had written the play in relation to the Garter ceremony and here we have proof that Neville witnessed this royal ritual (Nash 1928, 375). Neville would also have known about any problems with getting horses because in 1597-98, he sat on Parliamentary committees on horse stealing and "abuses committed by the lewd and licentious soldiery", both of which are themes in *The Merry Wives of Windsor* (Hasler 1981, vol 3: 123). The play was written between 1597 and 1600 (Casson & Rubinstein 114).

Neville's authorship of the play explains an obscure joke:

> *Slender:* In the County of *Glocester*, Iustice of Peace and Coram.
> *Shallow:* I, (Cosen *Slender*) and *Cust-alorum.*
> *Slender:* I, and *Rato lorum* too…
> (*First Folio* spelling, 1.1.4)

Neville was a Justice of the Peace from 1583. In 1605, he became *Custos Rotulorum* of Berkshire (keeper of the rolls: the county records). This joke about "*Cust-alorum… Rato lorum*" is not in the first quarto of 1602, which was printed before he took office, but does appear in the *First Folio* of 1623. Melchior (2000, 43), editor of the Arden edition of the play, wondered, "how a Justice of the Peace … could have owned a deer park in Windsor". With Neville as the Bard this question is answered: he was both a J.P. and a keeper of the royal Windsor forest.

In August 1592 Queen Elizabeth I, on her summer progress, visited Elizabeth Russell at Bisham Abbey (Laoutaris 2014, 171). To entertain the Queen, Lady Russell composed a masque, *The Lady of the Farm* which bears a remarkable resemblance to the Herne's Oak scene in *The Merry Wives of Windsor.* In *The Lady of the Farm*, two virgins are tempted by Pan, half-man-half goat, before being interrupted by the Queen. In *The Merry Wives of Windsor*, two women are tempted by a man disguised as half-man-half stag before being interrupted by a Fairy Queen. In the masque a wild man led the Queen to Pan and the girls, whereas in the play Sir Hugh, as the satyr, leads the Fairy Queen to Falstaff, the stag-man. In the masque, Elizabeth Russell ended the ceremony, disguised as Queen Ceres accompanied by nymphs, while in the play, Mistress Quickly ends the revel at Herne's Oak, disguised as the Fairy Queen accompanied by fairies. In the masque, Pan was converted from his lust by the Queen, just as Falstaff is by the Fairy Queen. Billingbear is eleven miles from Bisham Abbey and as Lady Russell was Neville's mother-in-law's sister, it is reasonable to suggest that he could have been present. In order to escape from the irate husband Ford, Falstaff is disguised as a woman, Mistress Page saying, "Let's go dress him like the witch of Brentford" (4.2.92). Brentford is a dozen miles east of Windsor. The witch is called "Gillian of Brainford" in the first quarto (Spain-Savage 2016, 229). Gillian was probably a real woman who was an innkeeper. She first appeared in a 1563 comic poem by Robert Copland, *Jyl of Breyntford's Testament* (reprinted by Frederick James Furnivall in 1871) and again in a lost 1599 play, *Friar Fox and Gillian of Brentford.* Other real people may also be behind this incident in the play.

Richard Gallys, an alderman and mayor of Windsor, was M.P. for New Windsor in 1563 and 1572. He was the landlord of the Garter Inn. In the play the Host of Garter Inn is a significant character. Gallys was believed to have been cursed to death by witches. His son, Richard, claimed to be bewitched and visited Neville's father (1572-9) to seek support and relief. He also had several meetings with Neville's mother. He became a witch hunter and terrorised women with a cudgel. One, Mother Dutton, was so frightened she hid in a chest. In the play, before he escapes, Falstaff refuses to hide in a chest (4.2.57) and, disguised as a woman, is beaten by Ford who is armed with a cudgel. Richard left a record of his difficulties and how he visited "the lodging of the said Sir Henry Neuel béeing in the Castel"[12] at Windsor. Richard's account continues:

12 For Richard Galis' account see <http://quod.lib.umich.edu/e/eebo/A72130.0001.001/1:3?rgn=div1;view=fulltext> accessed 23/10/2016.

> I went to the sayde Elizabeth Stiles house, charging her to goe with mée vnto Sir Henry Neuelles, … I came vnto the lodging of Sir Henry Neuell, vnto whome in the presence of a companie of Gentlemen at that time talking with him, I offered vp my present, saying, behold here rigth worshipfull, I haue brought you héer a monster, … Then shée began to curse, banne and sweare, foming at the mouth like a bore, to the great astonishement of all the beholders, which amased with that horrible sight (more for feare I thinke then for any good wyll) suffered her to escape (Galis 1579).

Richard described the witch as a monster. In the play, Ford invites his friends home to dinner to see a monster: Falstaff (3.2.73). Ford wants to hang the witch (4.2.181). Elizabeth Stiles, after being arraigned before Neville's father, was tried and executed. This is evidence that the Nevilles spent time at Windsor castle, knew the host of the Garter Inn, and that the young Neville would have known about witch hunting in Windsor. The French and Italian elements in the play are also explained when we know that Neville was in Italy in 1581 and in France three times in 1578, 1582 and 1599-1600, including, indeed, at the time the play was written. In Paris, in March 1600, Neville wrote and signed a comic poem about an assertive wife troubling her husband and indirectly referred to Adam and Eve (see Casson & Rubinstein 115). In *The Merry Wives* Mistress Page tells of a husband who, "so rails against all married mankind, so curses all Eve's daughters…" (4.2.20).

Another example of Neville's poetic wit is a couplet recorded by Sir John Oglander:[13]

> Sir Henry Nevill on Kinge James
> Nevor man wrought moore and did les;
> Nevor man spoke bettor and did woorse.

It seems Neville was musing on his disappointment with James I after the latter declined to offer him the role of Secretary of State. This would date the couplet to 1614-15: after Shakespeare's last play (*The Two Noble Kinsmen*, 1613) and after the political treatise Neville had offered to James I in 1614, *An Advice Touching the Holding of a Parliament* (James 2011, 23). Neville had kept his authorship of this treatise secret until forced by Parliament to acknowledge he had written it.

13 The spelling may be Oglander's: (see Long 1888, 126).

Let us conclude this case for *our* Shakespeare, then. There are many and varied types of evidence that support Neville's authorship. No single piece of evidence may be convincing on its own but the growing mass of evidence is now so great that it has become compelling. The case for Neville's authorship grows stronger as the study of his literary paper trail alongside the historical and geographical data brings ever more evidence to light.

Images of books annotated by Henry Neville are published with the permission of the owners: Private Collection.

Chapter 6

Mary Sidney Herbert, the Countess of Pembroke

Robin Williams

Mary Sidney's family background provides for the education and worldliness expected of the author of the Shakespearean works. She was born into a powerful family in 1561, three years before William Shakespeare was born; she died five years after Shakespeare, just as the *First Folio* went to press. Her mother, Mary Dudley Sidney, was sister to Robert Dudley, the Earl of Leicester. The Dudley and Sidney families had been members of the English royal court for generations. Before Mary was a teenager, her family had consolidated into an alliance of faith and blood with power that controlled vast holdings throughout England as well as portions of Ireland and Wales, equaling about two-thirds of the land under Elizabeth's rule. When Mary Sidney married and established her home at Wilton House, it became a base away from London for the Herberts, Dudleys, and Sidneys: "In such a group, so closely knit by familial and marital bonds, it was difficult to spot where a family gathering ended and a political summit began" (Stewart 2000, 202). Shakespeare's ten British history plays are filled with historical figures from the Dudley family pedigree.

Mary grew up mainly on the Sidney family estate in Kent, called Penshurst Place, with most summers spent in Ludlow Castle on the border of Wales. While her older brother Philip attended Shrewsbury School for his primary education, Mary was tutored at home along with her younger brothers — Robert, who later enrolled in Oxford at age twelve, and Thomas — and her two surviving sisters, Elizabeth and Ambrosia. She read, wrote, and spoke Latin, French, and Italian; probably Greek as several dedications to her are in Greek; apparently some Hebrew learned in her versification of the Psalms; and some Spanish as her mother interpreted Spanish for the Queen and Mary had Spanish books in her library (Hannay *et al* 1998, 3). She is acknowledged as the most educated woman in England at the time, comparable only to Queen Elizabeth.

Mary was trained in poetry, rhetoric, history, and the classics, as was expected of every well-bred person, and medicine, as was expected of every female head of household, especially women who were to run large manors. Several medical remedies created in her own alchemy laboratory have been preserved, as well as her formula for invisible ink (Anonymous 1763, 131-133). She created exquisite needlework for which she was well known, she sang, read and composed music, and played the lute, virginals, and apparently the violin. It seems there was always music in the house — her father paid almost £67 for violins, the initial cost of establishing a violin consort in his household (Holman 2002, 125). The family had their own jester, or fool; her father paid for three yards of motley to make his coat (Somerset 1994, 645). Family records show that Mary grew up riding horses, hawking, hunting, using a bow and arrow, and later had a lawn bowling green on her own estate, the sport that is referred to most often in the Shakespearean plays, as in Hamlet's line, "Ay, there's the rub." Mary's father, Henry Sidney, was Lord President of the Marches of Wales and later the Lord Deputy Governor of Ireland. As Hannay tells us, "because Henry Sidney had a particular interest in geography and cartography, his children were probably better schooled in those fields than most" (1990, 27).

Music, medicine, language, rhetoric, writing, politics, even motley, are in her background, as one would expect of the playwright. Also as one would expect, Mary was exposed to and involved in theatre all her life. The account books of the Sidney family indicate that troupes of actors reenacted the adventures of Robin Hood and his merry men, singers celebrated May Day, and minstrels played at midsummer (*ibid*). At Ludlow Castle, a family seat during her lifetime, there were performances from a regular stream of acting companies. An elaborate Christmas season at the castle while Mary was in attendance included the nobility themselves performing in a production of *King Arthur's Knights of the Round Table.* Acting troupes sponsored by the Lords Stafford,

Bergavenny, Burghley, Berkeley, Hunsdon, Chandos, Essex, Darcy, the Earls of Worcester, Oxford, Pembroke, and Leicester, the Queen's Men from both Queen Elizabeth and Queen Anne, the Master of the Revels players, as well as sundry musicians, minstrels, and jesters all provided theatre and music (Somerset 395). Children's theatre troupes, the Lord of Sussex players, and Lord Stanford players were also in attendance at Ludlow for the Sidney and later the Herbert families (Witherspoon 1968, 69). The personal connections with some of the players were close: the famous Richard Tarlton was an actor in her uncle Leicester's company, and Philip Sidney stood godfather to Tarlton's son (Ringler Jr. 1962, 362). This active family interest and household participation in theatre was a lifelong passion. Even in her forties, the royal court records show that Mary Sidney was one of three women who participated in all four masques written by Ben Jonson.

Mary Sidney grew up surrounded by intelligent and highly educated women. Her mother's female friends were also well educated, including the five remarkable Cooke sisters who were among the first generation of female humanist scholars. Her mother's closest friend was Mildred Cooke, married to William Cecil, Lord Burghley, the Queen's chief minister. Another good friend, Anne Cooke, was the mother of Sir Francis Bacon. Mary's aunt Frances Sidney, the Countess of Sussex, was the founder of Sidney Sussex College at Cambridge in 1596. Mary grew up surrounded by intelligent, educated, powerful women in a country governed by a remarkable woman and, as Witherspoon reminds us, "there was probably never an age in which women held a greater sway physically and intellectually than during this period" (69).

The entire Sidney family produced literary works. Verses penned by her parents, Mary Dudley and Henry Sidney, are extant in Latin and English with French phrasing. Her younger brother Robert produced the largest collection of lyric poetry of the age, not discovered until 1973. Her oldest son William published a book of his own poetry, and her daughter Anne is known to have written poetry (Lamb 301–15). In Mary's newlywed years, her brother Philip lived in her home and turned to writing full-time during a self-imposed retirement from court. As Cerasano & Wynne-Davies write, "the numerous dedications to [Mary Sidney] portray a chaste, pious, gracious, and intelligent woman, the exact female counterpart of her famous brother: if Philip Sidney was depicted as the ideal Renaissance man, then Mary came to personify the ideal Renaissance woman" (1996, 13). At Mary's request, Philip composed *The Countess of Pembroke's Arcadia*, "the most important work of prose fiction in English of the sixteenth century" (Merriam-Webster 1995, 1030). Philip's essay, *The Defence of Poesy,* is considered "the finest work of Elizabethan literary criticism; Sidney's elegant essay suggests that literature is a better teacher than history or philosophy" (*ibid*). His lengthy sonnet sequence, *Astrophil and Stella,* popularized the sonnet form in England. In the 1590s, the publication of *Astrophil and Stella* was "followed by dozens of sonnet sequences, but it must be remembered that when Sidney wrote it there were no other sonnet sequences in English. . . . Sidney's is not only the earliest English sonnet sequence properly so described: it is also arguably the best, in terms of assured poetic technique, richness of tone, and subtlety of organisation" (Duncan-Jones 1989, xvii).

It is important to keep in mind that at this time the only country in which English was spoken was England — it was rarely used even in Wales, Ireland, or Scotland. At the beginning of the sixteenth century, as Roma Gill notes, the English "had a very poor opinion of their own language: there was little serious writing in English, and hardly any literature. Latin was the language of international scholarship, and Englishmen admired the eloquence of the Romans" (1996, 120). Yet when Philip Sidney turned to devote himself to his unelected vocation as a poet, he wrote entirely in English: "he hoped to lay the foundations of a body of literature in his own language which might ultimately stand comparison with the Greek and Latin classics" (Duncan-Jones, 143). This is a point that must be emphasised: there were great works of literature in Greek, Latin, Italian, and French, but few in English — it became Philip and Mary Sidney's purpose to create great literary works in the English language.

Through their own writing, as well as the patronage and encouragement of other writers, Mary and Philip developed the most important and influential literary circle in England, today referred to as the Wilton Circle. The developments at Wilton in the 1580s were an attempt on the part of the Sidneys to instigate a revival of English aristocratic culture. For her own part, in providing Wilton's hospitality and its unique atmosphere of these crucial years of Elizabethan literature, the Countess was also re-creating in her own, perhaps typically English, way a pattern of patronage by noble women that had flourished in Italy and France for a century or more. As Buxton states, "we remember how much the Florentine Renaissance owed to the Medici, but we forget that a similar debt was owed by the English Renaissance to the Sidneys" (1966, 31). It is relevant to note that in his writing, Philip's development of "women who are active and strong without being evil or dominant over men was something new in literary history" (Roberts 1993, 122). It is even more relevant, in light of the Authorship Question, that in Sidney's portrayals of women "as intelligent, capable, and morally responsible human beings, Sidney very likely paved the way for writers like Shakespeare who came after him to develop strong, active heroines and to alter, however slightly and gradually, cultural perceptions of women" (Waller 1979, 39).[1]

Albert Baugh describes three directions in which Philip Sidney's achievements rank him among the most stellar of the Elizabethan writers: 1) none but Shakespeare and Spenser produced a finer sonnet sequence; 2) none but Ben Jonson surpassed him as a literary critic; and 3) none of the writers of Sidney's age approached his influence in the field of prose romance. Baugh confirms the importance of Mary Sidney in these achievements: "yet if *Astrophil and Stella,* the *Defence of Poesy,* and the *Arcadia* had never been published, we should still have to regard Sidney as a cultural landmark. Seconded by his sister, he created through his personal efforts and his personal charm a new artistic atmosphere more stimulating than any other that then existed. Together . . . they first produced what in the highest sense may be called the academic spirit in English letters" (1948, 472).

This is precisely the sort of preparatory background as well as passionate interest and dedication that one expects from the writer of the Shakespearean canon. Success leaves a paper trail. Mary and her brother Philip laid a remarkable groundwork for the future of the English language and literature. Devoted to each other and to the literary arts, they stimulated excellence and perfected their craft while inspiring the writers of the Wilton Circle. When Philip died of a battle wound in early 1586, the literary mantle passed from Philip to Mary Sidney, and she wore it the rest of her life. As late as 1616 she developed another noted literary salon in Spa, the original Forest of Ardennes, while traveling abroad for several years, and letters between her friends Sir Edward Wotton and Sir Toby Matthew mention manuscripts that are now presumed lost (Brennan & Kinnamon 2003, 214-215).

Scholars such as Anne Ferry have long noted the remarkable influence that Philip Sidney had on the author of the Shakespearean sonnets, starting with the speaker's plea in Sonnet 21, "O let me true in love but truly write":

1 Waller compares Mary and Wilton House with Marguerite de Navarre's palace academy, which is said to be an inspiration for *Love's Labour's Lost.*

> The deliberate echo of the opening of [Philip Sidney's] *Astrophil and Stella* is verified by the poem as a whole, which assimilates many characteristic means invented by Sidney for representing Astrophil's struggle to show the truth of his love in verse. The issues involved in that effort about the relation of poetic language to inward experience are first raised in Shakespeare's sequence in this sonnet, which is so closely, complexly, and successfully patterned after a characteristic Sidneian model as to prove that Shakespeare there understood the issues in Sidney's terms, and learned his means for exploring them (1983, 170).

Ferry elaborates on how "Shakespeare" uniquely followed Sidney in making these explorations a central concern. The author of the Shakespearean sonnets assimilated their "most far-reaching implications for what amounts to a new conception of human nature. Other poets, by contrast, borrowed only details of phrasing from Sidney, or imitated his motifs and manner" (*ibid* 172). Ferry explores Philip Sidney's influence on "Shakespeare" in shared themes and motifs, his vocabulary about art, imitations of specific personifications such as an argumentative personal Muse or a careless Cupid, and even echoes of individual lines. She shows that the poet of the Shakespearean sonnets repeatedly turned to *Astrophil and Stella* for models, adapted individual poems, borrowed simultaneously from multiple poems, and combined "specific echoes with adaptations of devices more generally characteristic of Sidney's style" (177-78). Beyond influences of writing style and subject, Ferry demonstrates that "the fullness and power of Shakespeare's adaptations show how profoundly he understood what were Sidney's different assumptions" (205). It is inconsistent, unlikely, and even bizarre that William Shakespeare, who never met Philip Sidney nor was ever associated with the Wilton Circle, could have "understood" Philip and his work so intimately and completely. Only Mary Sidney among all the authorship candidates was in such close collaboration and discussion with Philip as to be able to explore and develop so deeply these new ideas in literature.

Mary Sidney has the profile of the author of the Shakespearean canon: extremely intelligent; superbly educated; literate in a number of modern and classical languages; holder of a celebrated library of books; politically involved; active in the sports, artistic, and intellectual pursuits that appear in the plays; living in the society about which the plays are written — and all of this well documented. Mary Sidney's most important biographer, Margaret P. Hannay, describes the countess: "Mary Sidney, like her brother Philip, was brilliant, learned, witty, articulate, and adept at self-presentation. . . . In an age when women were required to be chaste, silent, and obedient, she may have been chaste — but she was certainly eloquent and assertive. She was able to challenge the norms for women while appearing to follow them, empowered by her own clever self-promotion, her brother's legendary death, and her husband's money" (vix).

Mary, after Philip's death, gathered the poets and writers at Wilton House to persist in her brother's work to improve English literature. In fact, "the Countess took a more active part in the literary experiments of the Circle, and developed a much more highly organised salon, closer to its continental models" (Waller 71). If at first she felt it was her duty to further the revolution begun by her brother, she apparently discovered that her own talents lay in actively writing herself. Her Wilton estate became a collaborative "workshop for poetical experimentation, the seedbed of a literary revolution. Centred upon Wilton's congenial and hospitable lifestyle, on Sidney's example and on his sister's enlightened enthusiasm, it became the still centre of the rapidly turning world of late Elizabethan literature" (*ibid* 45). In awe and admiration, contemporaries called Wilton House a little university, an academy, and Mary Sidney's own court. For two decades she gathered the greatest writers around her, including Edmund Spenser, Fulke Greville, Samuel Daniel, Michael Drayton, Nicholas Breton, Thomas Watson, and Abraham Fraunce, who dedicated their common efforts to what they saw as the betterment of English letters. She acted as an active patron to many, requested specific works from various poets, and encouraged others to develop their writing talents and expand their skills. Her circle of writers became "one of the most dynamic cultural influences in late Elizabethan England, and at the centre were her writings"; the Wilton Circle "became one of the most interesting coteries in the history of English literature" (Witherspoon 68).

Mary Sidney dedicated herself to the discipline and craft of writing, and acted as mentor to other writers in her circle. Numerous documents refer to her indirectly or directly educating others. The poet Thomas Churchyard wrote "A Pleasant Conceit" in 1593 in which he celebrates twelve of the young ladies in Queen Elizabeth's court, and says of Mary Sidney:

> A gem more worth than all the gold of Ind,
> For she enjoys the wise Minerva's wit,
> And sets to school our poets everywhere,
> That doth presume the laurel crown to wear (Young 1912, 174).

The renowned and gentle poet Samuel Daniel was a lifelong friend of Mary's. In 1607 he wrote a dedication to her son and gave credit to Mary for having taught him to write: "Having been first encouraged and framed thereunto by your most worthy and honourable mother, and received the first notion for the formal ordering of those compositions at Wilton, which I must ever acknowledge to have been my best school and thereof always am to hold a feeling and grateful memory" (*ibid* 164).

Women were allowed to write religious pieces and translations. Translations were acceptable in part because they were originally written by a man and also because they were considered a defective form of writing. Within this public stricture, Mary's own work shows a constant study of the writing craft. In her versification of 127 Psalms of David, she used 126 different verse forms. An unpublished but well-known and lauded piece is her translation from Italian of Petrarch's *Triumph of Death,* the only version to reproduce Petrarch's *terza rima* verse form in English. Pushing the boundaries of what was acceptable for women, Mary Sidney is the first woman to publish a play in English, *Antonie,* a translation from French of a closet drama meant to be read aloud in a noble household. She is the first woman to publish original dramatic verse, *Thenot and Piers in Praise of Astrea,* barely permissible because it was written for the Queen. She also published a skillful, lengthy prose work translated from Mornay's French version, *A Discourse of Life and Death,* of which Diane Bornstein remarks: "at a time when English syntax was still in an unsettled state, the countess translated Mornay's sophisticated French prose into a smooth, idiomatic English that fully reflected its rhetorical ornaments" (1985, 134). Mary is also the first woman who did not apologise for publishing her work, as the few other published females felt obligated to do.

Mary Sidney was celebrated as a writer of the highest distinction in her own time. An indication of her reputation can be seen in the book of miscellaneous verse titled *Bel-vedére* (1600), in which she is ranked as a writer alongside Edmund Spenser, Philip Sidney and William Shakespeare — with no notice of her gender. Three quotations from one of Mary's works are cited in this book. Queen Elizabeth is the only other female writer mentioned. As Hanay *et al* remind us, "such presentation of a non-royal woman author was unprecedented in England, for women were admonished to be silent, not to write and publish" (Vol 1, 22). Mary is also the only woman, again besides Queen Elizabeth, mentioned as a writer in Francis Meres' *Palladis Tamia: Wits Treasury*, the 1598 publication so important to literary history because it lists nine Shakespearean plays. Meres, comparing Mary to Octavia as a patroness, exclaims that "she is a most delicate Poet," and finds her comparable to Sappho as the Tenth Muse (285). Mary was inventive with the language in her work. She is credited in the Oxford English Dictionary with the first recorded use of more than forty words, including *sea-monster* and *unpeopled* as used in the Shakespearean plays, plus four dozen words that she used for the first time in English in a particular sense, such as *eternise, measure, shallow,* and *winged* (as a ship with sails), which are used in the same sense in the plays. There are words that Mary used earlier than the citations in the OED, such as *thunder-strike,* and other words that she used in the same senses as in the Shakespearean plays before their recorded use, such as *candy, oblivion, unsounded,* and *void.* For instance, the OED lists Shakespeare first using *lonely* in *Coriolanus* in 1607, but it was used in the same sense by Mary Sidney in her play, *Antonie,* published in 1592. Mary invented words such as *feathery, heart-broken, head-long, re-become, empearl, powerfulness, surrounded, mix* as a noun, *wondered* as used in *The Tempest, soundless deep* as in Sonnet 80 (Hannay 65). Compound adjectives, an oft-used device in the Shakespearean plays, were introduced into English poetry by Mary's brother Philip: "Joseph Hall singled Sidney out for praise because of his introduction into English poetic practice of the French fondness for compound adjectives" (Woudhuysen 2004). Mary, as well, often uses compound adjectives in her work, such as *hunger-starvèd land, never-dying rhymes, brain-sick men, shadow-clothèd night, ghost-haunted tomb, angel-like delight.*

H. R. Woudhuysen states that it was the publication of Philip Sidney's work in the 1590s that paved the way for writers like Shakespeare to print their own works:

> Sidney's sudden availability in print also had an important influence on the production of literature. It is too simple to suggest that writers thought that if his work could be exposed to the public view their own could be as well, but there may be an element of truth in this. . . . Sidney became a standard author, as Daniel . . . Spenser, Drayton, Jonson, Shakespeare, and eventually Greville were all to do within the next

> few years. In this way, it could be argued that the 1598 folio [of Philip's literary works] served as a model for later writers and promoted the idea of a predominantly print-based literary culture (1996, 386-87).

Philip died in 1586 — it was Mary Sidney who published Philip's writing in the form and style appropriate to the work, establishing a permanent place for him in the literary world. Thus Woudhuysen's statement should be more specific: it was Mary Sidney who served as a model for writers to accept a print-based literary culture.

Lukas Erne shows that "Shakespeare", who wrote far fewer plays than the most popular dramatists of the time, became "the best-published dramatist with far more title page ascriptions than any other English playwright dead or alive" and was in many ways "the rising star of the English literary scene" (2013, 110-11). Publication of the plays is something Mary Sidney understood how to do and believed to be critical to the future of the English language. In this light it is interesting to remember that the first nine Shakespearean plays were published anonymously and the first four in print state on their titles pages they were acted by Pembroke's Men, an acting company she sponsored.[2]

The sonnets

The collection of 154 sonnets presents the most perplexing mystery about the man named William Shakespeare. Many are difficult to understand, the forms of address are inconsistent, and there has never been consensus on what an individual sonnet actually means. Most experts agree that the sonnets seem intensely autobiographical, but it is impossible to credibly explain how they fit into Shakespeare's life: "after nearly two hundred years of speculation and scholarship, we have made remarkably little progress toward uncovering the 'true story' behind Shakespeare's Sonnets, if indeed there is a story to be uncovered" (Foster 1999, 15). Experts also agree the sonnets were not meant for publication and were taken to press without the poet's cooperation. The biggest puzzlement of these passionate and often desperate love poems: most of them are written to a younger man.

Overall, the sonnets appear to show the poet's passionate affair with a younger man, but at some point the younger man has an affair

2 "That the countess herself had some responsibility for the players is indicated by the will of the actor Simon Jewell, which bequeathed 'my share of such money as shalbe givenn by my ladie Pembrooke or by her means.'" Hannay *et al* (vol. 1, 38).

with a dark-haired, dark-eyed woman close to the poet's heart. The dark-haired woman is newly married to a man who seems to be named Will. The sonnets that address this "Dark Lady" are not love poems, but verses berating the woman for lust and betrayal. No one has been able to identify the younger man or the dark-haired woman and her possible husband named Will in relation to William Shakespeare. This is an oversimplification of the general theme of the sonnets: W. Shakespeare > Younger Man? > Dark-haired Woman? > Will? Mary Sidney, however, was involved in precisely this romantic situation. It is well documented that after her 67-year-old husband died, Mary, 43 years old, had an affair with a younger man, Dr. Matthew Lister, 33 years old, whom she could not marry because of his lower social status, although she was with him for the rest of her life. At one point there was strife in their relationship when she believed that her younger lover was having an affair with her dark-haired, dark-eyed niece, Mary Wroth, 19 years old and newly married, whom Mary Sidney had helped raise. However, Mary Wroth was *not* having an affair with Dr. Lister, but with the newly married William Herbert, Mary Sidney's oldest son and thus Mary Wroth's first cousin. After Mary Wroth's husband died, she had two illegitimate children with William Herbert; due to a cover-up by the Herbert family, this was not discovered until 1935 (see Beese in Waller 1993, 122). The oversimplification is a precise match with Mary Sidney: Mary Sidney > Matthew Lister, Younger Man > Mary Wroth, Dark-haired Woman > Will Herbert, Mary Sidney's son.

This relationship between her son and his first cousin presents an emotional quandary of another kind for Mary Sidney. Is sonnet 135 written to Mary Wroth?

> Whoever hath her wish, thou hast thy Will,
> And Will to boot, and Will in over-plus. . . .
> So thou, being rich in Will, add to thy Will
> One Will of mine to make thy large Will more.

The first seventeen sonnets in this sequence, today called the procreation sonnets, implore a man to have a baby. Over and over and over the poet gives impassioned reasons for some man to marry and have a child. John Dover Wilson notes a remarkable coincidence between Philip Sidney's work and the Shakespearean procreation sonnets: "This marriage section had a source peculiar to itself . . . namely a famous passage in the *Countess of Pembroke's Arcadia*, which Sir Philip Sidney wrote for his sister . . . which consisted of a series of arguments virtually identical with those Shakespeare advances to the youth" (1969, 89). This possibility should be considered: perhaps the first seventeen sonnets were written by a young woman who is studying the art of writing along with her beloved brother who is educated, worldly, handsome, charming, almost thirty years old, unmarried, childless, and the sole heir to the entire fortunes of the two most powerful noblemen in England, his uncles Robert Dudley, the Earl of Leicester, and Ambrose Dudley, the Earl of Warwick. If a nobleman dies without heirs, his fortune and lands revert to the crown, so there is an extremely practical side to the desire for an heir, as well as the natural desire of a woman who is herself a mother to see the brother she cherishes fulfilled in this way. Sonnet 18, "Shall I compare thee to a summer's day," may be read as a shattered goodbye to a youthful Philip upon his death in war. Dover Wilson muses regarding this sonnet: "One recalls the weeping crowds in February 1587 when Sir Philip Sidney was carried to his grave leaving no son to perpetuate his name" (90). Marriage and babies are never mentioned again.

The sonnets are rich and complex and there are still many unanswered questions. But once Mary Sidney is considered as the author of the majority of the poems, we have the only authorship candidate documented as having a younger male lover who was believed to be in love with a dark-haired woman, while this Dark Lady was really in love with a man named Will. Mary is an author who had a legitimate reason to write procreation sonnets, sonnets that other critics have seen as connected to Philip Sidney. Acknowledging this strong possibility provides a chance at clarifying other issues in the sonnet collection.

Sources of the plays

For more than two hundred years scholars and critics have searched for not only contemporary references to current events incorporated into the Shakespearean plays, but specific plot lines, rare words, literary motifs, characterisations, and word-for-word lines taken from existing books. More than 220 works have been identified that we know the author read in the process of writing the plays. Two dozen of these source materials were available only in Latin, French, or Italian, languages in which Mary Sidney was fluent. It is remarkable to see the number of source materials that were written by Mary or by her brother Sir Philip or by someone else in her writing circle, how many were dedicated to Mary or written about her, and how many are known to have been owned by her family and included information about or have connections to her family. Here is a small sampling:

- Five plays use *The Countess of Pembroke's Arcadia* as a source. This book was written by Mary's brother Philip at her request; it was written in her home; it is dedicated to her; it was published by her.

- *Antonie,* written and published by Mary Sidney, is one of the sources for Shakespeare's *Antony and Cleopatra.*

- Samuel Daniel's play *Cleopatra* is also used as a source for *Antony and Cleopatra.* Daniel wrote this play at the request of Mary Sidney as a sequel for her *Antonie;* he wrote it in her home and it is dedicated to her.

- The small book *Of the Silkworms and their Flies* is one of the sources for *A Midsummer Night's Dream.* It was not in print until five years after the play was registered for printing, so the playwright must have read the original *Silkworms* manuscript, an impossibility for William Shakespeare because the author of the manuscript, Thomas Moffett, was Mary Sidney's estate physician. He wrote this manuscript in her home and dedicated it to her.

- An important source for *The Tempest* is a letter written by William Strachey to the Virginia Company about a shipwreck on Bermuda. The letter was not made public until nine years after Shakespeare died, but Mary Sidney was a founder and shareholder of the Virginia Company, her husband and sons were founders and shareholders, and her brother Robert was a manager. The letter was addressed to "Excellent Lady."

- Both the 1570 and 1583 editions of John Foxe's *Acts and Monuments of Martyrs* were sources for five of the history plays. Family records show that the Sidney family bought two copies of this book when Mary was a child. It includes tales of heroic deaths, including that of Mary's aunt, Lady Jane Grey.

- Family records show the Sidneys bought a copy of Lord Berner's translation of Jean Froissart's *The Chronicles of England,* which was used as a source for *Richard the Second.*

More than fifty other source materials have already been shown to be directly connected to Mary Sidney, but not one for William Shakespeare.

The *First Folio* eulogy and Mary's sons

The *First Folio* was printed seven years after William Shakespeare's death. Ben Jonson wrote a eulogy in this *Folio* praising the author of the plays, "To the memory of my beloved, the author." One of the most intriguing features of Jonson's poem is his own introduction to it in which he complains that there are those who might pretend to praise a woman, while actually trying to ruin her. He writes that this is how a Bawd (a pimp) or a Whore might treat a Matron:

> Or crafty malice, might pretend this praise,
> And think to ruin, where it seemed to raise.
>
> These are, as some infamous Bawd, or Whore,
> Should praise a Matron. What could hurt her more?

There is no explanation of why Ben Jonson, considered a protégé of Mary Sidney's, mentions a "Bawd" and a "Whore" and a "Matron" in the poem's introduction. But a close look at Mary's sons provides a clue.

Historical records document William Herbert's arrival at King James' royal court as a young man of twenty-three, where he immediately began working toward advancement: "the state papers and parliamentary records show an immensely detailed and patient building up of political power over the first decade of James's reign" (Waller 1993, 87). William's career started off well enough: King James awarded him the lucrative keepership of various lands and offices in the tin-mining districts; he was also appointed Lord Lieutenant of Cornwall and governor of Portsmouth. But William particularly desired the job of Lord Chamberlain, the person in charge of the public theatre, printing, and the court entertainments, a position held at the time by the King's favourite, Robert Carr. Carr was the Earl of Somerset and well entrenched in the opposing Howard faction. William Herbert created an opportunity through which he could change the power structure at court and gain for himself the position he coveted. Waller informs us what happened: "in 1614, seemingly resigned to a minor political role, Pembroke held one of the most significant factional supper meetings in British politics at Baynards Castle [the Herbert's London seat]. Pembroke, Abbott [the Archbishop of Canterbury], [Sir Ralph] Winwood, and Sir Thomas Lake decided to provide James with a new favourite to supplant Carr. The bait was Sir George Villiers, a Lancashire knight — handsome, sparkling, and —superficial" (*ibid* 89). The plan was that George Villiers would catch the eye and heart of King James, topple Carr as the King's favourite, with the result that William and his faction would then have the King's favourite in their own pocket and their advancements could be procured through him. They coached George how to walk, talk, dance, primp, curl his hair, tie his ribbons, and sweeten his breath to entice King James. Jonson wrote a masque specifically for the occasion, *The Golden Age Restored*, that included a dance to be performed by George to show off his dancing legs to the King (Riggs 1989, 215-18). It worked. King James fell madly in love, William Herbert became the Lord Chamberlain, and George Villiers eventually became the Duke of Buckingham. In securing the position, Herbert included the specific condition that the position of Lord Chamberlain be passed on to his brother Philip when William died, ensuring that the control of the theatre and printed plays stayed within the Sidney/Herbert family. Thus Mary's son, William Herbert, the 3rd Earl of Pembroke, went on to become the wealthiest and most powerful man in England, second only to the King himself. In 1617 Pembroke became Chancellor of Oxford University, and he did not forget those who did him favours: Ben Jonson was given an honorary degree from Oxford at the behest of Pembroke, plus he received £20 every New Year for books. Did William Herbert spend most of his career at court manoeuvring for the position of Lord Chamberlain out of fear that his mother would expose herself as an author of popular and potentially explosive plays for the public theater? Only as Lord Chamberlain would he have absolute control over their publication. In E. E. Willoughby's classic book on the printing of the *First Folio*, he notes that no new edition of the plays of William Shakespeare appeared since 1615 (1934, 166). The year 1615 is the year William Herbert became Lord Chamberlain.

Herbert acted as a bawd, as mentioned in the *First Folio* eulogy, but what about the whore? Mary's younger son Philip gained his power at court through a very different process than that of his older brother. Being a younger son, Philip had no chance at a hereditary title. As Lawrence and Jeanne Stone explain in *An Open Elite?*, a "distinctive feature of the English landed elite was the fact that their younger sons were downwardly mobile, with few career options . . . unless they should have the good fortune to marry an heiress. Because there were no special legal privileges or hereditary titles attached to them, younger sons had to make their own way in the world" (2001, 165). Nor did younger sons of the nobility have a history of accomplishing much: "they certainly had the opportunity of making large fortunes and buying their way back into the society into which they had been born, perhaps indeed at a higher level, but few of them seem to have made it" (*ibid* 185). Perhaps it was this automatic strike against Philip that made him so different from his older brother. The Earl of Clarendon describes William as endowed with "a good proportion of learning, and a ready wit to apply it," while Philip "pretended to no other qualifications than to understand horses and dogs very well, which his master loved him the better for" (1707, Vol 1: 24). Philip had other gifts. Clarendon carries on to note that Philip "had the good fortune, by the comeliness of his person, his skill, and indefatigable industry in hunting, to be the first who drew the King's eyes towards him with affection" (*ibid*). Wilder and handsomer than William, Philip was even more successful than his older brother in attracting James' notice. Before the King's coronation, Philip was appointed Gentleman of Queen Anne's bedchamber, made a Knight of the Bath, and received a grant for the transport of cloth worth not less than £10,000. By the time James was officially king, Philip "was familiar enough with the king to be able to get away with kissing him on the lips rather than the hand at the ceremony, and he had great influence with the king from the earliest days of the reign" (Kernan 1995, 11). Philip was nineteen years old. On the first New Year's night of King James's court, 1603-04, Philip exploited the effects that his physical charms obviously had on the King: when James asked Philip for an interpretation of his heraldic design, "a fair horse colt in a fair green field," Philip explained that it represented "a colt of Bucephalus's race and had this virtue of his sire that none could mount him but one as great at least as Alexander"; this caused James to "make himself merry with threatening to send this colt to the stable" (Brennen 1988, 107-09). In October 1604, Philip married Susan de Vere, the youngest daughter of Edward de Vere, the Earl of Oxford; they secretly arranged their own marriage six months after the Earl died. On their first morning after the wedding, with great glee, "the King in his shirt and nightgown gave them a Reveille Matin before they were up and spent a good time in or upon the bed, choose which you will" (letter from Dudley Carleton to Winwood; see Waller 1993, 83).

Philip's relationship with the King progressed; Robert Cecil's letters are full of references to Philip's intimacy with James. Finally, the pay-off: in 1605, Philip Herbert was granted an earldom, even though he was a younger son. Alvin Kernan is explicit: "James took up with Herbert's younger brother, the even more handsome Philip, who as a result of this intimacy was made Earl of Montgomery" (118). An earldom wasn't the only honour King James heaped upon Philip Herbert: he presented the handsome young man with lands worth £1,200 a year in rents and tithes; had Oxford University award him an M.A. although Philip had studied there only a few months; paid off Philip's debts accumulated from his loose living and extravagance; created him a Knight of the Garter, the highest order of knighthood in England, and outright gave him £6,000 as a gift (Akrigg 1968, 52). Essentially, Philip Herbert was a whore for the King. Although William and Philip received their awards through different means, by mid-1616 when the Earl of Pembroke as Lord Chamberlain presided over the arrangements for the King's summer progress, "the Herbert brothers were widely recognized as being among James's most intimate advisers and friends" (Brennen 1998, 167).

Now Jonson's odd reference to a Bawd and a Whore trying to ruin a Matron makes perfect sense. With both of her surviving children clawing their way up the factious court ladder, how could Mary Sidney, as their mother, engage publicly in any potentially subversive literary activity? In the world of the royal court, if Mary Sidney had been known to be writing inappropriate literary work, such as bawdy, licentious, politically insurgent plays for the public theatre, it would have caused a scandal easily capable of destroying both sons' careers. Hannay explains; "the lives of these aristocratic women, although less restricted in many ways than those of women in the lower classes, were still tightly constrained by an emphasis on the virtues of chastity, silence, and obedience" (1985, 10). Cerasano and Wynne-Davies agree: "as a female author/translator, not to mention a member of the nobility, Mary Sidney would have opened her reputation to considerable risk by involving herself in public theatre" (15). Any question of the mother's reputation would have been valuable material for the enemies of her sons. Indeed, Lukas Erne points out that between 1605 and 1608, fifty-two plays for the commercial stage were printed, more than during any other four-year period in Shakespeare's life, but while Shakespeare's published work accounts for eighteen percent of printed plays in the last decade of Elizabeth's reign, they only account for four percent in the first decade of James' reign (109).

Mary's sons became two of the wealthiest and most powerful men in the English court, and the self-proclaimed poet laureate Ben Jonson had a part in their success with his masque that featured George Villiers as bait for the King. The *First Folio* is dedicated to these two sons, the Earl of Pembroke and the Earl of Montgomery, although no personal or professional connection between William Shakespeare and

Mary's sons has been found. Campbell muses that Philip Herbert "was a generous patron of the arts, but he was habitually in debt, a fact which makes his selection as a dedicatee of such an expensive volume as the *folio* somewhat unusual" (1966, 620).

Printing the *First Folio*

The collected works were first taken to the press in August of 1621. William Shakespeare had been dead for five years. Mary's sons were by now well established and powerful, and she had felt "how sharper than a serpent's tooth it is to have a thankless child" (*King Lear,* 1.4.287-88). William had not spoken to her for more than a decade, even though many of the legal battles she fought were for his inherited estate. Philip had secretly married the daughter of the Earl of Oxford, who earlier had a bitter altercation with Philip Sidney, who retained "the uncomfortable distinction of being one of those the Earl of Oxford said he wanted to kill" (Duncan-Jones 1991, 174).[3] Philip had grown into an "intolerable and choleric" profligate who, along with his older brother, openly kept a mistress. Francis Osborne (1593-1659) describes an incident at court where Philip did not behave well, and noted that: "I have been told the Mother of [Philip] Herbert tore her hair at the report of her son's dishonour, who, I am confident, upon a like opportunity would have ransomed her own repute, if she had not redeemed her country's" (1673, 507). So at 60 years old, with ungrateful children, did Mary Sidney decide to publish her own plays? It was a process familiar to her. The *First Folio* went to press without being licensed — not an extremely rare occurrence, but it is unusual: "before a play could be printed, it had to be licensed. The licensing agent responsible for printed matter was a panel of London clergymen . . . and the Lord Chamberlain" (Bevington 2009, xcv). The Lord Chamberlain in 1621 was Mary's oldest son, William Herbert. It is possible Mary Sidney had to circumvent licensing a book that would have made the Lord Chamberlain take notice.

The title page of the *First Folio* falsely states, "Published According to the True Original Copies." The first four plays in the *Folio* were printed from copies made by a professional scribe; the others are cobbled together from a variety of sources. As Bevington writes, "if

3 Contrary to the belief of many Oxfordians, Philip never did reconcile with Oxford. Oxfordians claim that Philip was Oxford's second in the "Callophisus" tournament as the White Knight, but Duncan-Jones proves Philip was the Blue Knight. The White Knight was Oxford's nephew, Edward, Lord Windsor (1991, 202-03).

the editors had planned to continue this practice [of using fair copies] throughout the volume, however, they abandoned it after the fourth play and turned instead to a variety of sorts of copy" (xcvii). This suggests that Mary may have provided the printer with these first four plays, planning to supply the others as the project progressed. The timing is provocative. In July of 1621 she entertained King James at Houghton House near Ampthill, but she was back in her London home on Aldersgate Street in August of 1621. Did she come into London for the specific purpose of finally publishing her own collected works? The printer of the *Folio* was right down the street from her home. Several documented events intersect here: the printer began production of the book in August, 1621; Mary Sidney died in late September; production of the *Folio* stopped in October (Willoughby 166). Printing eventually resumed and the project was completed in November, 1623 — seven years after William Shakespeare died and two years after the death of Mary Sidney. It was licensed the day it came off the press. John Michell remarks on the finished book: "The editors of the *First Folio* hinted by two or three phrases that the author was the man buried at Stratford-upon-Avon, but they never openly stated it. There were no biographical notes on the great dramatist, nor any indications of where and when the plays were written. On the question of how they acquired authentic copies and the rights to plays previously published, the editors were secretive and mendacious. The originals from which they worked have never been seen since" (1996, 80).

The editors are assumed to be John Heminges and Henry Condell, although they had no previous experience in such a project, Condell being the son of a fishmonger and Heminges a full-time grocer throughout his intermittent acting career, even employing six of his ten grocer apprentices in plays, plus he built and operated a tap house at the Globe (Egan 2001, 72-77). It is difficult to explain why the King's Men would allow these two unqualified men to appropriate this valuable property and do what they wished with it, and there is no indication that the acting company contributed in any way. There is no record where they procured the small fortune necessary for publication, or why an investor would allow two unqualified part-time actors to find, collect, and edit thirty-six manuscripts from the previous thirty years and prepare them for the press. Charlton Ogburn sees a solution: "if we seek answers to the crucial questions the *First Folio* raises, I think we shall be forced to accept the indications that those primarily responsible for the publication were the Herbert brothers" (1984, 219).

The timing of Mary's death is curiously entwined with these Herbert brothers and the *First Folio*. She died shortly after the press began the lengthy process of publication. The parish records of Salisbury Cathedral state only that she was buried, but in 1621 John Chamberlain, a gentleman and scholar in the court of King James but unreliable in his reports, gossiped in a letter (to Sir Dudley Carleton on 13 October) from London; "the old Countess of Pembroke died here some ten days since of the smallpox, and on Wednesday night was carried with a great store of coaches [probably no less than a hundred] and torchlight toward Wilton where she is to be buried" (2: 400). Her death certificate does not confirm smallpox, and no will was found. This is an interesting note, that Mary Sidney Herbert, a countess, a woman of wealth and property, supposedly had no will — yet Dr. Matthew Lister, upon her death, was awarded £140 a year for the rest of his life (*ibid*). It is also notable that the Herbert brothers were unusually amicable in the division of property after her death, with William turning over most everything to his younger brother Philip. Were they trying to avoid an inquest?

Ben Jonson is also connected to the publication process of the *First Folio*. He had long been closely associated with Mary and her Wilton Circle, her sons, and her younger brother Robert, and wrote numerous poems and epigrams to and about members of the family. As Kay observes, "Jonson consistently portrays the Sidneys and the Herberts as members of a self-contained aristocratic community that is answerable only to its own ancestral traditions" (1995, 117). Understanding how the generally cantankerous Ben Jonson admired and respected the Sidney and Herbert families and was embedded in William Herbert's plot to change the power structure in the royal court, it is possible after Mary Sidney died and the *First Folio* was on the press that William Herbert confided to Ben Jonson that his mother was the author of these plays. Was Jonson the editor? It might explain why Jonson, in the *First Folio* eulogy, calls "the author" the "Star of Poets" and the "Sweet Swan of Avon" and points out the danger to a Matron from a Bawd and a Whore. Riggs believes that Jonson may well have been one of the editors. He notes that whoever prepared the *Folio* "remade Shakespeare in Jonson's image," describing how the prefatory letters and poems in the book "transform Shakespeare into a specifically literary figure whose works have achieved the status of modern classics; the closest analogue to these tributes are the poems prefixed to Jonson's 1616 folio" (276). Riggs describes how the *First Folio* follows the same method of punctuation that Jonson used in his own *Works* instead of that used in the previously published editions of the Shakespearean plays. The "extensive use of parentheses, semicolons, and end-stopped lines in the 1623 folio owes more to Jonson's example than to Shakespeare's habits of composition" (*ibid*). Even a line in *Julius Caesar* that Jonson had derided as ridiculous appears in the *First Folio* as corrected and logical. If Mary Sidney began the printing process in 1621, it is possible that after she died, the printer contacted her son the Lord Chamberlain about the unfinished project — and payment. Up until this time, William Herbert may have been the only person aware that Mary Sidney was the author. But now, to finish the project and attribute the plays to William Shakespeare for posterity, Herbert would have needed help; perhaps at this point he called on Ben Jonson.

Sweet Swan of Avon

Jonson's participation would explain why he calls the author of the plays the "Sweet Swan of Avon . . . upon the banks of the Thames." No one ever refers to William Shakespeare as a swan in any form. But Michael Drayton wrote of Mary Sidney in 1593:

> The lofty subject of a heavenly tale,
> Thames' fairest Swan, our summer's Nightingale (in Collier 1856, 98).

Samuel Daniel wrote of Mary Sidney in 1592 on the Avon River, seat of her Ivychurch estate:

> No, no, my Verse respects not Thames nor Theatres,
> Nor seeks it to be known unto the Great,
> But Avon, rich in fame, though poor in waters
> Shall have my song, where Delia [Mary Sidney] hath her seat.
> Avon shall be my Thames, and she my song;
> I'll sound her name the river all along (in Grosart 1885, 75)

Mary Sidney is noted to have written with a white swan quill pen, the most expensive and long-lasting quill available. She commissioned her portrait when she was 57 years old, shown below. Note the swans in her lace collar and wrist ruffs; the swan wings below her hand, the quill pens that border the portrait. A female swan is called a pen. She is buried in Salisbury Cathedral on the edge of the Avon. It is believed that she took on the swan motif partly because her adored brother, Philip Sidney, was immortalized by French poets as a swan — Sidney sounds very similar to the French *cygne*, which means swan. Another poignant symbol that connects Mary to the beautiful and elegant white swans is that they are mute until they die; the dying gasp makes a musical sound as the air travels through the "organ-pipe of frailty" (*King John*, 5.7.20–24).

This final portrait, just two years before her death, shows a woman who plans to go down in history as a writer: she holds a book she authored in her hand, *David's Psalms*; the portrait is bordered by quill pens in ink pots; the laurel wreath, symbol of a poet, crowns the image. The Sidney spearhead points to Mary, and the inscription uses her maiden name.

Mary Sidney, while ostensibly staying within the established limits of feminine convention, became "the most important woman writer and patron of the Elizabethan period, one who demonstrated what could and what could not be accomplished in the margins" (Hannay 1990, x). Of all the writers and potential authorship candidates during this specific time period, none others show the broad range of skill, the deep involvement in the world of literature that they are attempting to influence, the leadership in the field of writing and publishing, the support of a local community of like-minded artists, the known patronage of other professionals, the known ownership of source materials, and so much more. No other writer was referred to as a swan on the Thames, but Mary Sidney Herbert, the Countess of Pembroke.

Chapter 7

My Shakespeare – Francis Bacon

Barry Clarke

Francis Bacon (1561-1626) was an essayist, philosopher, and statesman who served as Solicitor General (1607), Attorney General (1613), and Lord Chancellor (1618). His academic reputation rests mainly on the three editions of his *Essayes* (published 1597, 1612, and 1625), and his critique of scientific practice in the *Novum Organon Scientiarum* (1620). The latter, along with Galileo's work, inspired the founding of the Royal Society of London in 1660 (see Scriba 1970, 39-41). This essay outlines the evidence for Bacon's contribution to three of the Shakespeare plays — *The Comedy of Errors*, *Love's Labour's Lost*, and *The Tempest* — and makes the point that unless the attribution method employed attempts to follow scientific principles then no real progress can be made in terms of authorship attribution.[1] In my view, more progress can be made by concentrating on a small number of plays for which there is strong evidence for contribution, than by indulging in unbridled speculation about a single alternative author of the entire Shakespeare canon.

Traditionally, the Shakespeare Authorship Question produces arguments to show that William Shakspere of Stratford did not originate most, if not all, of the works published under his name.[2] These demonstrations usually proceed by constructing a profile of a

1 Here "scientific" is meant in the Popperian sense that the method attempts to eliminate both the main subject of the test as well as other possibilities. It is the subject's survival of such a test that renders the subject's contribution "corroborated".

2 For clarity, a distinction is made between "Shakspere" the Stratford man who was assigned all credit in the *First Folio* (1623), and "Shakespeare" which will serve as a generic name for all the contributors to this work who were not assigned credit.

typical dramatist of the period and comparing the known facts about Shakspere against it. Having raised sufficient suspicion as to Shakspere's credentials for authorship, an alternative candidate, or a cooperating group of candidates, is then proposed as an alternative. The argument for a candidate's authorship of a Shakespeare work typically relies on supposed autobiographical allusions.

In contrast, traditional methods of authorship attribution depend on textual analysis, comparing aspects of writing style between a particular author's canon, and a piece of unknown provenance, known as the target text. Often, the method can offer a crucial insight into how well the thought processes correspond in the works under comparison, the attributed and the unattributed. However, it is important to emphasize the distinction between an "originator" and a "contributor". A stylistic test cannot say anything about the originator of a Renaissance play. For example, it is easily possible that a manuscript that was conceived by some unknown dramatist was later acquired by a known playwright for expansion and revision into a two-hour stage presentation. So unless there is additional documentary evidence such as an original manuscript copy,[3] the most that can reliably be claimed about this or that work is that a particular author made a "contribution" to it, and for this we rely on tests of style. The difficulty with Shakspere is that if one wishes to test his contribution to any play (or poem) under his name, there are no extant letters or prose works of his against which a comparison can be made. So traditional stylistic methods of attribution can never rule out Shakspere from having contributed to a work under his name.

In exploring Francis Bacon's contribution to the Shakespeare work, an examination of rare phrases and collocations is carried out.[4] Fortunately, there exists an online collection of pre-1700 books in the database "Early English Books Online" (EEBO) that can be searched. Here, a phrase can be typed into the search engine — it automatically covers spelling variations — and the number of texts containing this phrase before any chosen date is returned. In this way, an estimate of the rarity of a phrase can be estimated. To be informative, one hopes to discover a rare phrase that only the target text and some known author share.

While a stylistic test can deliver no verdict on the originator of a Shakespeare play, it is still possible to construct arguments

3 Even in this case it might still have been plagiarised and copied.

4 Here "rare" is defined as a phrase or collocation occurring in less than 0.17% of the records searched.

against Shakspere's origination by other means. For example, several Shakespeare plays appear to have been earmarked for performance at Inns of Court revels at a time when only Inn members — and Shakspere was not a member — were writing and performing plays there. We shall see that Francis Bacon was involved in the organisation and writing of entertainments for the 1594-5 Gray's Inn Christmas revels where *The Comedy of Errors* and *Love's Labour's Lost* were to be performed. In addition, *The Tempest* contains information about the Virginia colony that only an informed insider could have known. If Shakspere, who was not a member of the Virginia Company, originated this play then he would have needed assistance from a Virginia Company member. Again, Francis Bacon was a prominent member of the Virginia Company at the time *The Tempest's* main source event occurred, namely, the 1609 Sea Venture shipwreck at Bermuda.

In contrast to conventional discussions on the Shakespeare Authorship Question, the present essay makes no attempt to argue for Bacon's origination of the entire Shakespeare canon. In my view, the proposal that any particular candidate was the alternative originator of the Shakespeare work is untestable. Instead, the focus will be directed to three Shakespeare plays for which evidence of Francis Bacon's contribution is quite strong: *The Comedy of Errors*, *Love's Labour's Lost*, and *The Tempest.* A comparison of rare parallels will be applied, in which the evidence for the last two plays turns out to be particularly compelling. Bacon has 27 works in the EEBO database so it is possible to establish the extent to which he shares rare phrases with a given Shakespeare play or poem. What renders the method scientific is that the opportunity is also provided to eliminate Bacon from having made a contribution.[5]

There is a wide variation in the extent to which academics are willing to admit the presence of other hands in the Shakespeare canon. For *Titus Andronicus*, *1 Henry VI*, *Timon of Athens*, and *Pericles*, the Cambridge editors regard Shakspere as sole author.[6] In contrast, the Oxford editors of *Shakespeare: The Complete Works* are at least willing to accept a degree of collaboration.[7] In both cases, Shakspere is assumed

5 For example, Bacon's corpus shares only one rare phrase with the long poem *A Funerall Elygye* (1612); see Clarke (2013, sec. 4.3).

6 Hughes, ed., *Titus Andronicus* (1994); Hattaway, ed., *The First Part of King Henry VI* (1990); Klein, ed., *Timon of Athens* (2001); DelVecchio and Hammond, eds., *Pericles, Prince of Tyre* (1998).

7 Wells and Taylor *et al*, *William Shakespeare: A Textual Companion* (1987, 112 -15, 127-8, 130-1). The collaborators are taken to be George Peele, Thomas Nashe, Thomas Middleton, and George Wilkins, respectively. This point was made by Jackson (2003, 1).

to be a self-educated natural-achiever who, in the latter case, was charitable enough to delegate the writing of certain acts, scenes, or sub-plots to other grateful dramatists. Nevertheless, there only needs to be one work under the Shakspere name that is not his to justify a further investigation into attribution. Indeed, the 1619 quarto of *The first part Of the true & honorable history, of the Life of Sir John Oldcastle, the good Lord Cobham* has "Written by William Shakespeare" on the title page,[8] a name that by this time had appeared on several quartos. For 16 October 1599, Henslowe's diary records a receipt of "ten pownd" by "Thomas downton of phillipp Henchlow to pay m^r^ Monday m^r^ drayton & m^r^ wilsson & haythway for the first pte of the lyfe of Sr Jhon Ouldcasstell & in earnest of the Second pte for the vse of the company" (Greg 1904: F.65, 113). So the hypothesis that Shakspere is the principal author of this work does not fit the facts.

Supposed autobiographical allusions in a play provide a weak case for contribution and any serious attribution argument must employ a traditional comparison of style. This issue is addressed in section 2 where it is argued that rare collocation analysis using the EEBO database presents fewer opportunities for error than traditional stylometric counts. An examination of Francis Bacon's interest in drama will be treated in section 3, while section 4 looks at Inns of Court drama, important background material for two of the three case studies that follow. The case studies provide the main part of the present work, and are given in sections 5-7, covering Bacon's suggested contribution to *The Comedy of Errors*, *Love's Labour's Lost*, and *The Tempest.*

1. Attribution methods

1.1 Biographical connections

An attribution argument based entirely on autobiographical correspondences between the work of a proposed contributor and a target play is highly problematic. In the first place, assuming the validity of the correspondence, the writer might well be alluding to someone other than himself. Secondly, taken in isolation, biographical associations can seem highly persuasive. However, once one takes a wider view, and compares such an argument against those for other possible candidates,

8 However, the title page bears the year 1600. An earlier 1600 quarto has no attribution.

it soon becomes clear that they are all more or less equally credible. This suggests that this kind of argument, which is incapable of eliminating other possibilities, is unscientific. By building an ever-growing mountain of connections, and by ignoring similar constructions for others, the practice labours under the illusion of exclusivity. As Love informs us, "one would have to proceed with great caution in attempting to profile a dramatist through his or her characters (which has not stopped many attempts). Such a matching of profiles would not establish the matter on its own but would be a useful adjunct to other arguments" (2002, 87). The difficulty arises when there *are* no other arguments.

1.2 Stylometry

The most widely used test is a stylometric one, which involves word counts. In 1993, Gerald McMenamin defined stylometry as "the scientific comparison of written or spoken utterance habits in questioned [doubtful attribution] and authentic [known attribution] samples" (1993, 46). The key word here is "habits" because it relies on what an author repeatedly does and so its methods demand the examination of a large section of text to obtain a significant count. The following is an example of the stylometric method in operation. A section of text in the unattributed document is taken, and the number of occurrences per thousand words of some linguistic feature is counted, for example, the number of words with a "dis-" prefix. This process is carried out for several different features, for example, spellings, word endings, stressed/unstressed syllables, until one has a set of numbers. These totals are then compared with similar sets taken from other authors' work, and a comparison or correlation is used to suggest attribution. The problem with this method is that it relies on the dubious assumption that only one person has contributed to the document under examination, and that the counted words have not suffered later corruption by some scribe, editor, or compositor. In fact, there is no way of knowing. It is possible that what one might actually be counting is the average effect of several hands.

The main defects of current stylistic practice are that firstly, it is usually limited to the works of a small set of known dramatists, and secondly that the low cognitive content of the counted items render them vulnerable to editorial, scribal, and compositorial intervention. The first point is related to the fact that for a play, the method does not attempt to eliminate other possible writers. Inns of Court dramatists who have published prose works might also have made contributions. These are not usually examined. The second point relates to the assumption that the target text has only a *single* author. An illustration of the difficulty involved with compositor influence is afforded by John Cooke's *Greene's Tu Quoque, or the Cittie Gallant* (1614), which was not entered in the Stationers' Register, and was printed in two different sections by two different teams. One team used "quoque" and "you're" only, while the second team used "Quoque" and "y'are" instead (Lake 1975, 17). This clearly indicates intervention. However, the problem facing the application of stylometry to an unattributed target text is one that rare collocation analysis does not suffer from.

1.3 Rare collocation analysis

Since this process examines an individual phrase or collocation, the demand that the words in a large section of text should all have been supplied by a single author is superfluous. Instead, the method focuses on individual phrases and collocations which can each be examined independently of the rest of the text. Attributing a text to an outstanding writer is much easier than for a lesser pen: "[i]n the case of none [that is, in no case], however, is the judgment more certain than in the case of those whom strength of intellect, depth of knowledge, and matchless eloquence and other pre-eminent gifts place [him] beyond the range of imitation" (Brady and Olin 1992, 79). All scholarly attribution methods attempt to establish an exclusive match between a particular linguistic feature found in a target text and a particular author's canon. Collocations and phrases are more reliable as markers since a later reviser is less likely to amend meaningful expressions that convey the personality of the originator. By their very nature, phrases and collocations carry a greater meaning than words, parts of words, or the rhythm of words, so that their higher cognitive complexity provides them with a far lower frequency of occurrence. It is this rarity that can be used to suggest an exclusive match. Unless a parallel is sufficiently complex, the presentation of meaningful verbal parallels without an estimate of their rarity carries no weight, and for a contribution to be suggested, it is important that rare usage occurs both before and after the presumed date of the play.

We now turn to Francis Bacon and his interest in drama. In biographies of Bacon, what is almost never discussed is that he was producer for the Inns of Court acting companies.

2. Francis Bacon and drama

On 27 June 1576, Francis Bacon was admitted to Gray's Inn, one of the four Inns of Court. He obtained the privilege of attending Pensions [committee meetings] on 10 February 1586 (Fletcher 1901, 72), although without a voice and in the Lent term of the following year he obtained influence on being appointed a Reader (Stewart 2001, xxiii). Inns of Court members frequently wrote as well as enacted their own plays for Christmas revels. One such play was *The Misfortunes of Arthur* which was presented on 28 February 1587-8 "to her Maiestie by the gentlemen of Graies-Inn at her Highnesse court in Greenwich" (Hughes 1587 [1588], sig. G2). Although Thomas Hughes receives the main writing credit, on the last page of the 1587 printed edition we find that, "The [five] dumbe shows were partly deuised by Maister Christopher Yeluerton, Maister Frauncis Bacon [...]" along with at least two other Gray's Inn members. On 17 November 1592, Queen's Day, the Earl of Essex gave a device before the queen written by Bacon. In 1734, the Histiographer Royal, Robert Stephens, published "Mr. Bacon's discourse in prayse of his Soveraigne (Queen Elizabeth)" and "Mr. Bacon in Prayse of Knowledge" which "the Earl of Oxford [Robert Harley, (1661-1724)] was pleased to put into my hands" (1734, sig. a2). Stephens thought they had been "in the possession of Dr. Rawley, his Lordship's [Bacon's] Chaplain", and the Victorian editor of Francis Bacon's *Works*, James Spedding, went on to suggest that "both formed part of some fanciful device presented at the Court of Elizabeth in 1592" (1870, v-vi).[9]

Two treasurers were usually elected at Gray's Inn in the late sixteenth century and Bacon held the post until 26 November 1594 (Fletcher 1901, 101). This would have given him supervision over the organisation of the 1594-5 Gray's Inn Christmas revels. In 1688, a detailed account of these revels went on sale at the price of one shilling as the *Gesta Grayorum* (Affairs of Gray's Inn). It reports that on Innocent's Day, 28 December 1595, "a Comedy of Errors (like to *Plautus* his *Menechmus*) was played by the Players" (1688, 22). The *Gesta Grayorum*'s wealth of detail suggests that it was composed shortly after the revels had ended and we now examine some of the internal evidence that Bacon compiled it. This

9 The dating evidence arises from the fact that the first speech was extended into "Certain Observations upon a Libel" which Bacon published in 1592. Copies of both speeches also appear under the heading "Of Tribute, or giving what is dew" in the Northumberland Manuscripts Collection under the name of "M^r. ffrauncis Bacon" (see Burgoyne 1902), which dates to 1597.

relies on a list of rare parallels located using the EEBO database and the search details are provided in the footnotes. For example, for footnote relating to Parallel 2, the information 3/3521 before 1595 means that there were 3521 texts available for search dating to before 1595, and for the particular phrase or collocation typed into the search engine, only 3 records were returned that contained it.

Gesta Grayorum: Articles of the Knights of the Order

Parallel 1. There are no matches before the *Gesta Grayorum* for its use of "narrow observation" and none before Bacon first adopted it in his *Advancement of Learning* (1605) with "as men of narrowe obseruation may concyue them" (Bacon 1605, sig. Ff2).

Parallel 2. Pierre de La Primaudaye's *The French Academie* (1586) is mentioned in the *Articles* and it is the source for the *Gesta Grayorum*'s "selling of Smoak". This relates to the conduct of the Emperor Alexander Severus who smoked to death one of his officials at the stake for selling non-existent offices for gold. In Bacon's private waste book the *Promus* (1592-4), which at the time only he would have accessed, there is the Latin entry *Fumos vendere* [To sell smoke] (Bacon 1592-94, f.85).[10]

There are six speeches given by the mock Privy Counsellor's at the revels. Vickers notes that "[t]he ideas contained in these speeches have many parallels with Bacon's writings" (Vickers 2002, 532). However, a study of their rarity has not been carried out hitherto and so two examples will suffice here.[11]

Gesta Grayorum: Privy Counsellor's Speeches

Parallel 3. The Second Counsellor's speech has "Alexander the Great wrote to Aristotle, upon establishing the Physickes, that he esteemed more of excellent Men in Knowledge, than in Empire" (31). In Bacon's *Advancement of Learning* (1605) he writes "in his [Alexander's] letter to Aristotle after hee had set forth his Bookes of Nature [... he] gaue him to understand that himselfe esteemed it more to excel other men

10 EEBO has 3521 searchable documents dating to before 1595. With 3/3521 returns from EEBO before 1595, this predates the *Gesta Grayorum* as a rare occurrence.
11 For others, see Clarke (2013, table 5.2).

in learning & knowledge, than in power and Empire" (Bacon 1605, sigs K^v-K2). These two versions correspond better to each other than either does to their source in Plutarch (1597, 725).[12]

Parallel 4. Another example where Bacon precedes the *Gesta Grayorum* appears in the Third Counsellor's Speech. The *Gesta Grayorum* attributes to Augustus Caesar the line "I found the City of Brick, but I leave it of Marble". In "Mr Bacon's discourse in Praise of his Sovereign (Queen Elizabeth)" (1592) he has "as Augustus said, that he received the city of brick, and lefte it of marble" (Spedding *et al* 1861-74: Vol. 1, 131). With no returns from EEBO for "city of brick" prior to 1595, Bacon has priority.[13]

Gesta Grayorum: Final commentary

Parallel 5. The last paragraph of the *Gesta Grayorum* runs as follows:

> But now our Principality is determined; which, although it shined very bright in ours, and others Darkness; yet, at the Royal Presence of Her Majesty, it appeared as an obscure Shadow: In this, not unlike unto the Morning-Star, which looketh very chearfully in the World, so long as the Sun looketh not on it: Or, as the great Rivers, that triumph in the Multitude of their Waters, until they come unto the Sea. *Sic vinci, sic mori pulchrum.* [To be conquered is a beautiful death] (68).

In *A Brief Discourse touching the Happy Union of the Kingdom of England and Scotland* (1603), Bacon also employs this "greater lessens the smaller" figure making use of two of these exampddles, light and water: "[t]he second condition [of perfect mixture] is that the greater draws the less. So we see when two lights do meet, the greater doth darken and drown the less. And when a small river runs into a greater, it loseth both the name and stream" (Spedding *et al* Vol. 3, 98). Curiously, it also appears in *The Merchant of Venice*, again using light and water:

12 For details of the searches carried out see *ibid* (table 5.2, number 32).

13 "Mr Bacon's discourse" (1592) is not in the EEBO database.

> *Ner.* When the moone shone we did not see the candle
> *Por.* So doth the greater glory dim the lesse,
> A substitute shines brightly as a King,
> Untill a King be by, and then his state
> Empties it selfe, as doth an inland brooke
> Into the maine of waters: musique hark. (5.1.92-7)

For the Queen's Day celebrations of 17 November 1595, Bacon wrote a device for the Earl of Essex to present that included speeches for several fictional characters: an old Hermit, a Secretary of State, a Soldier, and a Squire. The first three characters attempt to convince the Squire that his master Erophilus should not demonstrate love for the queen. This was evidently a direct parody of Essex's own wooing of Elizabeth. The evidence for Bacon's authorship resides in an unfinished rough draft of a similar device in Bacon's hand kept at Lambeth Palace Library (Gibson Papers, vol. viii. No. 274) involving a "Heremite", "Counsellor of Estate", "Capitain" [sic], and a "Squire" (see Spedding *et* al Vol. 1, 367).

Bacon was also a producer of masques for the Inns of Court players. In an undated letter to Lord Burghley [prior to his death in 1598] he refers to two masques, one that was intended but failed, and another that he proposes as compensation:

> Yt may please your good Lordship I am sory the joynt maske from the fowr Innes of Cowrt faileth. Wherin I conceyue thear is no other grownd of that euent but impossibility. Neuerthelesse bycause it falleth owt that at this tyme Graies Inne is well furnyshed, of gallant yowng gentlemen, your lordship may be pleased to know, that rather then this occasion shall passe withowt some demonstration of affection from the Innes of Cowrt, Thear are a dozen gentlemen of Graies Inne that owt of the honour which they bear to your lordship, and my lord Chamberlayne to whome at theyre last maske they were so much bownden, will be ready to furnysh a maske wyshing it were in their powers to performe it according to theyr myndes (British Library, Burghley Papers, Lansdowne: MS 107, f.13).[14]

14 In Bacon's hand, no address, fly-leaf missing, docketed "Mr Fra. Bacon".

Part of the wedding celebrations for Frederick Count Palatine and Lady Elizabeth on 20 February 1612-13 involved a joint masque by Gray's Inn and the Inner Temple. Francis Beaumont is credited as the author but there is the following dedication to Bacon that reveals his role as producer: "Yee that spared no time nor trauell, in the setting forth, ordering, & furnishing of this Masque [...] as you did then by your countenance, and louing affection aduance it" (Beaumont 1613, sig.B).[15] The following year, on 9 December 1613, he receives credit for producing *The Masque of Flowers* (Coperario 1614, sig. A3). It inspired John Chamberlain to write to Sir Dudley Carleton; "Sir Francis Bacon prepares a mask which will stand him in above £2000, and although he has been offered some help by the House [Gray's Inn], and specially by Mr. Solicitor, Sir Henry Yelverton, who would have sent him £500, yet he would not accept it, but offers them the whole charge with the honour" (Nichols 1828: Vol. 2, 705). Even though George Chapman was assigned the writing credit (1614), Adams has doubts; "Bacon's writing style, his garden preferences, and his knowledge of flowers, visible in his two garden descriptions and *The Masque of Flowers* support other evidence presented here that he [...] was equipped to script and produce one [a masque] with a garden of flowers as its defining theme and visual focus" (2008, 53). The evidence for Bacon's involvement in *The Comedy of Errors* and *Love's Labour's Lost* relies, in part, on an estimation of who wrote and acted plays at the Inns of Court before these two plays were scheduled for performance at the Christmas 1594-5 revels. This will now be explored.

3. Inns of Court drama

The tradition of Inns of Court members writing and performing a play as part of their training into courtly practices is revealed in a report prepared for Henry VIII (c.1534-47); "in some of the houses ordinarily they have some interlude or Tragedy played by the Gentlemen of the same house, the ground, and matter whereof, is devised by some of the Gentlemen of the house" (Waterhouse 1663, 546). With this in view, a study has been carried out of writers and players at the Inns of Court prior to the 1594-5 Gray's Inn Christmas revels at which *The Comedy of Errors* had its first known performance (Clarke 2013, chp. 3). In *Records of Early English Drama: Inns of Court*

15 On the title page we find "By Francis Beamont [sic], Gent."

the claim is made that it was a visiting company that performed the play; "[a]ll Inns of Court plays subsequent to 1587-8 seem indeed to have been performed by professionals, including *Comedy of Errors* [...] and Shakespeare's *Twelfth Night"* (Nelson and Elliott Jr., 2010, xxii).[16] It is a conclusion that appears to rest on the assumption that a payment to players necessarily implicates the hiring of a professional company. We now examine the counter evidence.

There is a record of a payment from Christmas 1417–18 for Furnivall's Inn, one of the Inns of Chancery related to Lincoln's Inn, "For players and their play" who are unidentified (*ibid*, 819). There is also a record from the Steward's accounts at Lincoln's Inn up to October 1494-5 listing a "reward to players" (*ibid*, 829). However, no further information is available. At a Gray's Inn Pension dated 5 February 1594-5 we read, "the some of one hundryd marks to be layd out & bestowyd upon the gentlemen for their sports & shewes this Shrovetyde at the court before the Queens Majestie" (Fletcher 107). Here, Inns of Court players receive a gift for their performance at the royal court. There is a second example. From the Gray's Inn Ledger Book for 1587-8, we find, "Item deliuered to mr fflower 18 ffebruary ffor and towards the chardges of the Tragedie" (Nelson and Elliott Jr., 111). For the 1587-8 Christmas season, Francis Flower contributed two Choruses and parts of dumb shows to *The Misfortunes of Arthur*, a tragedy written and played by members of Gray's Inn.[17] Again, a payment is being made to players belonging to the Inns of Court, this time for expenses accrued in staging a play. So, a payment to players need not implicate a professional company. As far as precedent is concerned, in the period 1522-88, only Lincoln's Inn are on record as having hired outside companies.[18]

Around the time of the 1594-5 revels, there is no record of a payment to a professional company in either the Gray's Inn Pension Book or Ledger Book for *The Comedy of Errors* (Nelson and Elliott

16 Nelson elsewhere comments; "*Comedy of Errors* was famously acted at Gray's Inn in 1594-5, his *Twelfth Night* at Middle Temple in 1601-2, both presumably by Shakespeare's company," (in Zimmerman and Sullivan 2009, 67).

17 The title page in Hughes (1587 [1588]) states "Certaine deuises and shewes presented to her Majestie by the Gentlemen of Grayes-Inne at her Highnesse Court in Greenewich" and the last page attributes "Frauncis Flower" with two Choruses and contributions to dumb shows.

18 The Treasurer's Allowance at Lincoln's Inn records payments to the boys of the Queen's Chapel (1564-5, 1565-6, 1579-80) and Lord Rich's players (1569-70); see Nelson and Elliott Jr., (866-7, 871, 877).

Jr., 121-24).[19] There is even external evidence that Shakspere was not present when the play was introduced to the gathering of law students at Gray's Inn on Innocent's Day, 28 December 1595. An abstract of an entry in the Accounts of the Treasurer of the Chamber prepared by the auditors, records a payment for a performance by Shakespeare's company at Greenwich on the same night that *Errors* was being enacted at Gray's Inn: "To Willm Kempe Willm Shakespeare Richarde Burbage servants to the Lord Chamberlayne [...] dated at Whitehall xv^to^ [15th] Martij [March] 1594 [1595] for twoe severall comedies or Interludes shewed by them before her ma^tie^ [majestie] in xpmas tyme laste paste viz upon St Stephens daye & Innocents daye".[20] It would have been impractical to expect the Lord Chamberlain's Men to perform both at Gray's Inn after 9pm as the *Gesta Grayorum* suggests (22) *and* for the queen at Greenwich on the same day, "Innocents daye", since "the Court performances were always at night, beginning about 10pm and ending at about 1am" (Chambers 1945: Vol. 1., 225). So Chambers, who could not accept that players other than the Lord Chamberlain's Men were performing *Errors* at Gray's Inn, suggested that the "Innocents daye" recorded on the warrant really meant the 27th, a day earlier, freeing Shakespeare to appear at Gray's Inn on the 28th (1906, 10-11). The fact is, the administrator "Thomas Grene" explicitly wrote "Innocents daye" [28th] and so due respect should be given to his evidence.

Chambers' evidence also relies on the fact that in the *Gesta Grayorum* we find that "a company of base and common fellows" performed at Gray's Inn on the "Night of Errors", which typically means a professional acting company. However, the remark is part of a comic charge read by the Clerk of the Crown who refers to "a great Witchcraft used the Night before" at which time "a Sorceror or Conjuror" was accused of "foisting a Company of base and common Fellows, to make up our disorders with a Play of Errors or Confusions" (23). Chambers has presented his evidence out of context. If we also consider that the *Gesta Grayorum* states the proceedings "were rather to be performed by witty inventions than chargeable expenses" (2), then his case becomes weakened. In fact, the known revels contributors,

19 Payments were being recorded in the Gray's Inn Ledger Book at that time. For example, William Johnson of Gray's Inn was given £30 17s 10d to distribute to the gentlemen for a show before the queen at Shrovetide; see Nelson and Elliott Jr., (124).

20 A graphic of the document appears in Clarke (2013: Figure 5.1).

Francis Bacon,[21] Thomas Campion,[22] and Francis Davison,[23] were all Gray's Inn members.

Special admittance seems to have been necessary for an outside dramatist to write for an Inns of Court revels. Arthur Brooke's *Masque of Beauty and Desire* was performed at the Inner Temple in the 1561-2 season (see Leigh 1562). He was not an Inn member and a Latin entry in the Inner Temple Admissions Register translates as "Arthur Brooke of London specially (admitted) on 18 December, the pledges being Thomas Sackville (and) Thomas Norton" (Nelson and Elliott Jr., 865). An Inner Temple Parliament held on 4 February 1561-2 also recorded; "Order that Arthur Broke shall have special admission, without payment, in consideration of certain plays and shows at Christmas last set forth by him" (Inderwick 1895, 220).[24] During the Gray's Inn 1594-5 revels, a list of seven people were signed in by the mock Prince of Purpoole on 25 December 1594, and a further four on 6 February 1594-5 but William Shakspere was not one of them (Nelson and Elliott Jr., 124-5 and 886).

The first recorded association of Shakspere with the *The Comedy of Errors* is when Francis Meres mentions "Shakespeare" and "his *Errors*" in *Palladis tamia* (1598). His company are not on record as having played it until 28 December 1604 at court (see Whitworth 2002, 10). A correct summary of the known facts should therefore be documented as follows: "of the six known plays involving Gray's Inn in the 50 years leading up to the 1594-5 Gray's Inn revels, three were written by their members, at least three were acted by their members, all six were played at Gray's Inn, and none of them are on record as having involved an outside writer or playing company" (Clarke 2013: sec. 5.4). This suggests that *The Comedy of Errors* and *Twelfth Night* were most likely played and conceived by Inns of Court players without Shakspere being present. With the ground set, we shall now examine the evidence for Francis Bacon's contribution to three Shakespeare plays: *The Comedy of Errors*, *Love's Labour's Lost*, and *The Tempest*, the first two of which are associated with the 1594-5 Gray's Inn revels. It again takes examples from lists of rare parallels which have been located through use of the EEBO database. The strongest correspondences occur for the last two plays.

21 Apart from the evidence that Bacon compiled the *Gesta Grayorum*, he at least wrote the six Privy Counsellors' speeches.

22 He wrote "A Hymn in Praise of Neptune", credited to him in Davison (1602: sig. K8).

23 He wrote "Sonnet IIII" and perhaps also "The Masque of Proteus", although it contains a Squire, a character that Bacon had previously used. The former but not the latter piece appears in Davison (1602: sig. D3^{v})

24 See also Nelson and Elliott Jr., (85 and fn).

4. *The Comedy of Errors*

Dorsch has expressed the view that "the play was chosen, and the words of the *Gesta* devised, to complement each other" (2004, 33). Whitworth concurs, claiming that it was "purpose-written for the Christmas season, 1594" (4). The two main arguments that it was written specifically for these festivities are as follows:

> (a) In common with other Inns of Court plays such as *Gordobuc, Gismond of Salerne*, and *The Misfortunes of Arthur*, it appears to glance at the succession question. This it achieves through references to St. Paul's *Epistle to the Ephesians* with its theme of alienation (Clarke 2013, sec. 6.2). *The Comedy of Errors* is set in Ephesus, a Greek city on the coast of Asia Minor, where St Paul was trying to reconcile the Jews and Christians.[25] Plautus's *Menaechmus*, one of the two main sources for *Errors*, is actually set in Epidamnus.
>
> (b) Several commentators have pointed out that the dialogue surrounding the gold chain, which does not appear in its Plautine sources *Menaechmus* and *Amphitruo*, provides a test case for the developing law of contract (see for example Zurcher 2008). This consists of the tension between the traditional action of debt and the then recently introduced action of *assumpsit.* The complexity of the argument suggests that it was intended for trained legal minds (Clarke 2013, sec. 6.2).

Two rare parallels involving Bacon have been found that pre-date the play's first known performance.

Parallel 6. The first is "voluble and sharp discourse" (1.1.93), while Bacon has "no wise speech though easy and voluble" in his private waste book *Promus* (1592-4). Here the search was conducted for "voluble and *" or "* and voluble", where the "*" represents some other descriptor (Bacon 1592-94, f.85).[26]

Parallel 7. The second appears as "Apparell vice like vertues harbinger" (3.2.12). In the *Promus* (1592-4), in Bacon's hand, is the Latin "*Da mihi fallere da justume sanctumque viderj*" [grant me to escape detection; grant me to pass

25 It was also where Plautus set the action for *Milos Gloriosus.*

26 The EEBO search for "voluble and *" registered 3/3440 returns and "* and voluble" 2/3440 before 1595.

as just and upright]. Admittedly, this example loses some force due to there being no direct correspondence of words (Bacon 1592-94, f.91^{v}).[27]

Three correspondences that post-date the first-known *Errors* performance are as follows:

Parallel 8. The first is "creep in crannies" (2.2.31). In *Syluia syluarum*, Bacon has "the Species does passe through small Crannies" (1627, 68).[28] The locution "in crannies" was first used in the play and "crannies" had only appeared once before Bacon first used it.

Parallel 9. The second is the legal term "fine and recoverie" (2.2.74), which first appears in the play. Bacon has the next known use after the play in a manuscript copy of "Office of Compositions for Alienations" in 1598 (see Montagu 1831: Vol. XIII, 378).

Parallel 10. Third, there is the phrase "present satisfaction" (4.1.5). Only Richard Cosin's *An apologie* (1593), and William Cornwallis's *Essayes* (1600-01) precedes Bacon's use of "present satisfaction" in his unpublished "Valerius Terminus" of 1603 (see Spedding *et al.* Vol. 6, 40).

Parallels 7–10 were rare both when the play used them and when Bacon first inserted them in his known work, while Parallel 6 has two search returns that are each rare. So, there is some evidence here that Bacon made a contribution to this play, although not as strong as that which will now be presented for *Love's Labour's Lost* and *The Tempest.* Altogether, Bacon has nine rare parallels, two before 1594 and seven after. Thomas Heywood has seven, all after 1594, so he is a good candidate for having worked on a later revision. Thomas Nashe has four, which predate 1594 and suggest that his work acted as a source.

5. *Love's Labour's Lost*

On 23 January 1594-5, the new term started at Gray's Inn. Unfortunately, as recalled in the *Gesta Grayorum*, it disrupted the conclusion of the revels: "very good Inventions, which were to be performed in publick at his [the mock Prince's] Entertainment into the House again, and two grand Nights which were intended at his Triumphal Return, wherewith his reign had been conceitedly determined, were by the aforesaid Readers

27 Five different searches were carried out: "*da mihi fallere*", "sin near.8 saint", "just near.8 sin(s)", "just near.10 night", and "deceive near.15 just" with no returns before 1594 for any of them.

28 It occurs 1/7607 in EEBO before 1626.

and Governors made frustrate, for the Want of Room in the Hall, the Scaffolds [theatre galleries] being taken away, and forbidden to be built up again" (53). The presence of the scaffold and "two grand Nights" suggest that two plays were scheduled for performance but cancelled. It also suggests that a "play" is an example of an "Invention" mentioned above. Let us recall that the *Gesta Grayorum* states that the revels "were rather to be performed by witty inventions than chargeable expenses" (2). This points to the in-house creation of plays for the revels, as a professional company would certainly have demanded expenses. In what follows, we shall examine the rare parallels between the play and the *Gesta Grayorum*, before moving on to the ones between the play and Bacon's corpus. There are 5 rare parallels, Parallels 11-15, between *Love's Labour's Lost* and the *Gesta Grayorum* that suggest that this was one of the cancelled "Inventions".

Parallel 11. King Ferdinand opens the play by reminding his lords, Longaville, Dumain, and Biron, that they have sworn to be celibate for three years in order to devote themselves to study. He claims that in relation to their research "Nauar shall be the wonder of the world". The phrase "wonder of the world" was used to describe the "living art" or the ethics of the Stoics, whose aim was to reveal the secrets of the universe (Reid 1922, 226-7). At the 1594-5 revels, Francis Bacon's second Counsellor's speech in the *Gesta Grayorum* "Advising the Study of Philosophy" applies the same epithet to the Prince; "when all miracles and wonders shall cease, by reason that you shall have discovered their natural causes, yourself [the Prince of Purpoole] shall be the only miracle and wonder of the world" (35).[29]

Parallel 12. Biron then expresses his frustration that their devotion to study is too prohibitive:

> O, these barren taskes, too hard to keepe,
> Not to see Ladies, study, fast, not sleepe. (1.1.47-8)

The association of "tasks" and "ladies" does not appear before 1594, but occurs in Bacon's sixth Counsellor's speech at the revels; "[w]hat! nothing but tasks, nothing but working-days? No feasting, no music, no dancing, no triumphs, no comedies, no love, no ladies?" (41).[30]

---

29 An EEBO search returns 2/3440 records containing "wonder of the world" prior to 1594.

30 For the search "tasks near.20 ladies" EEBO returns no records before the play.

Parallel 13. Lord Boyet has been spying on the king and his lords, and reports back to the Princess that they are disguised "Like *Muscovites*, or *Russians*". Hibbard has suggested that "an even more precise dating [of the play] would be possible if only it could be shown conclusively that Shakespeare was indebted to the Gray's Inn revels of Christmas 1594-5 for the idea of the Masque of Muscovites in 5.2 of his comedy" (2008, 45). In *Love's Labour's Lost* (David 1956, xxvii), when the "blackamoors" musically herald the arrival of the four academy members dressed as Muscovites, it seems to echo the commentary of *Gesta Grayorum* when there arrived an "Ambassador from the mighty Emperor of Russia and Moscovy" (44),[31] who states that they "surprized another Army of Negro-Tartars" (46). These two terms "muscovites" and "Russians" find no connection in the 1598 quarto of *Love's Labour's Lost* but do so in the *First Folio* (1623) version.

Parallel 14. In *Love's Labour's Lost,* once the Princess and her ladies have exposed the Lords' disguises, Rosaline confronts Biron:

> *Rosaline.* Help hold his brows, he'll swoon. Why look
> you pale?
> Seasick, I think, coming from Muscovy. (5.2.391-3)

As recorded in the *Gesta Grayorum*, on 1st February, the mock Prince of Purpoole complains of seasickness on returning from his supposed journey to Moscow (Taylor 1932, 8-9). In the Prince's letter to Sir Thomas we find; "I found, that my Desire [to entertain the Queen at Greenwich] was greater than the Ability of my Body; which, by length of my Journey [from Russia] and my Sicknesse at Sea, is so weakened, as it were very dangerous for me to adventure it". This example from the *Gesta Grayorum* and the one in *Love's Labour's Lost* are the earliest two returns for the association of "seasick" and "Muscovy".[32]

Parallel 15. White has partially identified a further correspondence between the play and the *Gesta Grayorum.* Without elaborating, he notes that, "it [the *Gesta*] has various elaborate edicts couched in the legal terms of 'Items' that we find in *Love's Labour's Lost*" (White 1996, 150). An investigation reveals a similarity between the play and the

31 A search for "russians near.5 muscovites" produces only 4/3440 returns before the revels and none for "russia near.5 muscovy".

32 See "Prince's speech" items 69-71 and footnotes in Table 5.2, Chapter 5 in Clarke (2013). Two EEBO searches "seasick(e) near.80 muscovy" and "sea sick(e) near.80 muscovy" yield no returns before the play.

"Articles of the Knights of the Order" that were read out at the revels. One of these "Articles" is as follows: "*Item*, No Knight of this Order shall be inquisitive towards any lady or Gentlewoman [...] except such Knight have passed three Climacterical Years" (28). In *Love's Labour Lost* (1.1), Longaville reads out the following edict: "*Item*, Yf any man be seene to talke with a woman within the tearme of three yeares, hee shall indure such publique shame as the rest of the Court can possible deuise" (Shakespeare 1598, sig. A3^{v}).[33] Later, in Act 2 the Queen decides that

> Till painefull studie shall out-weare three yeares,
> No woman may approach his silent Court (*ibid*: sig. B4).

Both the play and the *Gesta Grayorum* frame the demand not to see a woman for three years as a legal "Item".

Aware of Parallels 12, 13, and 14, but without access to a test of their rarity, Woodhuysen has claimed; "there are few if any verbal links" between the *Gesta Grayorum* and *Love's Labour's Lost* (1998, 64). However, with a test for rarity included, the links become persuasive, especially when Parallels 11 and 15 are appended. A sample of connections between the play and Bacon's body of work will now be examined.

Parallel 16. First we take an example in Latin, where Bacon's use precedes the date of the play. In *Love's Labour's Lost* we have:

> You leere vpon me, do you? There's an eie
> Wounds like a leaden sword. (5.2.480-1)

It originates from Diogenes as "draweth forth a leaden swerd out of an Iuery skaberd" and was recorded by Desiderius Erasmus in *Flores aliquot sententiarum* (1540). Only one example before 1594 is in the context of a leaden sword causing injury and this appears as "you had with this your leadden sweard killed God haue mercie on his sowle" in Jerónimo Orsório's *A learned and very eloquent treatie* (1568). In Bacon's unpublished waste book *Promus* (1592-4), he has the Latin "*Plumbeo jugulare gladio* [to kill with a leaden sword]" which is closer to the play's version than Erasmus's version (Bacon 1592-94, f.98).[34] The following examples are of Bacon's correspondences that post-date the play.

---

33 EEBO returns no examples before the revels for the search "tasks near.20 ladies".

34 This is not in EEBO. The EEBO search for "leaden sword" returns 1/3440 before 1594.

Parallel 17. The king refers to "Anthony Dull, a man of good repute, carriage, bearing, & estimation" (1.1.266). In October 1621, Francis Bacon completed *The historie of the reigne of King Henry the Seuenth* in which we find, "But howsoeuer succeeded, by a moderate Carriage and bearing the Person of a Common-friend" (Bacon 1629).[35]

Parallel 18. Biron's following speech perhaps reveals the occasion that the play was intended for:

> I see the trick on't
> (Knowing aforehand of our merriment)
> To dash it like a Christmas comedy (5.2.460-2)

The earliest use is Bacon's "putting trickes vpon them" in his 1612 collection of essays (sig. C).[36] A similar locution appears in *The Tempest* (1611) as "Doe you put trickes vpon's with Saluages" (2.2.57-8).

Parallel 19. Biron has a speech "Behold the window of my heart, mine eie" (5.2.843).[37] In Bacon's then unpublished "Device of an Indian Prince" (1595) he has "Your Majesty shall obtain the curious window into hearts of which the ancients speak" and constitutes the first known use (Spedding *et al*, Vol. 1: 390).

Parallel 20. There are lines that appear in the *First Folio* (1623) version but not in the 1598 quarto:

> Follie in Fooles beares not so strong a note,
> As fool'ry in the Wise, when Wit doth dote. (5.2.75-6)

The idea of folly affecting a wise man more than an ordinary one is echoed in Spedding's translation of Bacon's Latin Proverb 11 in Book VIII of *De Augmentis Scientiarum* (1623) "*Itaque viro valde prudenti parva stultitia, valde probo parvum peccatum, urbano et moribus eleganti paululum indecori, de fama et existimatione multum detrahit*" (Spedding *et al*, Vol. 3: 69) [Hence a little folly in a very wise Man [...] detracts greatly from their character and reputation [...] which in ordinary men would be entirely

35 Three EEBO searches "repute near.5 estimation", "carriage near.5 estimation", "carriage near.5 bearing" produce no returns prior to 1594.

36 At present this is only in digital image format in EEBO and not as searchable text. For the searches "trick on it" and "put(ting) trick(s) upon" there are no EEBO returns before the revels and 1/5471 before Bacon's use in 1612.

37 No examples were returned by EEBO for "window fby.3 heart" prior to 1594.

unobserved] (*ibid*: Vol. 9, 246).[38] No EEBO record contained all three ideas of "folly", "fool", and "wise" in the required comparative sense. So Bacon's example, which is not in the EEBO database, is the best match found.

Thomas Dekker has eight and Thomas Heywood seven rare parallels with the play that all post-date the 1594-5 Gray's Inn revels. This suggests that they were hired for a later revision. Bacon has three that precede the revels and five that follow which renders him a good candidate for contribution. Thomas Nashe has six strong parallels that precede the revels, so his work could have been a source, or perhaps the play was originally his and was revised by others.

We now turn to a play that is not usually associated with the Inns of Court, but seems to have been conceived to advertise England's power and influence in the New World. Its first known performance was before King James's court and invited ambassador's from other lands would almost certainly have been present.

6. *The Tempest*

The first known performance of *The Tempest* was on 1 November 1611 by the King's Men at Whitehall (Chambers 1945, Vol. 4: 177). There is evidence that it relied partly on source documents connected with the Virginia colony around the first decade of the seventeenth century (see Clarke 2016, 71-93). One such document was *True Reportory*, a confidential company report sent back to England from the colony in July 1610 by the secretary William Strachey.[39] Two pamphlets that were in print before the play's first known performance also appear to have been sources: John Smith's *A true relation* (1608), and Richard Rich's *Newes from Virginia* (1610). Unpublished information about the colony that appeared in the play, later appeared in Ralph Harmor's *A True Discourse* (1615), and John Smith's *The general historie* (1624). William Shakspere was not a member of the London Virginia Company, so it is unlikely that he could have accessed this information without the assistance of a Virginia colony specialist (see Clarke 2011, 13-27).

In 1610, after Strachey's *True Reportory* arrived in England, the

38 A complex EEBO search strategy was carried out in an attempt to find other examples. All records returned were individually inspected for sense, and those returned for "folly near.15 fool(s)" (114/3440) were compared with those returned for "folly near.15 wise" (214/3440). The idea was to find a common return from the two sets but none occurred.
39 It was published in 1625 (Purchas 1734-58, Vol. IV).

"Counseil for Virginia" issued a propaganda pamphlet running to some 10,800 words under the title *A true declaration.*[40] There is evidence that it borrowed from the *True Reportory*, so that whoever compiled *A true declaration* had seen Strachey's report, a source for *The Tempest* (Clarke 2016, 82-84). Bacon was a leading member of the Virginia Company and sometime after January 1618, when he became Lord Chancellor, former secretary William Strachey sent him a manuscript copy of his *The Historie of Travaile into Virginia Britannia* with the following dedication: "Your Lordship ever approving himself a most noble fautor [supporter] of the Virginia Plantation, being from the beginning (with other lords and earles) of the principal counsell applyed to propagate and guide yt" (1612). In what follows, we shall examine rare phrase and collocation evidence that Francis Bacon contributed to *A true declaration*, with the consequence that he must have inspected the *True Reportory*, one of the sources for *The Tempest.* We shall also review some of the rare correspondences between Bacon's work and the play. First, we shall present two examples of Bacon's parallels with *A true declaration* (1610) before its publication.

Parallel 21. The pamphlet has "which is an infallible argument that" (56). John Lyly's *Euphues* (1578) has "which is an infallible argument that", and is the only example that precedes Bacon's "which is still an infallible argument, that our Industry is not awakened". This appeared in a speech concerning the general Naturalization of Scotland which he gave to the Lower House in 1606–7 (Spedding *et al*, Vol. 3: 313).[41]

Parallel 22. Also in *A true declaration* we have "when procrastinating delays and lingering counsels, doe lose the opportunity of flying time" (67).[42] It originates from Virgil's '*sed fugit interea, fugit irreparabile tempus*' [but time flies meanwhile, time irretrievable] (*Georgica*, Book III, lines 284-5). Bacon has Virgil's complete Latin tag in his *Advancement of Learning* (Montagu 1838, 303).

The next example is later than *A true declaration.*

Parallel 23. The locution "carried away by the tide of vulgar opinion" appears on the second page of the pamphlet. Bacon's *The Charge* (1614)

40 Counseil for Virginia, *A true declaration of the estate of the colonie in Virginia with a confutation of such scandalous reports as haue tended to the disgrace of so worthy an enterprise* (London 1610). It was entered for publication at Stationers' Hall on 8 November 1610 by Sir Thomas Smith, Sir Maurice Barkley, Sir George Coppin, and Master Richard Martin.

41 EEBO gives only 1/5268 return for this five-word string prior to 1610.

42 All 121 returns from the search "flies/flieth/flying near.10 time" were individually inspected for the context "time does not return" and only 4/5268 records available before 1610 satisfied it.

has "the stream of vulgar opinion" which is only the third use of "vulgar opinion" after *A true declaration* and Richard Rich's *Opinion deified* (1613).

Moving on to *The Tempest*, we now examine two Bacon parallels that pre-date it.

Parallel 24. There is the phrase "print of goodnesse" (1.2.352) and only two examples are returned by EEBO before *The Tempest* when searched as "good" or "goodness". One is John Jewel's *A replie* (1565) and the other is Bacon's "hath the print of Good" in his *Advancement of Learning* (1605).

Parallel 25. The line "The Mistris which I serue, quickens what's dead" (3.1.6) finds at least three related uses by Francis Bacon. In his essay "Of Sutes", there is "Secrecie in Sutes is a great meanes of obtaining, for voicing them to bee in forwardnes may discourage some kind of suters, but doth quicken and awake others" (1597). Also in a speech on "The Article of Naturalization" delivered on 17 February 1607 we have "whether it [denial of naturalisation] will not quicken and excite all the envious and malicious humours" (see Spedding *et al*, Vol. 3: 307 and 322). In the posthumously published *Sylva Sylvarum* written in English he writes "For as Butterflies quicken with Heat, which were benummed with Cold" (1627).

There are also some examples of Bacon's that follow the play.

Parallel 26. The Iesuites play at Lyons in France (1607) seems the most likely source for this excerpt from the play:

> that now he was
> The Iuy which had hid my princely Trunck,
> And suckt my verdure [health] out on't (1.2.86-7)

Bacon has "But it was ordained, that this Winding-Iuie of a PLANTAGANET, should kill the true *Tree* it selfe" in *The historie of the reigne of King Henry the Seuenth* which he finished in October 1621 (see Spedding *et al*, Vol. 11: 302).[43] The closest to Bacon's version is "like iuie [ivy] so long it hath embraced, that it hath eaten vp whole Monarchies" in Thomas Ireland's *The oath of allegiance* (1610). However, in the correspondences located, only Bacon and *The Tempest* combine the ideas of "ivy", "tree", and "royalty".

43 Bacon completed this work in October 1621. Five different searches were carried out to find examples; see Clarke (2013: Table 7.1, No. 15).

Parallel 27. There is the idea of a self-deception by repetition of a fabricated tale which appears in the play:

> Like one
> Who hauing into truth, by telling of it,
> Made such a synner of his memorie
> To credite his owne lie, he did beleeue
> He was indeed the Duke, out o' th' Substitution
> And executing th' outward face of Roialtie
> With all prerogatiue". (1.2.99-105)

Only Francis Bacon in *Henry the Seuenth* (1622) has anything resembling this when discussing the imposter Perkin Warbeck; "Insomuch as it was generally beleeued (aswell amongst great Persons, as amongst the *Vulgar*) that he was indeed *Duke* Richard. Nay, himselfe, with long and continuall counterfeiting, and with oft telling a Lye, was turned by habit almost into the thing hee seemed to bee; and from a *Lyer* to a *Beleeuer*" (Spedding *et al*, Vol.11: 210).[44]

Quiller–Couch and Dover Wilson (1961, 91) see the lines from *The Tempest* as counterfeit coining metaphors, and Bacon also made use of them in *Henry the Seuenth*; "To counterfeit the dead image of a King in his coyne, is an high Offence by all Lawes: But to counterfeit the liuing image of a King in his Person, exceedeth all Falsification" (Spedding *et al*, Vol. 11: 219). Altogether Bacon has three rare parallels that pre-date, and eight that post-date *The Tempest* (see Clarke 2013: Table 7.3). No other returned author in EEBO has more than three and they all post-date the play. As stated earlier, Bacon produced masques and devices, having later been commended in print for producing two masques at Whitehall: "20 February 1612-13: Elizabeth-Palatine marriage celebrations, jointly played by Gray's Inn and Inner Temple players, writing credited to Francis Beaumont" (sig. B) and "6 January 1613-14: Earl of Somerset-Lady Frances Howard marriage celebrations, played by Gray's Inn members, writing credited to George Chapman" (1614). The first of these was about eighteen months after *The Tempest* was played at Whitehall in November 1611 at a time when Bacon was also a close adviser to King James.

There are other lines of enquiry that are worth investigating in relation to Bacon's contribution. In *Measure for Measure*, Melsome has pointed out that the conflict between the terror of the law and the need

44 EEBO searches were made for "warbeck near.20 duke" and "indeed fby.2 duke" but none of the 5 returns were in context.

to show mercy is echoed in Bacon's comments on these two positions (1945). Two further plays might have been intended for the Inns of Court: Elton has highlighted the correspondences between *Troilus and Cressida* and the Inns of Court revels (2000), and Gras has suggested that *Twelfth Night* was designed for performance at the Middle Temple (1989, 545-64). Finally, a comprehensive catalogue of research topics has been compiled by Cockburn, one that investigators into Bacon's contribution might find profitable (1998).[45] This concludes what seem to me to be the main arguments for Francis Bacon's contribution to certain Shakespeare plays. I suggest that in addressing only three such plays, a clearer picture has emerged from a focus of evidence than would have been obtained from a superficial survey of the entire Shakespeare canon. More emphasis than is usual has been placed on the method of attribution in the Shakespeare Authorship Question, but if real progress is to be made I suggest this is unavoidable. Unless the attribution method allows the possibility of eliminating a candidate then the claim for contribution has not been put to a critical test. Is our interest merely confined to collecting facts for our favourite candidate in order to massage our beliefs, or do we wish to find a way to make progress in what is known? If the latter, then I suggest some thought must be given as to how a candidate's contribution to a play can be allowed the possibility of negation, for it is the possibility of elimination that makes a case scientific.[46]

45 Available from *The Francis Bacon Society*.

46 In the absence of documentary evidence, if a candidate has insufficient works to conduct a critical test of style then the claim is untestable. I suggest that the motive for holding a belief in the candidate is then purely psychological.

Chapter 8

My (amalgamated) Shakespeare

William Leahy

The year 2016 was a fascinating one in many ways, not least for the global Shakespeare community, as it saw the 400th anniversary of Shakespeare's death celebrated in many festivals and events around the world. The epicentre of these celebrations was, appropriately enough Stratford-upon-Avon, the birthplace of the playwright and were led by the United Kingdom's most celebrated Shakespearean scholar, Sir Stanley Wells, CBE, Chairman of the Trustees of Shakespeare's Birthplace in Stratford and Emeritus Professor of Shakespeare studies at the University of Birmingham. These celebrations were reported widely and, in the month of April (the month in which Shakespeare died), dominated the world's media on a daily basis. This moment was, in many ways the apotheosis of the place of Shakespeare in our global culture, celebrated as the greatest genius the world has ever seen and is ever likely to see. It was, one could say the moment in which the unparalleled cultural capital of Shakespeare was both captured and displayed in all its glory. However, in terms of impact within Shakespeare studies itself and, furthermore impact upon the dominant and orthodox perception of Shakespeare, an event which occurred later in the year, but which was well in train as the party was underway, has had and will continue to have a much more profound effect than the celebrations in April.

I refer here to the publication in late October 2016 of *The New Oxford Shakespeare: Modern Critical Edition: The Complete Works* by the Oxford University Press and edited by Gary Taylor (Taylor *et al*). The significance of this edition, particularly when considered in tandem with its sister publication *The New Oxford Shakespeare: Authorship*

Companion (Taylor and Egan) which appeared some months later in February 2017 mark a breach in the traditional attribution of the plays of Shakespeare to the man from Stratford. These publications are, in effect the initial universal step in the disintegration of Shakespeare of Stratford as the author of the plays and poems traditionally attributed to him from within the orthodox academic Shakespeare community itself. They are not the first orthodox scholars to do this, but their text is certainly the most mainstream and will therefore have the greatest impact. It is worth noting that in the *Critical Edition*, where many of the plays are attributed (at least partially) to other authors than Shakespeare, a number of them have been edited by Sir Stanley Wells himself. The significance of this in the current context — that is, in the context of *my* Shakespeare — is that this move towards mainstream disintegration is one which I have been, from the margins as it were, championing for many years and which will I believe lead eventually to an acknowledgement that our traditional understanding of Shakespeare has been simplistic, erroneous and based in what I have called elsewhere "a will to mythologise" (Leahy 2016, 32).

I have articulated in a number of scholarly books (Leahy 2010), academic papers (Leahy 2008, 2009a, 2009b, 2014, 2016a) and journalistic articles (Leahy 2013, 2015, 2016b and 2016c) over the years my own journey in terms of understanding the "difficulty" of Shakespeare. I have argued that the orthodox, traditional narrative of the authorship of Shakespeare's plays is fundamentally flawed and that the many biographies of him which appear every year and which argue that the man from Stratford wrote all the plays and poems traditionally attributed to him are, to a great extent little more than works of "fictional narcissism" (Leahy 2016, 46-50). In this scenario I argue, "we see the 'nothing' of Shakespeare's recorded writing life filled with the 'everything' of the respective biographer's narcissistic urges" (33). The very basic problem with this scenario is the lack of evidence for Shakespeare's writing life, as captured so brilliantly by Diana Price in her book *Shakespeare's Unorthodox Biography* (2001) and which I have also written about at length in my own earlier paper "'Exit pursued by a Zombie': The Vampire we Desire, the Shakespeare we Reject" (Leahy 2014, 29-44). Here, I argue that there are essentially two Shakespeares in our culture; one captured in contemporary records ("Will of the Records") and one created from the study of his plays and poems ("Will of the Works"). I come to this conclusion, as there are essentially no records in existence that help us to understand Shakespeare's life *as a writer.*

We have no records for Shakespeare at all between his baptism and his marriage some eighteen years later; no records of his receiving payment for writing; no manuscripts, diaries or letters; no personal references to him as a writer. In short, there exists no writer's profile for him. As Diana Price has shown, when we examine the records of Shakespeare's life, we generally find him deeply involved in business dealings and not in literary pursuits. Given this, I have tried to understand why the traditional, orthodox narrative exists and why it is so compelling and convincing for the vast majority of not only scholars, but also people interested in Shakespeare generally. This exploration, which I will now discuss, has led me to what I can describe as *my* Shakespeare; a Shakespeare with no individual identity but rather one who is "an amalgamation of authors". Furthermore, I will show how, through the use of new technologies in relation to attribution studies the gap between this amalgamated Shakespeare and the orthodox version of him has narrowed considerably.

Since 2005, I have been developing the view, ever evolving and never static, that the traditional narrative of Shakespeare is wildly inaccurate and have captured this evolution in a number of published articles and one collected edition referred to above. It is worth saying here that getting such essays and articles published has been extremely difficult due to the fact that each of them was challenging received "knowledge" and articulating views which questioned orthodox methodologies and practice. Trying to bring this evolution of ideas all together in one short article would be an impossible task, so allow me instead to present a portrait of a moment in time which in many ways articulates ideas which had formed regarding the reality of my Shakespeare but also, due to the forum in which this presentation took place allowed me to speculate on this theme and consider ideas that have since come to take on a more concrete reality. In order to do this, I want to go back to a particular moment in June 2011. This was the month that saw the release of the film *Anonymous*, directed by Roland Emmerich and which argued that Edward De Vere, the seventeenth Earl of Oxford was, among other things the author of the plays and poems traditionally attributed to William Shakespeare, who, the film claimed was merely a "front" for the true author. Riding upon a great deal of public interest in the film and the theory it controversially articulated, the English Speaking Union in Mayfair, London set up a debate between those arguing for Shakespeare as the unquestioned author of the plays and poems traditionally attributed to him and those against. One side comprised three scholars from the Shakespeare Birthplace Trust and the Shakespeare Institute in Stratford-upon-Avon, Professors Stanley Wells and Michael Dobson and Doctor Paul Edmondson and, on the other side along with Roland Emmerich, sat Charles Francis Topham de Vere Beauclerk, Earl of Burford, an advocate for his ancestor Edward de Vere as author of the works of Shakespeare and myself, self-described at the time as a "skeptical Stratfordian". Each speaker was given five minutes to address the motion; "This House believes that William Shakespeare of Stratford-upon-Avon wrote the plays and poems attributed to him", followed by questions and a final vote from the (120 strong) audience gathered there. Below, I reproduce (for the first time) my five-minute argument exactly as presented in 2011 and which captured my thoughts up until that time and speculated on other, related possibilities.

This House believes that William Shakespeare of Stratford-upon-Avon wrote the plays and poems attributed to him.

Surely nobody believes this motion anymore. It is accepted that at least five other playwrights collaborated with William Shakespeare on some of his plays and many more are being investigated. Indeed, it is now accepted that, for example, William Shakespeare perhaps contributed just one Act to *1 Henry VI* — essentially then, this play is not a Shakespeare play. Yet, it was included in the *First Folio*. This being the case, we cannot trust the *First Folio* as an accurate register of what William Shakespeare wrote. As stated, this along with many other plays is regarded as a collaborative work and therefore the motion of this House cannot stand. There is much more, however.

Specific things are absolutely certain about William Shakespeare of Stratford-upon-Avon and are clearly documented:

1. He was a moneylender
2. He was litigious; he was prepared to sue for the return of his loans plus interest at the drop of a hat.
3. He was a theatre shareholder.
4. He was a theatre broker; he bought and sold plays.
5. In his lifetime he was accused of plagiarism; theft of others' work; pomposity; arrogance; stupidity; of doing anything underhand to make a buck.

6. Oh, and did I mention that he was constantly pursued for tax evasion? Oh, and that he was fined by the authorities for hoarding grain during a famine?

We know other things for certain:

a) He left no manuscripts; no letters; no poems; nothing.

b) He left no library — strange for such a clever chap!

c) The six signatures he left — that's all he left and they are from the last 4 years of his life — are written in a hand unlike that of someone who made their living by writing; they look like they were written by a chimpanzee wearing oven gloves.

d) The one drawing we have of him — the Droeshout engraving from the *First Folio* — is hilarious. As though drawn by the same chimpanzee now trapped in a sack and tied at the neck.

e) As far as we know he never travelled, well, anywhere! Yet twelve of the plays are set in Italy.

f) At most, he spent six years at school.

Record after record tells us we are dealing here with a rather unpleasant, not particularly well educated, but very successful and opportunistic businessman and not with a writer of many great works. That is not snobbery — that is sociology!

Yet, we are told this can all be easily explained. How?

It is simple — he was a genius. That accounts for everything.

But, it explains nothing. Or rather, it explains everything mythologically. It is not a rational or logical explanation. The Tower of Babel story explains why there are different languages in the world; but not rationally, not scientifically. It is a mythical explanation. You accept it if you buy into that kind of theological or religious way of seeing the world. The concept of genius exists in the same place as the Tower of Babel story — it ends the need for rational explanation by providing a mythical one. In the end, it explains nothing about William Shakespeare, but everything about those who hold to the view that he was a genius. For the genius of William Shakespeare is totally untraceable.

So, then, how was William Shakespeare so wise? How did he know so much about so many subjects? How did he know so many languages?

How did he acquire such a massive vocabulary? Depending on who you listen to, his vocabulary was four, five, six, seven, eight times that of the normal person.

Let me posit a rational and logical explanation for all of this. William Shakespeare is not an author — William Shakespeare is an *amalgamation* of authors, of various playwrights writing in his time. His is a complex and multifaceted identity — not a simple one. So, my view is this:

1. William Shakespeare wrote *bits* of plays himself.
2. William Shakespeare *changed* bits of plays too, as he saw to improve them.
3. William Shakespeare *paid* playwrights to write plays for him — that eventually became attributed to him.
4. William Shakespeare *stole* the work of some around him and passed it off as his own.

This is not snobbery — this is business!

William Shakespeare was a mover and shaker, a moneylender, a paymaster, an opportunist and an entrepreneur. He made a living from the writing of others. He held the power and he used it to enrich himself. This is a complex and uncomfortable truth. There is a simple and comfortable alternative. Which will you choose?

It came as no surprise to us on my side, given the tone of the questions which followed our presentations that when the audience was indeed asked that final question in the form of a vote, the orthodox view won out and Shakespeare retained his crown as the recognised single author of the plays and poems attributed to him.

A five-minute speech prepared for a debate is not a context that allows for subtleties in terms of argumentation and I concede of course, that many of the statements I made on that day were provocative and that some were speculative. However, I felt I was debating against the entire Shakespeare establishment, embodied by the members of the panel on the other side and also by the well-known faces in the audience, many of whom were orthodox Shakespeare scholars. The final vote confirmed this for me; as it was reported this was a "victory for Shakespeare" and from then on I began to be referred to by many in the establishment as an "anti-Shakespearean" (Edmondson and Wells 2013). I was arguing against many things that day, from what I regarded as the mythologising dynamic that characterised orthodox Shakespeare studies to the wilful misrepresentation of the properties held by the Shakespeare Birthplace Trust and portrayed as genuine Shakespeare houses and which I subsequently wrote about some years later (Leahy 2016d). But the thrust of my argument was much deeper and a couple of examples will allow me to explain this more clearly.

In the last few years I have become fascinated by Shakespearean biography and I have become particularly intrigued with a specific manifestation of this sub-genre in the following passage in an article entitled "What Was He Really Like" by Stanley Wells:

> As a boy he howled and wept, smiled and laughed. He played games with his siblings and was irritated when they could not keep time in their recorder playing. He walked to and from school with his satchel on his back, he learned to read and write, to swim and to ride a horse, and he struggled with Latin grammar. He went regularly to church, and thought, as any intelligent boy would, about what he heard there. He ate and drank, belched and farted, urinated and defecated (you can substitute the Anglo-Saxon terms if you wish). As adolescence came on he began to experience erections and to feel desire. He masturbated and, earlier than most of his contemporaries, copulated (Wells 2009, 110).

I have written about this at length in an article, the title of which sums up for me this passage by Wells; "'the dreamscape of nostalgia' Shakespeare Biography: Too Much Information (but not about Shakespeare)" (Leahy 2016). What there is not in the Wells paper, despite the claim in his title is any information about Shakespeare; everything that he writes here and continues to write in the article is fiction. Now let's just ponder the significance of this for a moment — in an academic article entitled "What Was He Really Like" we are provided with an entirely fictional account of Shakespeare growing up by the foremost orthodox Shakespearean scholar in the UK. Accepted practice in biography as a genre naturally allows for the biographer to interpret the actions of his/her subject in relation to known events. In this case, this accepted practice is ignored; it is pure fiction as there are *no* events to interpret here. Remember there are absolutely no known records in existence for Shakespeare between his baptism and his marriage at eighteen. As such, this is surely not biography at all; or at best it is biography in a vacuum. Rather, this is what I have termed "Bardography". As I wrote at the time:

> What Wells has produced here and the motivation for its production is, I would suggest, a microcosm of the entire sub-genre of Shakespearean biography. The vast majority of biographers of Shakespeare admit that there is "nothing" (or almost nothing) in the records in biographical terms to explain Shakespeare's life as a writer, and then proceed, normally over hundreds and hundreds of pages to produce a "comprehensive" biography of Shakespeare that delineates this writing life in detail (Leahy 2016, 34).

The list is almost endless, but just over the last few years such biographies include those by Michael Wood (2003), Stephen Greenblatt (2004), Peter Ackroyd (2005), Bill Bryson (2007), René Weis (2007), Jonathan Bate (2008), James Shapiro (2010) and Lois Potter (2012). As I said earlier, all of this led me to propose that we have in fact two Shakespeares, "Will of the Records" and "Will of the Works" (Leahy 2014). And I proceed to state that it is at the interface of these two Wills, as the profundity and the complexity of the works meet the vacuity of the recorded life, where the richness of the plays and poems meets the emptiness that is the life of the author, that the sub-genre of Shakespeare Biography ("Bardography") is born (Leahy 2016, 40). As I brought this perception into the debate in 2011, one strain of my argument was based in the notion that the orthodox version of Shakespeare the author, the dominant version in our global culture, is essentially a *constructed* one; enormously complex and dense biographies of him are written around just a few, mostly unrelated facts, none of which relate to his writing life.

Much of this theorisation and understanding stems from one aspect of Michel Foucault's ideas on authorship as expressed in his essay, "What is an Author?" (Foucault 1987). In this essay, Foucault makes many points, the most relevant of which for this current context being where he says (as, in another way did Roland Barthes in his essay "Death of the Author" (1967)) that the author is a "system of constraint" (Foucault, 119). By this, he means that the author's name has a classificatory function which by its very nature constrains interpretation. Here, the author's name acts in the same way as any system of classification; call something an amphibian and a naturalist will examine and research that animal in the way that it is and relates to "amphibianness"; call a piece of music "classical" and musicologists will research it in terms of its relation to the tradition of classical music; call a person a teenager or a student and all sorts of cultural concepts regarding "teenageness" and "studentness" are brought to bear on that person. In this sense, the classificatory function constrains and indeed determines what is theorised and said about that animal, that piece of music or those persons. In the case of the author, it manifests itself in this way; these plays were written by this author, Shakespeare and we therefore read those plays in terms of their "Shakespeareness". Further, this Shakespeare was a genius and we therefore read these plays in terms of that "geniusness". This is how the orthodox Shakespeare is constructed and it leads to all sorts of strange and irrational outcomes, though ones which due to the power of the orthodox construction are not viewed as strange or irrational. Let me provide an example.

In September 2006, Professor John Sutherland, though not a Shakespeare specialist, certainly one of the best known academics in the UK, wrote an article for the *Guardian* newspaper, entitled "Is this a pint I see before me?" (2006) in which he pondered the imponderable: why are there bits in Shakespeare's plays that are bad? Why, he asks in these plays which contain such sublime poetry are there sections which are so poor, so pedestrian, so second-rate? He theorises that as Shakespeare lived in the middle of London, a wild and exciting urban environment at a hugely creative moment in time, he spent many evenings in the tavern with his playwriting friends drinking and experiencing life to the full. Given this, Sutherland's answer to his question regarding the quality of writing produced is that Shakespeare must have written such poor sections of his plays when he had a *hangover*. There is, of course absolutely no evidence to support this reading. But, one could ask; is this really, as an academic pondering the variable quality of the writing in many of the plays, the first resort in terms of an answer? Surely not? Surely, one would think of many possibilities before coming up with this, such as, for example, that sections of the plays may have been written by different authors. This may also not be true, but it is surely more scholarly and more rational to posit such a possibility given that co-authorship was very common in the London theatre at the time Shakespeare was writing.

Why Sutherland posits such a thesis in this matter is it seems clear because he wishes to fit all of the works and words attributed to Shakespeare into the classificatory category "Shakespeare". That is, he is certain that all of these plays were, without doubt written by

Shakespeare alone (who was a genius) and we must account for the poor sections, the "non-genius parts" and thus he finds that Shakespeare must have written them when he was not at his best. And, as (according to this approach) no one else was involved this means he wrote them with a hangover. If Sutherland were to broaden his horizons and decline the constraining classificatory category of orthodoxy then other possibilities would come to the fore; such as, for example that many hands were involved in the plays. This could also help explain the highly unusual scope of Shakespeare's vocabulary and the unbelievable range of his knowledge and breadth of the sources he used. Perhaps a number of university-educated and erudite individuals were involved in the writing of the plays, each with his own special talents and knowledge to contribute. But Sutherland's approach is the same constraining one used by those writers producing the endless streams of enormous orthodox biographies, similarly built around the "knowledge" that Shakespeare alone is the author.

One therefore witnesses a highly visible system of constraint in action, which Foucault termed the "author function" and his desire was to analyse and track how such an ideological construction as the author (not just Shakespeare) came into being. He found it to be a discursive construct, arising as it does from these discourses of classification. But he shows it also has another function:

> the author . . . is a certain functional principle by which, in our culture, one limits, excludes, and chooses; in short, by which one impedes the free circulation, the free manipulation, the free composition, decomposition, and recomposition of fiction. In fact, if we are accustomed to presenting the author as a genius, as a perpetual surging of invention, it is because, in reality, we make him function in exactly the opposite fashion. One can say that the author is an ideological product, since we represent him as the opposite of his historically real function . . . . The author is therefore the ideological figure by which one marks the manner in which we fear the proliferation of meaning (Foucault, 119).

Identifying the author therefore limits meaning, limits interpretation. Furthermore, it stops the "proliferation" and is therefore culturally comforting, as it stabilises and unifies meaning. It provides a simple answer like Sutherland's, rather than producing complexity and uncertainty. It denies ambiguity and allows all Shakespeare's works to be read in relation to Shakespeare the individual, prioritising that one version of Shakespeare that is unambiguous over other possibilities.

The work of Foucault in this regard is invaluable, as it clarifies and reveals the discursively contracted nature of the author and, given his status as the primary author it helps enormously in understanding the contingency of the dominant, orthodox version of Shakespeare in our culture. This becomes particularly clear when placed into the context of the "two Wills" argument I have been making previously. For what is apparent in this scenario is that "Will of the Records" lacks any kind of purchase when related to "Will of the Works" and thus the received knowledge concerning the relationship between these two Wills is deeply flawed. For, despite the fact that it is accepted as knowledge, it is a relationship that is impossible to construct rationally and in fact can only be constructed (as Stanley Wells clarifies for us) *fictionally*. Considering these two Wills, one is a real man who existed but in terms of a writing life is invisible (Records). The other, the one who gives rise to all biography (Works) does not exist and is equally invisible. The reality of Shakespeare therefore is captured where the plenitude of the works meets the emptiness of the life, forced together to bring an end to the proliferation of potential meanings (and thus potential authors). We are therefore left with just one conclusion when considering the dominant, orthodox delineation of Shakespeare; it is a category that constrains meaning to the extent that only a *fictional* Shakespeare can be regarded as the real Shakespeare. Or, perhaps more accurately it leads us to say that Shakespeare in fact *does not exist*, other than as a means to bring order to the chaos that orthodoxy envisages in a world without Shakespeare.

***

With hindsight, it was all of this that I was arguing in the English Speaking Union in June 2011 and all of this that has led me to be labelled an "anti-Shakespearean". This nomenclature was coined by two of my opponents in the debate at the ESU, Dr Paul Edmondson and Professor Stanley Wells, both of the Shakespeare Birthplace Trust. In their book of 2013, *Shakespeare Beyond Doubt: Evidence, Argument, Controversy*, they commissioned a number of orthodox scholars to produce essays which challenged the arguments of those who questioned the traditional attribution of the plays and poems to Shakespeare, one outcome of which was to call such scholars and individuals who disagreed with them and their orthodox views of Shakespeare's authorship of the plays, "anti-Shakespeareans." As well as myself, this led them, rather strangely it must be said to the delineation of two of the universally recognised greatest interpreters of Shakespeare's plays for the stage, Sir Derek Jacobi and Sir Mark Rylance, the latter being Artistic Director of Shakespeare's Globe theatre in London for ten years, as also being "anti-Shakespeareans." This unseemly name-calling is probably best captured in an essay in the collection entitled "Fictional treatments of Shakespeare's Authorship" by Paul Franssen, who writes; "Rylance, [is] a prominent Shakespeare actor who has never made a secret of his anti-Shakespearean sympathies…" (189-200: 198). This statement is made in an academic book, published by Cambridge University Press about one of the most respected interpreters of Shakespeare's works in our lifetimes. For my own part, one of the collection's editors, Paul Edmondson devoted a number of pages of his contribution, "The Shakespeare 'Establishment' and the Shakespeare Authorship Discussion" to the debate itself, as he had presented in support of the motion. The tone of Edmondson's essay reveals his distaste with the subject in hand, perhaps best captured in this passage, which follows a lengthy criticism of the work I had done up to that moment in time:

> The antagonism in the Shakespeare authorship discussion then, expresses itself between those who participate in the focused enjoyment and understanding of Shakespeare and those who want to prevent Shakespeare of Stratford-upon-Avon from playing a major part in that equation, or to remove him from it altogether. Another perspective on the discussion shows a clash between the professional Shakespeare scholar and the anti-Shakespearean amateur. The former employs often highly specialized knowledge; the latter denies it, choosing to act on instinct rather than on evidence …. The difficulty here is that the anti-Shakespearians, whose cause is parasitic, need always to oppose something, so the "Shakespeare establishment" is construed as an edifice for them to contradict and challenge. When anti-Shakespeareans are labelled as conspiracy theorists, they see their accusers as part of that conspiracy. Shakespeareans

> are then forced into a position of taking the moral high-ground, often an unenviable and unpopular place (227).

This tone continues as Edmondson considers my input into the debate. He finds it difficult to ponder the issues raised and rather (like Franssen in relation to Rylance) decides instead to take the "unenviable and unpopular ... moral high-ground", saying "Leahy did academia a public disservice by endorsing the slippery, unsubstantiated and impressionistic narratives of anti-Shakespearians" (230). He then speaks for the entire audience as he continues:

> One of my abiding memories of the evening is the way in which the dozen or so Shakespeare scholars present in the audience seemed to find it too incredible to engage in questions from the floor. Anti-Shakespearian arguments can often overwhelm the established intellectual methodologies of their audience, creating the effect of a vacuum in which the anti-Shakespearian can go on speaking, while the Shakespearean is left gasping in incredulity at the folly of what is being said (230).

It should be remembered that Edmondson's role at the debate was to present a case for the motion. In his essay, he feels there is no need to repeat what this case was, merely to make a personal attack on those who hold a different view to him. The great misfortune in this entire project of Edmondson and Wells is that they convinced many highly respected orthodox Shakespeare scholars to join them in this identification of "anti-Shakespearians", such as MacDonald P. Jackson, Kathleen McLuskie, Andrew Murphy, Eric Rasmussen and Carol Chillington Rutter each of whom provided a chapter for the book, and James Shapiro who provided an "Afterword" (236-40).

This prolonged discussion about the debate and its aftermath is important in the delineation of *my* Shakespeare in two particular ways. Firstly, it is to clarify that my version of Shakespeare cannot be separated from the "institution" of Shakespeare; it cannot be isolated from the dominant, orthodox cultural producers of the traditional narrative of Shakespeare. This institution is so strong and their narrative relating to Shakespeare so all-pervasive that one cannot put forward an alternative without it being in some way oppositional. The institution of orthodox Shakespeare adheres to certain parameters or constraints which they have defined, to realms of truth of their making that are so overwhelming, that any deviance from those realms can be identified as "untruth". Given this, my version of Shakespeare cannot stand-alone and must be placed in the context of the types of criticism levelled at it by the likes of Edmondson *et al.* The second important point, the one I made earlier and which now, in the context of this criticism of my ideas seems unjust, is that many of the suggestions I made then have been accepted and are now regarded as either correct or at least highly plausible. The sharp criticisms of my views articulated in Edmondson and Wells' book now seem to be the product of a past era. They seem, even though written just four years ago, somewhat outmoded and simplistic. They seem to come from a time when people believed that the *First Folio* is the uniform and straightforward work of just one man. How quickly all this has changed.

And so, I would say now, some six years after the debate in London and four years after the related book which identified certain "anti-Shakespearians", the profile of Shakespeare has moved on and the place that he is inhabiting in our culture is now one which sees (or at least is beginning to see) that the *First Folio* is indeed the work of an amalgamation of authors and that, given the dearth of biographical information that exists relating to Shakespeare's life *as a writer*, the man himself is losing the identity which orthodoxy has defined for him. Now, he is an "unstable" Shakespeare. This is most clearly demonstrated in the pages of the recently published *New Oxford Shakespeare: Modern Critical Edition: The Complete Works* alluded to above. It is worth spending some time considering this text, given it is (at least partly) responsible for this burgeoning shift in our culture's understanding and consumption of Shakespeare. However, it will also be seen that it is in fact just the latest book to delineate the "new" Shakespeare that is forming before our eyes.

This edition, edited by Gary Taylor *et al*, updates the *Oxford Shakespeare: The Complete Works* edited by Taylor and Stanley Wells and published in 1988. The distance travelled in this twenty-eight year period reveals how much has changed in terms of our perception of Shakespeare as the author of the plays and poems attributed to him. The "Contents" pages of the 1988 edition (ix-xii) are wholly straightforward, the plays and poems listed without any author contribution, regarded no doubt as unnecessary given that this is simply an edition of the works of William Shakespeare. Emphasising this wholly orthodox approach, the "General Introduction" begins with a statement that could not be more straightforward and confident; "This volume contains all the known plays and poems of William Shakespeare, a writer, actor, and man of the theatre who lived from 1564 to 1616" (xv). Compare this with the opening statement of the "General Editors' Preface" in the 2016 edition:

> When our investigations began, almost a decade ago, we did not know that the *Complete Works* would include the 1602 additions to *The Spanish Tragedy* or the 1599 verses "To The Queen"; we did not know that we would identify Christopher Marlowe as a major collaborator on the *Henry VI* plays, or that we would date *Hamlet* in 1602-03; we did not know how we would handle the editorial problems posed by *The History of Cardenio/Double Falsehood* .... Our new work on questions about the canon and chronology of Shakespeare's plays and poems is included in the *Authorship Companion.* Our new work on questions about texts, editing and book history is included in the *Critical Reference Editions* (and such questions will be explored further in the forthcoming *Complete Alternative Versions*) (iv).

This is an articulation of enormous complexity when considering the plays and poems, that is in stark contrast to the simplicity and uniformity of the 1988 edition. This statement follows the "Contents" page where, along with the normal attributions the following titles are interspersed with the other works:

The Tragedy of M. Arden of Faversham; or, *The Tragedy of M. Arden of Fevershame*, by Anonymous and Shakespeare

The Most Lamentable Roman Tragedy of Titus Andronicus, by Shakespeare and Peele, with an added scene (by Thomas Middleton?)

The Second Part of Henry the Sixth; or *The First Part of the Contention*, by Shakespeare, Marlowe, and Anonymous; revised by Shakespeare

The Third Part of Henry the Sixth; or *The Tragedy of Richard Duke of York*, by Shakespeare, Marlowe, and Anonymous; revised by Shakespeare

The Reign of King Edward the Third, by Anonymous and Shakespeare

The First Part of King Henry the Sixth; or *Harry the Sixth*, by Marlowe, Nashe, and Anonymous, adapted by Shakespeare

The Passionate Pilgrim, by Shakespeare, Barnfield, Griffin, Deloney, Marlowe, Raleigh, and Anonymous

The Tragedy of Sejanus; A Lost Version by Jonson and Anonymous (Shakespeare?)

Measure for Measure, by Shakespeare, adapted by Middleton

All's Well That Ends Well, by Shakespeare, adapted by Middleton (?)

The Life of Timon of Athens, by Shakespeare and Middleton

The Tragedy of Macbeth, by Shakespeare, adapted by Middleton

Pericles, Prince of Tyre, by Shakespeare and Wilkins (vii-viii).

The authorship of these plays is anything but straightforward, perhaps best captured not by the naming of various co-writers or even the pervasive "Anonymous", but by the various question marks linked to a number of plays. This is a confusing and "messy" situation (which I will presently consider). Finally, all of this is set beside an accompanying text, *The New Oxford Shakespeare: Authorship Companion* (Taylor and Egan), published in February 2017 which, over 776 pages discusses the authorship of the plays and poems that under thirty years before they had, without thought or hesitation attributed solely to William Shakespeare of Stratford-upon-Avon.

What is clear from *The New Oxford Shakespeare* and its accompanying volumes is that orthodox Shakespearean scholars acknowledge, perhaps for the first time in the modern era in mainstream publications that the authorship of the plays and poems traditionally attributed to Shakespeare of Stratford is an enormously complex issue, rife with uncertainty and ambiguity and that, essentially it is a field in which it is difficult to speak with any kind of authority. As such, what is beginning to develop in orthodox Shakespeare studies — and we seem merely to be at the very start of this process — is an author that begins to resemble much more *my* Shakespeare, the one I called in 2011 "an amalgamation of authors". But how did this happen? What has changed? If I reached my conclusions some years ago that the orthodox conceptualisation of Shakespeare was one born out of a desire to constrain a "proliferation of meanings" and a related "will to mythologise," how did the orthodox editors of the *New Oxford Shakespeare* reach their conclusions that the *First Folio* is the work of many hands? The answer is both simple and unsurprising; they found a different Shakespeare through the use of technology.

***

My first exposure to the (then) emerging field of attribution analysis steeped in the uses of computer software was the genre-defining *Shakespeare Co-Author: A Historical Study of Five Collaborative Plays* written by Brian Vickers and published in 2002. As the title suggests, this seminal text not only analysed the authorship of five Shakespeare plays, but also, in great detail provided a lucid exploration of the whole tradition of author attribution studies as they related to Shakespeare. Vickers explains the important early twentieth century contributions made to the genre by the likes of F. G. Fleay, E. H. Oliphant, F. L. Jones and others and proceeds to demonstrate that he, Vickers is in many ways the latest scholar to publish analyses that spring from a whole tradition of such academic work. He shows how he is working in a field that has, since the 1980s produced and is continuing to produce cutting edge work that is the result of the mobilisation of certain computer software and its ability to analyse in detail to a degree hitherto impossible without it. He refers to current work by the likes of MacDonald Jackson, Ward Elliott, Jonathan Hope, Marina Tarlinskaya and Tom Merriam (among others), which by the use of various forms of software in their analyses have been producing all sorts of new and quite astonishing conclusions. For his part, Vickers used software to do verse tests, analyse parallel passages, examine vocabulary and linguistic preferences, identify function words and so on in a hugely complex fashion which required computer analysis of all words and phrases in extant plays written between 1570 and 1650.

The conclusions this analysis lead to in this particular study are these: that *Titus Andronicus* was co-written by Shakespeare with George Peele; that *Timon of Athens* was co-written with Thomas Middleton; that *Pericles* was co-written with George Wilkins; that *Henry VIII* and *The Two Noble Kinsmen* were written with John Fletcher. Naturally, these references to Fletcher as co-author were already known, but Vickers identifies, as he does in all of these analyses exactly which parts of the various plays were written by each of the co-authors. In many ways, the conclusions reached here by Vickers are not revolutionary. Each of the plays he analysed had previously been touted as collaborations of one sort or another. What was new however, was the sheer scale and complexity of the analysis undertaken by Vickers and his ability to identify the contributions of each of the co-authors to each of the plays. His findings were difficult to counter because these analyses were so complex to reproduce and the scale was beyond the means of most scholars. Yet certain scholars were undertaking their own computer analyses of various Shakespeare's plays and it is worth considering these in the light of Vickers next, truly revolutionary intervention.

Five years after he had published his *Shakespeare Co-Author* book, in the *Shakespeare Quarterly* autumn edition of 2007, Vickers published a long article entitled "Incomplete Shakespeare: Or, Denying Coauthorship in *1 Henry VI*" (311-352). In this article, which I believe to be a "game changer" in terms of authorship attribution as related to Shakespeare, Vickers opens with a statement which signals this significant change:

> The notion of a "complete" Shakespeare, as I understand it, means a collection of all plays and poems that he wrote. But if we turn our attention from his works to the way that we look at Shakespeare in his time, a complete view would recognise that, as a commercial dramatist in the hugely competitive London theatre world, he undoubtedly shared the writing of some plays in his canon. In the judgement of those scholars who have kept up with authorship studies in the last twenty years, a title such as *The Complete Works of William Shakespeare* should now be followed by the words "Assisted by Thomas Nashe, George Peele, Thomas Middleton, George Wilkins, John Fletcher, John Davies of Hereford, and Others." A scholarly consensus now exists as to the scope of Shakespeare's dependence on his coauthors (311).

The "scholarly consensus" Vickers alludes to includes (his footnote); "Cyrus Hoy, MacDonald P. Jackson, David J. Lake, M.W.A. Smith, Ward E. Y. Elliott, R. V. Holdsworth, Jonathan Hope, Gary Taylor, Marina Tarlinskaja, and others …" (311). These researchers, who by using computer software have along with Vickers "validated the findings of scholars dating back to the nineteenth century" (311), are called upon to be the vanguard of this new movement in Shakespeare studies. Vickers realises that many within the Shakespeare scholarly community will not be pleased with this announcement however: "Some readers will have read my opening paragraph with approval, others with dismay or indignation. The latter group, those who categorically deny the presence of any hand other than Shakespeare's in the canon of 38 plays, are in fact setting him on an illusory pedestal, as a genius who never needed assistance" (312). This has echoes, of course of the "will to mythologise" reached through an entirely different tradition of scholarship from that of Vickers and which I articulated in my debate paper at the English Speaking Union. Vickers' view is, of course more scholarly and founded in evidence rather than in my speculative ruminations reached through an approach founded in critical theory; but the resemblances in terms of trajectory are clear and knowledge needs both pillars to be sustainable, practice and theory.

In his paper, Vickers begins his analysis of *1 Henry VI*, by stating that there are so many incongruences in the play, it is clear that "the play text which survives in the *First Folio* was written by two or more dramatists and never properly edited" (325). Following his extensive and complex computer analysis of the play, Vickers concludes, referring to the work of Gary Taylor and Marina Tarlinskaja that "we can attribute two segments of *1 Henry VI*, with a high degree of probability; to Shakespeare and [Thomas] Nashe" (345) and one other playwright. More specifically, he feels that Tarlinskaja is probably correct when "she divides the play into three segments: Nashe (Act 1), Shakespeare (2.4, 4.2-4.5), and Y (the remainder of the play)…" (344). I do feel that this conclusion, if correct does justify the statement I made in the debate that the *First Folio* is not an accurate record of what Shakespeare wrote given that the logic of Vickers' findings (though he does not say so) is essentially that, as he wrote so little of it (not even 10%), *1 Henry VI* is not really a Shakespeare play at all. However, the important point I wish to make for now is that this group of scholars is essentially changing our understanding of Shakespeare and they are, in my view "disintegrating" him as the author of the plays and poems traditionally attributed to him. This is the true outcome of the work being undertaken by these scholars, as technology provides us with a more coherent picture of the amalgamation of authors that contributed to the production of the plays in the *First Folio*.

Vickers does not feel that his project and that of his fellow attribution analysts produces anything negative in terms of Shakespeare's place in our culture. At the end of his article he writes: "To wish to identify the playwrights who worked together with Shakespeare on some projects, making their own special talents available, is a simple instance of justice. Identifying his coauthors does not diminish Shakespeare's achievement: on the contrary, it helps us to define that achievement more clearly, and to distinguish it from his collaborators" (352). He is confident in making such a statement as his theoretical approach to his entire project is one which sees Shakespeare as a kind of master-craftsman in a "Michaelangelo model" and that his co-authors were put to work by him much like the Italian painter's understudies. Despite this fact, given that many of his findings continue to complicate and dissipate the authorship of the plays and poems of Shakespeare, it is a wonder that he has not been identified as an "anti-Shakespearian" by the likes of Paul Edmondson who, let us not forget argued unequivocally in 2011 for the motion; "This House believes that William Shakespeare of Stratford-upon-Avon wrote the plays and poems attributed to him." Indeed, it is perhaps strange that Gary Taylor, the editor of the recent *The New Oxford Shakespeare* has also not received such an honour. His and Vickers' findings are increasingly producing conclusions that undermine the notion of the single author/genius Shakespeare and posit instead a Shakespeare who could be considered an amalgamation of authors. However, there is one further observation to make in this context which relates clearly to the speculative nature of some of my comments in the debate at the English Speaking Union. And this observation arises not from the similarities but in fact from the differences between the important findings of Brian Vickers and those of Gary Taylor.

In the burgeoning field of authorship attribution studies using computer technology, many fascinating and complex analyses are being produced in what has become a highly active and important branch of Shakespeare studies. In a follow up to his 2007 article on *1 Henry VI* discussed above, Brian Vickers identified the author "Y" who both he and Marina Tarlinskaja feel wrote the majority of the play. In a piece for the *Times Literary Supplement* of April 18 2008, he makes a strong case, following further analysis using the software programme "Pl@giarism" for the author "Y" being the obscure Thomas Kyd (13-15). We have no cause to doubt Vickers' conclusions of course as he has undertaken such extensive analysis. However, we should remind ourselves that in *The New Oxford Shakespeare* Gary Taylor and his fellow editors attribute this play to Nashe (as does Vickers) and to Marlowe and Anonymous with Shakespeare as an adaptor. Thus, using complex software, Vickers has Kyd, Nashe and Shakespeare as authors while Taylor *et al*, using other, complex software have Marlowe, Nashe and Anonymous, with Shakespeare only having some kind of subsequent role adapting what came to him. Naturally, both of these cannot be correct. Indeed, this difference is indicative of the findings currently being produced in this field of study as each analyst publishes their own conclusions, which are often in conflict but which the computer analysis demonstrates to be accurate. Thus, Taylor *et al* also see a contribution from Middleton in *Titus Andronicus* which Vickers does not see. Furthermore, the identification of the Shakespeare sections of the various plays he collaborated upon are also the source of much disagreement despite again being the result of such computer analysis.

A good comparison is Vickers' chapter on *Henry VIII* in *Shakespeare Co-Author* (333-402) and Tom Merriem's 2005 analysis of the same play in his *The Identity of Shakespeare in Henry VIII.* That such differences exist in a relatively new field of study, one which mobilises extremely complex analysis, is perhaps no surprise. Indeed, Joseph Rudman, one of the pioneering experts of such analysis based in the US has written persuasively about the constraints of current approaches, concluding that "there cannot be a valid non-traditional authorship attribution study of the Shakespeare canon using the present day state of the science" (2016, 324). The use of the term "science" here is in itself both questionable and controversial, but the important point to make in the current context and one which I again wish to link back to the thrust of the debate in 2011 is that essentially the authorship attribution of the plays and poems traditionally assigned to Shakespeare is a "mess"; it is contingent, is unstable, is impossible to speak about with a convincing air of authority. There is so much that is unknown, so much that is guesswork, so much that is speculation and it is likely to remain so not despite but *because of* the complexity of the computer software analysis. And let us not forget that an added complication is the ever-evolving functionality of the software. Though not immersed in a deep knowledge of this field of study at the time, this is essentially the point I was making back in 2011 to those who subsequently proceeded to call me an "anti-Shakespearian." I was attempting to say that the experts did not know for sure when it came to attributing authorship of the plays and poems traditionally ascribed to Shakespeare; that they were, essentially operating in a field of speculative knowledge and that I was operating in the same field. I was saying that this field was enormously complex, was currently a "mess", that facts were hard to come by and that, as such, as scholars we had a duty to clarify what was known and what was not known, what was speculation and what was fact, what could be said with certainty and what could not. Furthermore, I was saying that the refusal to admit to this and to portray those who were trying to say it as deviants and amateurs was unscholarly, unintellectual and a true "disservice to academia."

This then is the basis and outline of *my* Shakespeare. My Shakespeare is unstable, provisional, contingent and largely unknown. On one side he is essentially an invention that has emerged and continues to emerge from the interface of the individual human mind and the pages of the *First Folio*. He lives as a collection of plays infused with centuries of views and opinions of scholars, laypeople, institutions, ideologies, political forces and hegemonies. Simply put, he is an unstable amalgamation of centuries of cultural considerations of the writings attributed to him. It is the book that exists and we each conjure our own author from that book. As a real author, he does not exist at all. But the conjuring that takes place, that has taken place and that will always take place is quintessentially complex and unstable. The author is ungraspable for this very fact; he exists differently for all of us and is of our own invention in any case. Thus, the debate concerning whether the author is the man from Stratford or not is irrelevant. For in reality, as I said in 2011 and as I repeat now, this author does not exist; it is the book that exists and that is the product of an amalgamation of authors. This is a complex and difficult scenario, but we must embrace such complexity and reject simplistic and comforting systems of constraint wherever they operate; not least in relation to Shakespeare and not least because they do not give rise to truth. And in this scenario, no one can ever be "anti-Shakespearian"; they can only have their own, equal Shakespeare. It will be different to yours. Celebrate that fact.

Bibliography

Introduction

Brecht, Bertolt (1980). *Life of Galileo.* Eds. John Willett & Ralph Mannheim. London; Methuen.

Chapter 1

Arber, Edward, ed. (1875-94). *A Transcript of the Registers of the Company of Stationers of London; 1554-1640 A.D.*, 5 vols. London: privately printed.

Bennett, H. S. (1965). *English Books and Readers 1558 to 1603.* Cambridge: Cambridge University Press.

Foakes, R. A., ed. (2002). *Henslowe's Diary*, 2nd ed. Cambridge: Cambridge University Press.

Nelson, Alan. H. (1998). 'George Buc, William Shakespeare, and the Folger George a Greene,' *Shakespeare Quarterly*, 48, 74-83.

Nelson, Alan. H. http://socrates.berkeley.edu/~ahnelson/

Pollard , Alfred W. and G. R. Redgrave, eds., (1976-91). *A Short-Title Catalogue of Books Printed in England, Scotland, and Ireland...1475-1640*; 2nd edn. ed. Katharine F. Pantzer, 3 vols.

Walker, Ralph W. (1953). *Ben Jonson's Timber or Discoveries.* Syracuse NY: Syracuse University Press.

Chapter 2

Albright, Evelyn May (1927). *Dramatic Publication in England, 1580-1640: A Study of Conditions Affecting Content and Form of Drama.* Reprint, New York: Gordian Press, 1971.

Blayney, Peter W. M. (1982). *The Texts of 'King Lear' and their Origins. Volume I. Nicholas Okes and the First Quarto.* Cambridge: Cambridge University Press.

Blayney, Peter W. M. (1997). 'The Publication of Playbooks', in John D. Cox and David Scott Kastan, eds., *A New History of Early English Drama.* New York: Columbia University Press, 383-422.

Bloom, Harold (1994). *The Western Canon.* New York: Harcourt Brace.

British Library website at <https://www.bl.uk/shakespeare/articles/

shakespeares-life> accessed August 2017

Brooks, Alden (1943). *Will Shakspere and the Dyer's Hand.* New York: Charles Scribner's Sons.

Bulman, James C., ed. (2016). *2 King Henry IV. The Arden Shakespeare* Third Series. London: Bloomsbury Arden Shakespeare.

Chambers, E. K. (1923). *The Elizabethan Stage*, 4 vols. Reprint, Oxford: Clarendon Press, 1961.

Chambers, E. K. (1930). *William Shakespeare: A Study of Facts and Problems*, 2 vols. 1930. Reprint, London: Oxford University Press, 1963.

Craig, Hugh (2012). 'Authorship', in Arthur Kinney, ed., *The Oxford Handbook of Shakespeare.* New York: Oxford University Press, paperback ed. 2014, 15-30.

Craik, T. W., ed. (1997). *Henry V. The Arden Shakespeare* Third Series. 1995. Reprint, Surrey, UK: Thomas Nelson and Sons Ltd.

Crockett, Bryan (2015). 'Shakespeare, Playfere, and the pirates', *Shakespeare Quarterly* 66:3, 252-85.

Davidson, Adele (2009). *Shakespeare in Shorthand: The Textual Mystery of 'King Lear'.* Newark: University of Delaware Press.

Downs, Gerald E. (2000). 'Hand D & The Book of Sir Thomas More: By the Nature of Your Error', pamphlet privately printed at The 2nd Shakespearean Research Symposium, Detroit, October 2000. A later version was published in 2007 without permission but is accessible at <www.oxford-shakespeare.com/Oxmyths/AQuestion.pdf> accessed March 2017.

Downs, Gerald E. (2007-8). 'Memorial transmission, shorthand, and *John of Bordeaux*', *Studies in Bibliography* 58, 109-34.

Duthie, George Ian (1949). *Shakespeare's 'King Lear': A Critical Edition.* Oxford: Basil Blackwell.

Dutton, Richard (1989). *William Shakespeare: A Literary Life.* New York: St. Martin's Press.

Foakes R. A., ed. (1997). *King Lear. The Arden Shakespeare* Third Series, Reprint, London: Thomson Learning, 2000.

Furness, Horace Howard, ed. (1880). *King Lear. A New Variorum Edition of Shakespeare.* Philadelphia: Lippincott.

Gossett, Suzanne, ed. (2004). *Pericles. The Arden Shakespeare* Third Series. London: Thomson Learning.

Greg, W. W. (1928). Review of Evelyn May Albright's *Dramatic Publication in England, 1580-1640*, in *The Review of English Studies* 4:13, 91-100.

Greg, W. W. (1942). *The Editorial Problem in Shakespeare: A Survey of the Foundations of the Text*, 2nd Edition, Oxford: Clarendon Press, 1951.

Greg, W. W. (1955). *The Shakespeare First Folio*, Oxford: Clarendon Press.

Gurr, Andrew (2009). 'Did Shakespeare Own His Own Playbooks?', *The Review of English Studies* 60, 206-29.

Hadfield, Andrew (2012). *Edmund Spenser: A Life*. Oxford: Oxford University Press.

Hadfield, Andrew (2014). 'Why Does Literary Biography Matter?', *Shakespeare Quarterly* 65:4, 371-78.

Hays, Michael L. (2016). 'Shakespeare's hand unknown in *Sir Thomas More*: Thompson, Dawson, and the futility of the paleographic argument', *Shakespeare Quarterly* 67:2, 180-203.

Hinman, Charlton (1965). 'Note to Second Impression' in W. W. Greg, ed., *King Lear: The Quarto of 1608. Malone Society Reprint*. 1939, Reprint: Oxford: Clarendon Press.

Honigmann, E. A. .J., ed. (1954). *King John. The Arden Shakespeare* Second Series. 1954. Reprint, New York: Metheun, 1984.

Honigmann, E. A. J. (1982). *Shakespeare's Impact on His Contemporaries*. London: Macmillan.

Hooks, Adam G. (2012). 'Bad Shakespeare' in Arthur Kinney, ed., *The Oxford Handbook of Shakespeare*. New York: Oxford University Press, paperback ed. 2014, 138-39.

Hoppe, Harry R. (1948). *The Bad Quarto of 'Romeo & Juliet: A Bibliographical and Textual Study*. Ithaca: Cornell University Press.

Humphries, A. R. ed. (1966). *2 Henry IV. The Arden Shakespeare* Second Series, Reprint, New York, Routledge, 1989.

Ioppolo, Grace (2006). *Dramatists and Their Manuscripts in the Age of Shakespeare, Jonson, Middleton, and Heywood: Authorship, Authority and The Playhouse*. London and New York: Routledge.

Ioppolo, Grace (2012). 'Revision' in Arthur Kinney, ed., *The Oxford Handbook of Shakespeare*. New York: Oxford University Press, paperback ed. 2014, 85-99.

Jowett, John (1999). 'After Oxford: Recent Developments in Textual Studies' in *The Shakespeare International Yearbook*, Aldershot, UK: Ashgate, 65-85.

Jowett, John (2007). *Shakespeare and Text.* Oxford: Oxford University Press.

Jowett John, ed. (2011). *Sir Thomas More, The Arden Shakespeare* Third Series, London: Methuen Drama.

Kirschbaum, Leo (1938). 'A census of bad quartos', *The Review of English Studies* 14 (January): 20-43.

Knowles, Richard (1985). Review of *The Division of the Kingdoms*, ed. Taylor and Warren, Oxford: Oxford University Press, 1983 in *Shakespeare Quarterly* 36:1, 115-120.

Knutson, Roslyn L. (1997). 'The Repertory' in John D. Cox and David Scott Kastan, eds., *A New History of Early English Drama.* New York: Columbia University Press, 461-80.

Maguire, Laurie E. (1996). *Shakespearean Suspect Texts: The "Bad" Quartos and Their Contexts.* Cambridge: Cambridge University Press.

McEachern, Claire, ed. (2006). *Much Ado About Nothing. The Arden Shakespeare* Third Series, Reprint, London: Methuen, 2007.

Miller, Edwin Haviland. (1959). *The Elizabethan Professional Writer in Elizabethan England: A Study of Nondramatic Literature.* Cambridge, MA: Harvard University Press.

Mowat, Barbara A. (1997). 'The Theater and Literary Culture' in John D. Cox and David Scott Kastan, eds., *A New History of Early English Drama.* New York: Columbia University Press, 213-30.

Mowat, Barbara A. (1998). 'The Problem of Shakespeare's Text(s)' in Laurie E. Maguire and Thomas L. Berger, eds., *Textual Formations and Reformations.* Cranbury, NJ: Associated University Presses, 131-48.

Murphy, Andrew. (2010). 'The Transmission of Shakespeare's Texts' in Margreta de Grazia and Stanley Wells, eds., *The New Cambridge Companion to Shakespeare*, 2nd Ed. Cambridge: Cambridge University Press, 61-75.

Price, Diana. (2013). *Shakespeare's Unorthodox Biography: New Evidence of An Authorship Problem.* Paperback edition with corrections and additions. Cleveland, OH: shakespeare-authorship.com, 2013.

Price, Diana. (2016). 'Hand D and Shakespeare's unorthodox literary paper trail' in *Journal of Early Modern Studies JEMS* 5, 329-352 and at <http://www.fupress.net/index.php/bsfm-jems/article/view/18095/16849>.

Rosenbaum, Ron. (2006). *The Shakespeare Wars: Clashing Scholars, Public Fiascoes, Palace Coups.* New York: Random House.

Sisson, C. J. (1942). 'Shakespeare quartos as prompt-copies', *The Review of English Studies* 18, 129-143.

Smeaton, Oliphant, ed. (1905). *The Return from Parnassus or The Scourge of Simony.* London: J. B. Dent.

Stone, P. W. K. (1980). *The Textual History of* 'King Lear'. London: Scolar Press.

Syme, Holger S. (2016). Review of Brian Vickers, *The One King Lear. Los Angeles Review of Books* (6 September) at <https://lareviewofbooks.org/article/text-foolish-brian-vickerss-one-king-lear/> accessed March 2017.

Taylor, Gary. (1983). '*King Lear*: The Date and Authorship of the Folio Version' in Gary Taylor & Michael Warren. eds., *The Division of the Kingdoms.* New York: Oxford University Press, 351-468.

Thomas, Sidney. (1984). 'Shakespeare's supposed revision of *King Lear*', *Shakespeare Quarterly* 35:4, 506-511.

Times Higher Education (June 6, 2016) at <www.timeshighereducation.com/news/shakespeare-scholar-vents-500-tweet-bitterly-sarcastic-attack-book> accessed March 2017.

Weis, René, ed. (2012). *Romeo and Juliet. The Arden Shakespeare* Third Series, Reprint, London and New York: Bloomsbury, 2013.

Wells, Stanley. (1983). 'Introduction: The Once and Future *King Lear*' in Gary Taylor & Michael Warren, eds., *The Division of the Kingdoms.* New York: Oxford University Press, 1-22.

Wells, Stanley, ed. (2000). *King Lear.* Paperback re-issue, Oxford: Oxford University Press, 2008.

Wells, Stanley (2013). Review of Diana Price's *Shakespeare's Unorthodox Biography* at <http://bloggingshakespeare.com/an-unorthodox-and-non-definitive-biography> and exchange at <http://bloggingshakespeare.com/beyond-doubt-for-all-time>, accessed 15 February 2015. See also Price's website at <www.shakespeare-authorship.com/?page=current> accessed March 2017.

Wells, Stanley, Gary Taylor with John Jowett and William Montgomery (1987). *William Shakespeare: A Textual Companion.* Reprinted with corrections, New York: Norton, 1997.

Werstine, Paul (1998). 'Touring and the Construction of Shakespeare Textual

Criticism' in Laurie Maguire. ed., *Textual Formations and Reformations.* Cranbury, NJ: Associated University Presses, 45-66.

Werstine, Paul (1999). 'A Century of "Bad" Shakespeare Quartos', *Shakespeare Quarterly* 50:3, 310-33.

Werstine, Paul (2013). *Early Modern Playhouse Manuscripts and the Editing of Shakespeare.* Cambridge: Cambridge University Press.

Wilson, John Dover (1923). 'Bibliographical Links Between The Three Pages and The Good Quartos' in A. W. Pollard, ed., *Shakespeare's Hand In The Play of Sir Thomas More.* Cambridge: Cambridge University Press, 113-41.

White, Richard Grant (1880). '*King Lear*: The Text', in *The Atlantic Monthly: A Magazine of Literature, Science, Art, and Politics.* Boston: Houghlin, Mifflin and Company, 824-836.

Chapter 3

Alberge, Dalya (2016). 'Christopher Marlowe credited as one of Shakespeare's co-writers', *The Guardian* online, (23 October).

Altrocchi, Paul H., (2014). *Shakespeare Fellowship Quarterly*, vol. 6.

Anderson, Mark (2006). *Shakespeare By Another Name.* New York: Gotham Books.

Anderson, Mark, Alexander Waugh & Alex McNeil, eds. (2016). *Contested Year: Errors, Omissions and Unsupported Statements in James Shapiro's '1606 Year of Lear'.* Kindle edition.

Anonymous (1589).*The Arte of English Poesie Contrived into three Bookes.* London: Richard Field.

Anonymous (1590). *The First Part of Pasquils Apologie.* London.

Anonymous (1605). *Sir Thomas Smithes Voiage and Entertainment in Rushia.* London: Nathaniel Butter.

Appleton, Elizabeth (2001). 'Examining Pasquill's imaginary and actual background', *An Anatomy of the Marprelate Controversy*, *Renaissance Studies*, vol. 5. Lewiston: Edwin Mellen Press, 295-301.

Armstrong, Charlotte (1969). *Seven Seats from the Moon.* London: Collins.

Baldwin, T.W. (1944). *William Shakspere's Small Latine & Lesse Greeke.* Vol. 1. Urbana: University of Illinois Press.

Baluk-Ulewiczowa, Teresa (2016). 'The Bad Quarto of *Hamlet* and the Polish

Connection', in Marta Gibinska & Agnieska Romanowska, eds., *Shakespeare in Europe: History and Memory*. Kracow: Jagiellonian University Press.

Baxter, Nathaniel. (1606). 'To the Right Noble, and Honorable Lady Susan Vera Mongomriana', *Sir Philip Sydneys Ourania*. London: Edward White.

Beane, Connie J. (2016). 'Reconsidering the Jephthah Allusion in Hamlet', *The Oxfordian*, Vol. 18.

Benezet, Louis O. (1937). *Shakspere, Shakespere and de Vere*. Manchester N.H: Granite State Press.

Billington, Sandra (1998). 'Was *Timon of Athens* performed before 1604?' in *Notes and Queries*, no. 45.

Bodenham, John, ed. (1600). *Bel-vedére or The Garden of the Muses*. London: Hugh Astley.

Bohun, Edmund (1693). *The Character of Queen Elizabeth*. London: Richard Chiswell.

Bradley, J. F. & J. Q. Adams, eds. (1922). *Ben Jonson Allusion Book*. New Haven: Yale University Press.

Brooke, John, trans. (1577). *The Staffe of Christian Faith*. London.

Brown, C. A. (1838). *Shakespeare's Autobiographical Poems*. London: J. Bohn.

Buckley, W. E., ed. (1882). *Cephalus and Procris, Narcissus*. London: Roxburgh Club.

Byrd, Samuel (1580). *A friendlie communication or dialogue betweene Paule and Damas*.

Chambers, E. K. (1930). *William Shakespeare: Facts and Problems*. Vol. 1. Oxford: Oxford University Press.

Chapman, George (1639). *The Tragedie of Chabot, Admirall of France*. London: Andrew Crooke & William Cooke.

Chiljan, Katherine, ed. (1998). *Letters and Poems of Edward Earl of Oxford*. California: First Edition.

Clegg, Cyndia Susan (1997). *Press Censorship in Elizabethan England*. Cambridge: Cambridge University Press.

Cole, Jan (2014). 'Who was the "late English Ovid"?' in *De Vere Society Newsletter* (May): 24-28.

Coryat, George (c. 1585). '*Ad illustrissimum Comitem Oxoniensem*', appended to Thomas Coryat's *Crudities* (1611), reprinted as 'George Coryat's Poems' in *Coryat's Crudities*, vol. 2, Glasgow: James MacLehose, 1905.

Cotgrave, Randle (1611). A *dictionarie of the French and English tongues.* London: STC 5830.

Craig, Hardin (1934). 'Hamlet's Book Cardan's *De Consolatione*', *Huntington Library Bulletin* (November).

Crawford, Charles (1910-11). 'Belvedere, or The Garden of the Muses', *Englische Studien*, vol. 43.

Crewe, Jonathan (2009). 'Believing the Impossible: *Aethiopika* and Critical Romance', *Modern Philology*, vol. 106, no. 4 (May).

Davenant, William (1638). *Madagascar with other Poems.* London: Thomas Walkley.

Davies of Hereford (1616). *Seculum Proditori.* London.

Delahoyde, Michael (2006). 'De Vere's Lucrece and Romano's Sala di Troia', *The Oxfordian*, vol. 9: 51-66.

Delahoyde, Michael with Coleen Moriarty (2016). 'New Evidence of Oxford in Venice', *Shakespeare Oxford Newsletter*, vol. 52, no. 1 (Winter).

Detobel, Robert (2004). 'The Testimony of Ben Jonson in re-dating *The Tempest, Othello,* and *Timon of Athens*', *Shakespeare Oxford Newsletter*, vol. 40, no 2.

Detobel, Robert and K. C. Ligon (2009). 'Francis Meres and the Earl of Oxford', *Brief Chronicles*, 1.

Detobel, Robert (2014). 'Idle Hours in Historical Context', unpub. paper delivered at Shakespeare Oxford Fellowship Conference, Madison, Wisconsin (October).

Detobel, Robert & Elke Brackmann (2016). 'Teaching Sonnets and de Vere's Biography at School' — Opportunities and Risks', *Brief Chronicles*, vol. 7.

de Heere, Lucas (1572), *Tableaux Poetiques.* MS f.4[r], Arbery Hall, Warwickshire.

de Vere, Edward (1573). 'To my louing frende Thomas Bedingfeld Esquyer, one of her Maiesties gentlemen Pentioners', in *Cardanus Comforte tyranslated into Englishe.* London: Thomas Marshe.

Dietz, Frederick (1923). 'The Exchequer in Elizabeth's Reign' *Smith College Studies in History*, Vol VIII, No. 2, (Jan).

Douce, Francis (1839). *Illustrations of Shakespeare.* Vol. 2. London: Thomas Tegg.

Duncan-Jones, Katherine (2011). *Shakespeare: Upstart Crow to Sweet Swan: The Evolution of His Image: 1592-1623.* The Arden Shakespeare. London: A & C Black.

Eccles, Mark (1934). *Christopher Marlowe in London.* Cambridge, MA.: Harvard University Press.

Edmondson, Paul and Stanley Wells, eds. (2013). *Shakespeare Beyond Doubt: Evidence, Argument, Controversy.* Cambridge: Cambridge University Press.

Ellis, David (2016). *1606: William Shakespeare and the Year of Lear*, review in *Cambridge Quarterly*, (March).

Elze, Karl (1874). *Essays on Shakespeare.* London: Macmillan & Co.

Farmer, John (1599). *The First Set of English Madrigals: to Four Voices: Newly composed by John Farmer.* London: Thomas Morley.

Feldman, Abraham Bronson (1947). 'Shakespeare's Jester — Oxford's Servant', *Shakespeare Fellowship Quarterly*, vol. 8, no. 3: 39-43.

Fowler, Alastair (1970). *Triumphal Forms.* Cambridge: Cambridge University Press.

Freeman, Arthur (1967). *Thomas Kyd: Facts and Problems.* Oxford: Clarendon.

French, George Russell (1869). *Shakespeareana Genealogica.* Kessinger Publishing (2008).

Furness, H. H., ed. (1901). *Twelfe Night.* Shakespeare New Variorum Edition. Philadelphia: J. B. Lippincott.

Golding, Arthur (1564). *Thabridgmente of the histories of Trogus Pompeius.* London: Thomas Marshe.

Goldstein, Gary (2016). *Reflections on the True Shakespeare.* Buchholz: Uwe Laugwitz.

Gollancz, Israel, ed. (1898). *Hamlet in Iceland.* London: Northern Library.

Gosson, Stephen (1582). *Plays Confuted in Five Actions.* STC 12095.

Greville, Fulke (1651).*The Life of Renowned Philip Sidney.* London.

Griffiths, Mark (2015). 'I know who the fourth man is — it's Shakespeare', *Country Life* (20 May): 121-38.

Grosart, Alexander, ed., (1872). '*Miscellanies of the Fuller Worthies*', *Library*, vol. IV, Private Circulation.

Grosart, Alexander, ed. (1878). *Poems of George Daniel.* Vol. II, Private Circulation.

Harris, Jesse W. (1940). 'John Bale: A Study of the Minor Literature of the Reformation', *Illinois Studies in Language and Literature*, 25:4.

Harvey, Gabriel (1578). 'Apostrophe ad eundum', in *Gratulationis Valdinensis ad nobilissumum, praeclarissumumque Domminum, Comitem Oxoniennsem.* 4th book. London.

Harvey, Gabriel (1580). 'Speculum Tuscanismi', *Three Proper and Wittie, familiar Letters.* London: H. Bynneman.

Harvey, Gabriel (1592). 'The thirde Letter', in *Foure Letters and Certain Sonnets.* London: John Wolfe.

Harvey, Gabriel (1593). *Pierces supererogation.* London: John Wolfe.

Heywood, Thomas (1612). *Apology for Actors.* London: Nicholas Okes.

Honigmann, E. A. J. (1987). *John Weever: A Biography of a Literary Associate of Shakespeare and Jonson, Together With a Photographic Facsimile of Weever's Epigrammes/1599.* Manchester: Manchester University Press.

Hotson, Leslie (1977). *Shakespeare by Hilliard: a Portrait Deciphered.* Berkeley & Los Angeles: University of California Press.

Hötteman, Benedikt (2011). *Shakespeare and Italy.* LitVerlag: Vienna and Berlin.

Hunter, Joseph (1845). *New Illustrations of Shakespeare.* Vol. 2. London: J. B. Nichols & Son.

I. G. (1615). *A Refutation of the Apology for Actors.* London.

Jolly, Eddi (2004). 'Dating the Plays: *Hamlet*', in R. Malim, ed., *Great Oxford.* Tunbridge Wells: Parapress.

Kathman, David (2012). 'de Vere, Edward Earl of Oxford', *Encyclopedia of English Renaissance Literature.* Vol. 1. Oxford: Wiley-Blackwell.

Knight, Charles, ed., (1839). *Pictorial Edition of the Works of Shakspere.* Vol. 1. London: Routledge.

Koppelman, George & Daniel Wechsler (2014). *Shakespeare's Beehive.* New York: Axeltree Books.

Kreiler, Kurt, trans., (2013). *Der Zarte Faden.* Berlin: Insel Verlag.

Lee, Sidney (1920). *The French Renaissance in England.* New York: Charles Scribner.

Lewis, C. S. (1944). *Poetry and Prose in the Sixteenth Century.* Oxford: Clarendon Press.

Lok, Henry (1597). 'To the Right Honorable, the Earle of Oxford', in *Ecclesiastes.* London.

Looney, J. T. (1922). *"Shakespeare" Identified.* London: Cecil Palmer.

Lyly, John (1597). 'Prologus', *The Woman in the Moone*. London: William Jones.

Macray, W. D., ed. (1886). *Returne from Parnassus Part 1* (c. 1600). London.

Magri, Noemi (2004). 'The Influence of Italian Renaissance Art on Shakespeare's Work: Titian's Barberini Painting: the Pictorial Source of Venus and Adonis", in R. Malim, ed., *Great Oxford.* Tunbridge Wells: Parapress, 79-90.

Magri, Noemi (2014). *Such Fruits Out of Italy: The Italian Renaissance in Shakespeare's Plays and Poems.* Buchholz: Laugwitz Verlag.

Markham, Gervase. (1624). *Honour in his Perfection.* London: Benjamin Fisher.

Marston, John (1599). *Metamorphosis of Pigmalions Image.* London: Edmond Matts.

McCrea, Scott (2005). *The Case for Shakespeare.* London: Praeger.

Mothe-Fénelon, Bertrand de Salignac de la (1840). 'Letter to Henri III (24 January 1574)', in C. P. Cooper, ed., *Correspondance diplomatique de Bertand de Salignac de la Mothe Fenélon.* Vol. 6, Paris & London.

Moore, Peter R. (2009). *The Lame Storyteller, Poor and Despised. Studies in Shakespeare.* Buchholz: Verlag Uwe Laugwitz.

Moray, James H. (1994). 'The Death of King John in Shakespeare and Bale', *Shakespeare Quarterly*, Vol 45/3.

Morris, Carolyn (2016). 'An Arrogant Joseph Hall and an Angry Edward de Vere in *Virgidemiarum* [1599]', *Brief Chronicles*, VII.

Mundy, Anthony (1580). *Zelauto.* London: John Charlewood.

Nashe, Thomas (1589). 'To the Gentleman Students of Both Universities', from Robert Greene's *Menaphon.* London: Sampson Clarke.

Nashe, Thomas(1592). *Pierce Penilesse his supplication to the diuell. Written by Tho. Nash, Gent.* London: Abell Jeffes.

Nashe, Thomas (1592). *Strange Newes.* London.

Nashe, Thomas (1596). *Have with you to Saffron Walden.* London: John Danter.

Nelson, Alan H. (2003). *Monstrous Adversary.* Liverpool: Liverpool University Press.

Nichols, John, ed. (1823). *Progresses and Public Processions of Queen Elizabeth.* Vol 1. New York: AMS Press.

Nowell, Lawrence. 'Tutor to the yong Earl of Oxon', L. to William Cecil (*et meum operam haud fore diu Oxoniensi comiti necessariam facile intelligam*); MS British Library, Landsdowne 6/54, f. 135.

Peacham, Henry (1622). 'Of Poetry', *The Compleat Gentleman*. London: F. Constable.

Peck, Francis (1732). 'Received of the Reverend Mr Abraham Fleming…A pleasant Conceit of *Vere* Earl of Oxford, discontented at the Rising of a mean Gentleman in the English Court, circa MDLXXX. MS. Manu Flemingi', *Desiderata Curiosa*, Liber VI.

Phillips, Gerald William (1936). *Lord Burghley in Shakespeare*. London: Butterworth.

Roe, Richard Paul (2011). *The Shakespeare Guide to Italy: Retracing the Bard's Unknown Travels*. London: Harper Perennial.

Severn, Charles, ed. (1839). *Diary of the Rev John Ward, A. M, Vicar of Stratford-upon-Avon, extending from 1648 to 1679*. London: Henry Colburn.

Shapiro, James (2010). *Contested Will — Who Wrote Shakespeare?* London: Bloomsbury.

Shapiro, James (2015). *1606: William Shakespeare and the Year of Lear*. London: Faber & Faber.

Showerman, Earl. (2009). '*Timon of Athens*: Shakespeare's Sophoclean Tragedy', *The Oxfordian*, 11.

Soothern, John (1584). *Pandora*. London: Thomas Hackette.

Steinburg, Steven (2013). *I Come to Bury Shakspere*. Café Padre Publishing.

Stritmatter, Roger (2001) *The Marginalia of Edward de Vere's Geneva Bible*, PhD thesis, University of Massachusetts.

Stritmatter, Roger (2010). 'Spenser's Perfect Pattern of a Poet and the 17th Earl of Oxford', *Cahiers Élisabéthains*, 77:1 (Spring): 9-22.

Strype, John ed., (1822). *The Life and Acts of John Whitgift*. Vol. 1. Oxford: Clarendon.

Stubbes, Phillip (1583). *The Anatomy of Abuses*. London: Richard Jones.

Turner Clark, Eva (1931). *Hidden Allusions in Shakespeare's Plays*. New York: Farquhar Payson.

Underdowne, Thomas, trans. (1569). Dedication to *Heliodorus: An Aethopian History*, London: Fraunces Cauldrocke.

Ward, B. M., ed. (1926). *A Hundreth Sundrie Flowres*. London: Frederick Etchells and Hugh Macdonald.

Ward, B. M. (1928). *The Seventeenth Earl of Oxford 1550-1604*. London: John Murray.

Ward, Robert Plumer (1827). *De Vere: Or, The Man of Independence*. Vol. 1. London: Henry Cockburn.

Warner, G. F. (1881). *Catalogue of MSS. and Muniments of Alleyn's College, Dulwich*. London: London Spottiswoode & Co.

Warner, William (1584). *Pan his syrinx*. London: Thomas Purfoote.

Warren, John (1640). 'Of Mr. William Shakespeare', *Poems; Written by Wil. Shake-speare. Gent.* London: John Benson.

Watson, Thomas (1582). '*Authoris ad Libellum suum Protrepticon*' in *Hekatompathia*. London: John Wolfe.

Waugh, Alexander (2013). 'Keeping Shakespeare out of Italy,' in J. Shahan & A. Waugh, eds., *Shakespeare Beyond Doubt?* Tamarac, Florida: Llumina Press, 72-85.

Waugh, Alexander (2014). 'Waugh on Jonson's Sweet Swan of Avon', *The Oxfordian*, vol. 16: 97-103.

Waugh, Alexander (2016). 'Shakespeare's Pole', *DVS Newsletter*, vol. 23, no. 4 (October).

Waugh, Alexander (2017). 'Hidden Truths', *De Vere Society Newsletter*, vol. 24, no. 2 (April): 14-46.

Webbe, William (1586). *A discourse of English poetrie Together, with the authors iudgment, touching the reformation of our English verse*. London: Robert Walley.

Wells, Stanley (2003). *Shakespeare for all Time*. Oxford: Oxford University Press.

Whalen, Richard (1994). *Shakespeare: WHO WAS HE?* Connecticut: Praeger.

White, Richard Grant (1859). 'William Shakespeare, Attorney and Solicitor', *The Atlantic Monthly*, (May).

Whittemore, Hank (2016).*100 Reasons Shake-speare was the Earl of Oxford*. Somerville: Forever Press.

Williams, Gordon (1994). *A Dictionary of Sexual Language and Imagery in Shakespearean and Stuart Literature*. Vol. 2, London: Athlone Press.

Wood, Anthony A., (1691). *Athenae Oxoniensis*. Ed., Philip Bliss. London: F. C. & J. Rivington, 1813.

Woudhuysen, H. R. (1981). *Leicester's Literary Patronage*. D.Phil: University of Oxford.

Chapter 4

Primary

1587 'Letter from the Privy Council to the Cambridge University Authorities', Privy Council Registers PC2/14/381.

1593a 'Remembrannces of wordes & matter againste Ric Cholmeley', Harley MS 6848 f.190r,v.

1593b 'Bayns Marlow of his blasphemyes', Harley MS 6848 ff 185-86.

1593c 'Copy of Marloes blasphemyes As sent to her H', Harley MS 6853 ff.307-8.

Secondary

Acheson, Arthur (1903). *Shakespeare and the Rival Poet.* London & New York: John Lane.

Ackroyd, Peter (2005). *Shakespeare: the Biography.* London: Chatto & Windus.

Bakeless, John Edwin (1942). *The Tragicall History of Christopher Marlowe.*, 2 vols. Cambridge: Harvard University Press.

Barber, R (2009). 'Shakespeare Authorship Doubt in 1593', *Critical Survey*, 21 (2): 83-110.

Barber, R (2016). 'Christopher Marlowe and Gervase Markham', *Notes & Queries*, 63 (3): 390-93.

Bate, Jonathan (1993). *Shakespeare and Ovid.* Oxford: Clarendon.

Bate, Jonathan (1997). *The Genius of Shakespeare.* London: McMillan.

Bloom, Harold (2002). *Christopher Marlowe.* 2nd edn., Bloom's Major Dramatists; New York: Chelsea House.

Boas, Frederick Samuel (1923). *Shakespeare & the Universities, and other studies in Elizabethan drama.* Oxford: Blackwell.

Cheney, Patrick (2008). *Shakespeare's Literary Authorship.* Cambridge: Cambridge University Press.

Cross, Claire (2004). 'Penry, John (1562/3–1593)', in H. C. G. Matthew and Brian Harrison, eds., *Oxford Dictionary of National Biography.* Online ed., ed. Lawrence Goldman, January 2008: Oxford: OUP.

Duncan-Jones, Katherine (1997). *Shakespeare's Sonnets.* The Arden Shakespeare. London: Thomson Learning.

Duncan-Jones, Katherine and Woudhuysen, H. R., eds. (2007). *Shakespeare's*

Poems, eds., Richard Proudfoot *et al.* The Arden Shakespeare. London: Thomson Learning.

Eder, Maciej (2015). 'Does Size Matter? Authorship Attribution, Small Samples, Big Problem', *Literary and Linguistic Computing*, 30 (2): 167-82.

Edmondson, Paul and Wells, Stanley W. (2004). *Shakespeare's sonnets.* Oxford Shakespeare. Oxford & New York: Oxford University Press.

Farey, Peter (2017). 'A Deception In Deptford', <http://rey.myzen.co.uk/title.htm>, accessed 10th October.

Farey, Peter (2017). 'Marlowe's Sudden and Fearful End', <http://rey.myzen.co.uk/sudden.htm>, accessed 10th October.

Feasey, Lynette & and Feasey, Eveline (1949). 'The Validity of the Baines Document', *Notes and Queries*, 26th November.

Greenblatt, Stephen (2004). *Will in the World : how Shakespeare became Shakespeare.* London: Jonathan Cape.

Hammer, Paul, E. J. (1996). 'A Reckoning Reframed: the "Murder" of Christopher Marlowe Revisited', *English Literary Renaissance*, 26 (2): 225-42.

Harvey, Gabriel (1884). *The Works of Gabriel Harvey*, ed., Alexander B. Grosart. The Huth Library.

Howard, Jennifer (2010). 'A Shakespeare Scholar Takes on a "Taboo" Subject', *The Chronicle of Higher Education*, <http://chronicle.com/article/A-Shakespeare-Scholar-Takes-on/64811/>, accessed April 10.

Hughes, Ted and Christopher Reid (2007). *Letters of Ted Hughes.* London: Faber.

Joyce, James (1980). *Ulysses.* Rev.ed 3rd imp. edn. London: Bodley Head.

Kendall, Roy (2003). *Christopher Marlowe and Richard Baines : journeys through the Elizabethan underground.* Madison, N.J.: Fairleigh Dickinson University Press; London: Associated University Presses.

Kingsley-Smith, Jane (2003). *Shakespeare's Drama of Exile.* Palgrave Shakespeare studies. Basingstoke, Hampshire; New York: Palgrave Macmillan.

Kuriyama, Constance B. (2002). *Christopher Marlowe : a Renaissance life.* Ithaca, London: Cornell University Press.

Logan, Robert A. (2007). *Shakespeare's Marlowe : the influence of Christopher Marlowe on Shakespeare's artistry.* Aldershot, England; Burlington, VT: Ashgate.

Lyon, John Henry Hobart (1919). *A Study of the Newe Metamorphosis.* Columbia

University Studies in English and Comparative Literature. New York: Columbia University Press.

McDonald, Russ (2004). 'Marlowe and Style', in Patrick Cheney, ed., *The Cambridge Companion to Christopher Marlowe.* Cambridge: Cambridge University Press: 55-69.

Merriam, Thomas V.N. and Robert A. J. Matthews (1994). 'Neural Computation in Stylometry II: an application to the works of Shakespeare and Marlowe', *Literary and Linguistic Computing*, 9: 1-6.

Minto, William (1874). *Characteristics of English Poets from Chaucer to Shirley.* Edinburgh, London: William Blackwood.

Moore, Hale (1926). 'Gabriel Harvey's References to Marlowe', *Studies in Philology*, 23 (3): 337-57.

Nashe, Thomas (1958). *The Works of Thomas Nashe.* Eds., Ronald Brunlees McKerrow and F. P. Wilson, 5 vols. Oxford: B. Blackwell.

Nicholl, Charles (2002). *The Reckoning: the Murder of Christopher Marlowe.* Revised edn.; London: Vintage.

Pinksen, Daryl (2009). 'Was Robert Greene's "Upstart Crow" the Actor Edward Alleyn?' *The Marlowe Society Research Journal*, 06: 18.

Riggs, David (2004). *The world of Christopher Marlowe.* London: Faber and Faber.

Robertson, John Mackinnon (1926). *The Problems of the Shakespeare Sonnets.* London: G. Routledge & Sons.

Segarra, Santiago, *et al.*, (2016). 'Attributing the Authorship of the Henry VI Plays by Word Adjacency', *Shakespeare Quarterly*, 67 (2): 232-56.

Sheils, William Joseph (2004). 'Whitgift, John (1530/31?–1604)', in H. C. G. Matthew and Brian Harrison, eds., *Oxford Dictionary of National Biography.* Online ed., ed. Lawrence Goldman, January 2008: Oxford: OUP.

Weis, René (2007). *Shakespeare Revealed : a biography.* London: John Murray.

Chapter 5

Antiquary, The (1903). Vol. XXXIX. January-December, London: Elliot Stock, 62, Paternoster Row.

Brockbank, P., ed. (1994). *Coriolanus.* The Arden Shakespeare. London: Routledge.

Burgoyne, F. J. (1904). *Collotype Facsimile and Type Transcript of An Elizabethan*

Manuscript preserved at Alnwick Castle, Northumberland. London: Longmans, Green and Co.

Casson, J. (2017). 'A Newly Discovered Seventeenth Century Sonnet', *Notes and Queries*, Vol 64, Issue 3: Sept. Oxford: Oxford University Press.

Chambers, E. K. (1966). *William Shakespeare, A Study of Facts and Problems, Volume II.* Oxford: Clarendon Press.

Clarke, B. C. (2011). *The Virginia Company and The Tempest,* Journal of Drama Studies, Vol. 5, July: available on-line <http://barryispuzzled.com/VirginiaCoTempest.pdf> accessed 5/1/2017).

Cole, J. (2014). *'The English Swain', the un-named Poet in Britannia's Pastorals, 1616.* The De Vere Society Newsletter, January, 20-28: <http://deveresociety.co.uk/articles/NL-2014jan.pdf>.

Daniell, D. (2005). *Julius Caesar.* The Arden Shakespeare. London: Thomson Learning.

Dowden, E. (1875). *Shakspere: A Critical Study of His Mind and Art.* Cambridge: Cambridge University Press.

Donaldson, I. (2011). *Ben Jonson A Life.* Oxford: Oxford University Press.

Duncan, O. L. (1974). *The Political Career of Sir Henry Neville.* Unpublished PhD Thesis: Ohio State University.

Falk, D. (2014). *The Science of Shakespeare, A New Look at the Playwright's Universe.* New York: Thomas Dunne Books.

Galis, R. (1579). *A brief treatise containing the most strange and horrible cruelty of Elizabeth Stile alias Rockingham and her confederates, executed at Abingdon, upon* R. *Galis.* London: J. Allde, London.

Gingerich, O. & Westman, R. S. (1988). *The Wittich Connection: Conflict and Priority in Late Sixteenth-Century Cosmology.* Philadelphia: American Philosophical Society.

Goulding, R. (1995). *Henry Savile and The Typhonic World-System. Journal of the Warburg and Courtauld Institutes*, Vol. 58, 152-179. Available on JSTOR: <http://www.jstor.org/stable/751509>: accessed 22/11/2016.

Hall, E. (1809). *Hall's Chronicle; Containing the History of England, During the Reign of Henry the Fourth and the Succeeding Monarchs to the end of the Reign of Henry the Eighth, in which are particular described the manners and customs of those periods. Carefully collated with the editions of 1548 and 1550.* London: Printed for

J. Johnson; F. C. And J. Rivington; T. Payne; Wilkie and Robinson; Longman, Hurst, Rees and Orme; Cadell and Davies; and J. Mawman.

Harding, A. *Biography of Sir Henry Neville, M. P. 1584-1603.* History of Parliament, On-line: <http://www.historyofparliamentonline.org/volume/1558-1603/member/neville-henry-1562-1615>: accessed 28/10/16.

Hansen, A. J. D. (1977). *Shakespeare and the Lore of Precious Stones.* College Literature, Vol 4, No. 3, Shakespeare Issue, Fall: 210-219, Baltimore, Maryland: John Hopkins University Press.

Hasler, P. W. (1981). *House of Commons 1558-1603.* London: HMSO for the History of Parliament Trust.

James, B. (2011). *Understanding the Invisible Shakespeare.* Bognor Regis: Cranesmere Press.

Keen, A. & Lubbock, R. (1954). *The Annotator.* London: Putman.

Kunz, G. F. (1916). *Shakespeare and Precious Stones.* London: J. B. Lippincott Co.

Laoutaris, C. (2015). *Shakespeare and The Countess: The Battle that Gave Birth to the Globe.* London: Fig Tree, Penguin Books.

Long, H. (1888). *The Oglander Memoirs.* London: Reeves and Turner.

Lytton, E. B. (1891). *The Last of the Barons.* London: Routledge and Sons Ltd.

McClure, N. E., ed. (1939). *The Letters of John Chamberlain.* Philadelphia: The American Philosophical Society, Memoirs XII, part 1, Vol 1.

Nash, T. H., trans. (1928). *Queen Elizabeth and Some Foreigners.* ed. Victor Von Klarwill, London: John Lane, The Bodley Head Ltd.

Newbery, E. (1824). *A Notable Berkshire Printer and* Publisher. available on-line: <http://archaeologydataservice.ac.uk/archiveDS/archiveDownload?t=arch-787-1/dissemination/pdf/BAJ050_PDFs/BAJ050_A05_newbery.pdf>: accessed 5/1/2017.

Peck, D. C., ed. (1985). *Leicester's Commonwealth, The Copy of a Letter Written by a Master of Art of Cambridge (1584) and Related Documents.* London: Ohio University Press.

Peck, D. C. ed., (2006). *Leicester's Commonwealth, The Copy of a Letter Written by a Master of Art of Cambridge (1584) and Related Documents.* Athens, Ohio: Ohio University Press, reprinted in PDF format: <http://www.dpeck.info/write/leic-comm.pdf>: accessed 5/1/2017.

Roe, R. P. (2011). *The Shakespeare Guide to Italy.* New York: Harper Perennial.

Rye, W. B. (1865). *England as Seen by Foreigners in the Days of Elizabeth & James the First, Comprising Translations of the Journals of the Two Dukes of Würtemberg in 1592 and 1610; Both Illustrative of Shakespeare.* London: John Russell Smith.

Sawyer, E., ed. (1725). *Memorials of State in the Reigns of Q. Elizabeth and K. James I Collected from the Original Papers of the Right Honourable Sir Ralph Winwood.* 3 Volumes, London: T. Ward.

Schurink, F. (2006). *An Unnoticed Early Reference to Shakespeare. Notes and Queries,* March. Oxford: Oxford University Press.

Sherman, W. H. (2008). *Used Books, Marking Readers in Renaissance England.* Philadelphia, University of Pennsylvania Press.

Spain-Savage, C. (2016). *Reimagining Gillian: The Merry Wives of Windsor and the Lost Friar Fox and Gillian of Brentford*: chapter 12 in in McInnes, D. & Steggle, M., eds., *Lost Plays in Shakespeare's England.* Basingstoke: Palgrave, Macmillan, available online <http://www.palgraveconnect.com/pc/doifinder/view/10.1057/9781137403971.0020>: accessed 22/10/2016.

Stoddard, R. E. (1985). *Marks in Books, Illustrated, and Explained.* Cambridge, MA: Harvard University Press.

Thrush, A. *Biography of Sir Henry Neville, M. P. 1604-1615: History of Parliament*, available on-line: <http://www.historyofparliamentonline.org/volume/1604-1629/member/neville-sir-henry-i-1564-1615>: accessed 28/10/2016.

Woolfson, J. (1998). *Padua and the Tudors: English Students in Italy, 1485-1603.* Cambridge: James Clarke & Co Ltd.

Books on Neville

Bradbeer, M. & Casson J. (2015). *Sir Henry Neville, Alias William Shakespeare: Authorship Evidence in the History Plays.* Jefferson, North Carolina: MacFarland.

Casson, J. (2010). *Enter Pursued by a Bear, The Unknown Plays of Shakespeare-Neville.* Bognor Regis: Music for Strings; republished from Tatcham, Berkshire: Dolman Scott.

Casson, J. (2010). *Much Ado About Noting, Henry Neville and Shakespeare's Secret Source.* Tatcham, Berkshire: Dolman Scott.

Casson, J. & Rubinstein, W. D. (2016). *Sir Henry Neville was Shakespeare: The Evidence.* Stroud: Amberley.

James, B. (2008). *Henry Neville and the Shakespeare Code.* Bognor Regis: Music for

Strings.

James, B. (2011). *Understanding the Invisible Shakespeare.* Bognor Regis: Cranesmere Press.

James, B. & Rubinstein, W. D. (2005). *The Truth Will Out: Unmasking The Real Shakespeare.* Harlow, Pearson Longman.

Leyland, B, & Goding, J. (2015). *The Map in Shakespeare's Sonnets.* Leanpub, available on-line: <https://leanpub.com/shakespearesirhenrynevilleandthesonnets>: accessed 21/4/2017.

Rubinstein, W. D. (2012). *Who wrote Shakespeare's Plays?* Stroud: Amberley.

Chapter 6

Akrigg, G. P. V. (1968). *Shakespeare and the Earl of Southampton.* Cambridge: Harvard University Press.

Anonymous (1763). *The Rare SECRETS of the English Countess Mary of Pembroke preserved in a Melodic Written Script of the Art of painting and stippling.* Nuremberg: Gabriel Nicolaus Raspe Publishers.

Baugh, Albert C., ed. (1948). *A Literary History of England.* New York: Appleton-Century-Crofts, Inc.

Beese, M. A. (1935). *A Critical Edition of the Poems Printed by John Donne the Younger in 1660, As Written by William Herbert, Earl of Pembroke, and Sir Benjamin Ruddier.* Unpublished dissertation: Oxford University.

Bevington, David, ed. (2009). *The Complete Works of Shakespeare,* 6th ed. New York: Pearson Longman.

Bornstein, Diane (1985). 'The Style of the Countess of Pembroke's Translation of Philippe de Mornay's "Discours de la vie et de la mort,"' in *Silent but for the Word: Tudor Women as Patrons, Translators, and Writers of Religious Works.* Ohio: Kent State University Press.

Brennan, Michael (1988). *Literary Patronage in the English Renaissance: The Pembroke Family.* London & New York: Routledge.

Brennan, M. and N. Kinnamon (2003). *A Sidney Chronology: 1554*-1654. London: Palgrave, 2003.

Buxton, John (1966). *Sir Philip Sidney and the English Renaissance.* New York & London: St. Martin's Press.

Campbell, Oscar James., ed. (1966). *The Reader's Encyclopedia of Shakespeare.* New

York: MJF Books.

Cerasano, S. P. and Marion Wynne-Davies, eds. (1996). *Renaissance Drama by Women: Texts and Documents.* London: Routledge.

Chamberlain, John (1939). *Letters of John Chamberlain.* Philadelphia: The American Philosophical Society.

Collier, J. Payne, ed. (1856). 'Shepheards Garland, Fashioned in nine Eglogs', in *Poems by Michael Drayton.* Printed for the Roxburghe Club. J. B. Nichols and Sons: London.

Duncan-Jones, Katherine, ed. (1989). *Sir Philip Sidney: A Critical Edition of the Major Works.* Oxford: Oxford University Press.

Duncan-Jones, Katherine (1991). *Sir Philip Sidney, Courtier Poet.* New Haven and London: Yale University Press.

Dover Wilson, John (1969). *The Sonnets.* Cambridge: Cambridge University Press.

Edward, Earl of Clarendon (1707). *The History and the Rebellion and Civil Wars in England.* Oxford: Oxford University Press.

Egan, Gabriel (2001). 'John Heminges' Tap-house at the Globe', *Theatre Notebook* 55.

Erne, Lukas (2013). *Shakespeare the Literary Dramatist.* Cambridge: Cambridge University Press.

Ferry, Anne (1983). *The "Inward" Language: Sonnets of Wyatt, Sidney, Shakespeare, Donne.* Chicago, London: University of Chicago Press.

Foster, Donald (1999). 'Master W. H., R.I.P.' in *Shakespeare's Sonnets: Critical Essays,* ed., James Schiffer. New York: Garland Publishing, Inc.

Gill, Roma, ed. (1996). *The Taming of the Shrew.* Oxford: Oxford University Press.

Grosart, Alexander B., ed. (1885). 'Sonnet LVIII', *The Complete Works in Verse and Prose of Samuel Daniel,* vol. 1. London: Hazell, Watson, and Viney.

Hannay, Margaret P., ed. (1985). 'Introduction', in *Silent but for the Word: Tudor Women as Patrons, Translators, and Writers of Religious Works.* Ohio: Kent State University Press.

Hannay, Margaret P. (1990). *Philip's Phoenix: Mary Sidney, Countess of Pembroke.* Oxford: Oxford University Press.

Hannay, Margaret P., Noel J. Kinnamon, and Michael G. Brennan (1998). *The*

Collected Works of Mary Sidney Herbert, Countess of Pembroke, vol. 1. Oxford: Clarendon Press.

Holman, Peter (2002). *Four and Twenty Fiddlers: The Violin at the English Court, 1540–1690*. Oxford: Clarendon Press.

Kay, W. David (1995). *Ben Jonson, A Literary Life*. New York: St. Martin's Press.

Kernan, Alvin (1995). *Shakespeare, the King's Playwright*. New Haven: Yale University Press.

Lamb, Mary Ellen (1984). 'Three Unpublished Holograph Poems in the Bright Manuscript: New Poet in the Sidney Circle', *Review of English Studies* 35, 301–15.

Meres, Francis (1978). *Palladis* Tamia. 1598; reprint. New York: Scholars' Facsimiles & Reprints.

Merriam-Webster, eds. (1995). *Merriam-Webster's Encyclopedia of Literature*. Springfield: Merriam-Webster.

Michell, John (1996). *Who Wrote Shakespeare?* London: Thames and Hudson.

Ogburn, Charlton (1984). *The Mysterious William Shakespeare: The Myth and the Reality*. McLean, Virginia: Dodd, Mead & Co./EPM Publications, Inc.

Osborne, Francis (1673). 'Memoirs on Q. Elizabeth and K. James', in *The Works of Francis Osborne, Esq.*, seventh ed. London: R. D.

Riggs, David (1989). *Ben Jonson: A Life*. Cambridge, London: Harvard University Press.

Ringler Jr. William A., ed. (1962). *The Poems of Sir Philip Sidney*. Oxford: Clarendon, 1962.

Roberts, Katherine J. (1993). *Fair Ladies: Sir Philip Sidney's Female Characters*. New York: Peter Lang Publishing, Inc.

Somerset, J. Alan B. (1994). *Records of Early English Drama, Shropshire*, vol. 2: *Editorial Apparatus*. Toronto: University of Toronto Press.

Stewart, Alan (2000). *Philip Sidney: A Double Life*. New York: St. Martin's Press.

Stone, Lawrence and Jeanne C. Fawtier Stone (2001). *An Open Elite? England 1540–1880*, abridged ed. 1986; reprint. Oxford: Clarendon Press.

Waller, Gary F. (1979). *Mary Sidney, Countess of Pembroke: A Critical Study of Her Writings and Literary Milieu*. Salzburg: Universität Salzburg.

Waller, Gary (1993). *Sidney Family Romance*. Detroit: Wayne State University Press.

Willoughby, E. E. (1934). *A Printer of Shakespeare*. London: Philip Allan & Co. Ltd.

Witherspoon, Alexander Maclaren (1968). *The Influence of Robert Garnier on Elizabethan Drama*. New York: Phaeton Press.

Woudhuysen, H. R. (1996). *Sir Philip Sidney and the Circulation of Manuscripts, 1558–1640*. Oxford: Oxford University Press.

Woudhuysen, H. R. (2004). 'Sidney, Sir Philip (1554–1586)', *Oxford Dictionary of National Biography*. Oxford: Oxford University Press.

Young, Frances Berkeley (1912). *Mary Sidney, Countess of Pembroke*. London: David Nutt.

Chapter 7

Adams, Christine (2008). 'Francis Bacon's Wedding Gift of "A Garden of a Glorious and a Strange Beauty" for the Earl and Countess of Somerset', *Garden History*, 36, No. 1. Spring: 36–58.

Bacon, Francis (1592-4). *The Promus of Formularies and Elegancies*. British Library, Harley 7017.

Bacon, Francis (1597). *Essayes*. STC: 1137.

Bacon, Francis (1605). *The two books of Francis Bacon, of the Proficience and Advancement of Learning*. STC: 1164.

Bacon, Francis (1612). *The essaies*. STC: 1141.

Bacon, Francis (1614). *The charge of Sir Francis Bacon touching duels*. STC: 1125.

Bacon, Francis (1627). *Sylua syluarum*. STC: 1168.

Bacon, Francis (1629). *The historie of the reigne of King Henry the Seuenth*. STC: 1161.

Beaumont, Francis (1613). *The Masqve of the Inner Temple and Grayes Inne*. London. STC: 1664.

Brady, James and John C. Olin., eds. (1992). *Collected Works of Erasmus*. Toronto: University of Toronto Press.

Burgoyne, Frank J., ed. (1902). *Northumberland Manuscripts*. London: Longmans, Green & Co.

Chambers, E. K. (1906). *Modern Language Review*, 2: 10–11.

Chambers, E. K. (1945). *The Elizabethan Stage*, 4 vols. Oxford: Clarendon Press.

Chapman, George (1614). *The memorable masqve of the two honovrable Hovses or Innes of Court, the Middle Temple and Lyncolnes Inne*.

Clarke, Barry R. (2011). 'The Virginia Company and *The Tempest*', *Journal of Drama Studies*, July: 13–27.

Clarke, Barry R. (2013). *A linguistic analysis of Francis Bacon's contribution to three Shakespeare plays: The Comedy of Errors, Love's Labour's Lost*, and *The Tempest*. PhD thesis, Brunel University London.

Clarke, Barry R. (2016). 'The Virginia Company's role in *The Tempest*', in Petar Penda, ed., *The Whirlwind of Passion: New Critical Perspectives on William Shakespeare*. Cambridge: Cambridge Scholars Publishing.

Cockburn, Nigel (1998). *The Bacon-Shakespeare Question*. private publication, *The Francis Bacon Society*.

Coperario, John (1614). *The maske of flowers. Presented by the Gentlemen of Graies–Inne, at the court of White-hall, in the Banquetting House, vpon Twelfe night, 1613*. London. STC: 17625.

Counseil for Virginia (1610). *A true declaration of the estate of the colonie in Virginia with a confutation of such scandalous reports as haue tended to the disgrace of so worthy an enterprise*. London. STC: 24833.

David, R. W., ed. (1956). *Love's Labour's Lost*. The Arden Shakespeare. London: Methuen.

Davison, Francis (1602). *A poetical rhapsody*. London. STC: 6373.

DelVecchio, Doreen and Anthony Hammond (1998). *Pericles, Prince of Tyre*. Cambridge: Cambridge University Press.

Dorsch, T. S. (2004). *The Comedy of Errors*, revised by Ross King. Cambridge: Cambridge University Press.

Elton, W. R. (2000). *Shakepeare's Troilus and Cressida and the Inns of Court revels*. Aldershot: Ashgate.

Fletcher, Reginald J., ed. (1901). *The Pension Book of Gray's Inn, 1569–1669*. London: Chiswick Press.

Gesta Grayorum: or, the History of the High and mighty Prince, Henry. (1688). London: Printed for William Canning. Wing: C444.

Gras, Henk (1989). 'Twelfth Night, Every Man Out of His Humour, and the Middle Temple Revels of 1597–8', *Modern Language Review* 84. July: 545–64.

Greg, Walter, ed. (1904). *Henslowe's Diary*. London: A. H. Bullen.

Harmor, Ralph (1615). *A True Discourse of the present estate of Virginia, and the successe of the affaires there till the 18 of Iune. 1614*. London. STC: 12736.

Hibbard, G. R. (2008). *Love's Labour's Lost.* Oxford: Oxford University Press.

Hughes, Alan, ed. (1994). *Titus Andronicus.* Cambridge: Cambridge University Press.

Hughes, Thomas (1587 [1588]). *Certain deu[is]es.* STC: 13921.

Hattaway, Michael, ed. (1990). *The First Part of King Henry VI.* Cambridge: Cambridge University Press.

Inderwick, F. A., ed. (1896). *A Calendar of the Inner Temple Records*, Vol. 1. London.

Jackson, MacDonald P. (2003). *Defining Shakespeare, Pericles as Test Case.* Oxford: Oxford University Press.

Klein, Karl, ed. (2001). *Timon of Athens.* Cambridge: Cambridge University Press.

Lake, David (1975). *The Canon of Thomas Middleton's Plays: Internal Evidence of the Major Problem of Authorship.* Cambridge: Cambridge University Press.

Leigh, Gerard (1562). *Accedens of Armoury.*

Love, Harold (2002). *Attributing Authorship: An Introduction.* Cambridge: Cambridge University Press.

McMenamin, Gerald R. (1993). *Forensic stylistics.* Amsterdam: Elsevier.

Melsome, William (1945). *The Bacon-Shakespeare Anatomy.* London: George Lapworth.

Montagu, Basil, ed. (1831). *The Works of Francis Bacon*, Vol. XIII. London: William Pickering.

Montagu, Basil, ed. (1838). *Of the Proficience and Advancement of Learning (1605).* London: William Pickering.

Nelson, Alan H. (2009). 'Emulating Royalty: Cambridge, Oxford, and the Inns of Court', in Susan Zimmerman and Garrett Sullivan, eds., *Shakespeare Studies*, Vol. XXXVII. Rosemont Publishing.

Nelson, Alan H. and John R. Elliott Jr., eds. (2010). *Records of Early English Drama: Inns of Court*, 3 vols, Vol. 1. Cambridge: D. S. Brewer.

Nichols, John (1828). *The Progresses, Processions, and Magnificent Festivities, of King James the First*, 4 vols, Vol. II. New York: AMS Press Inc.

Plutarch, Lucius Mestrius (1597). *The lives of the noble Grecians and Romans.* STC: 20066.

Purchas, Samuel (1625). *Purchas his pilgrimes*, 4 vols, Vol. IV. London: W. Stansby.

Quiller-Couch, Arthur and John Dover Wilson (1961). *The Tempest.* First edition 1921. Cambridge: Cambridge University Press.

Reid, J. S. (1922). 'Shakespeare's "Living Art"', *The Philological Quarterly*, 1. July: 226-7.

Rich, Richard (1610). *Newes from Virginia.* London: STC: 21005.

Scriba, Christoph J. (1970). 'The autobiography of John Wallis, F.R.S.', *Notes and Records of the Royal Society of London*, 25: 17-46.

Shakespeare, William (1598). *Love's Labour's Lost.* STC: 22294.

Smith, John (1608). *A true relation.* STC: 22795.5.

Smith, John (1624). *The generall historie of Virginia.* London. STC: 22790.

Spedding, James (1870). *A Conference of Pleasure, composed for some festive occasion about the year 1592 by Francis Bacon.* London: Whittingham and Wilkins.

Spedding, James, Robert Leslie Ellis, and Douglas Denon Heath, eds. (1857-59). *The Works of Francis Bacon*, 7 vols. London: Longmans.

Spedding, James, Robert Leslie Ellis, and Douglas Denon Heath, eds. (1861-74). *The Letters and Life of Francis Bacon*, 7 vols. London: Longmans.

Spedding, James, Robert Leslie Ellis, and Douglas Denon Heath, eds. (1882). *The Works of Francis Bacon,* 15 vols. Boston: Houghton, Mifflin, and Co.

Stephens, Robert, ed. (1734). *Letters and Remains of the Lord Chancellor Bacon.* London: W. Bowyer.

Stewart, Alan, ed. (2001). *The Oxford Francis Bacon, Vol. 1: Early Writings 1584–1596.* Oxford: Oxford University Press.

Strachey, William (1612). *Historie of Travaile*: London: for the Hakluyt Society, 1849.

Taylor, Rupert (1932). *The Date of Love's Labour's Lost.* New York: Columbia University Press.

Vickers, Brian, ed. (2002). *Francis Bacon: The Major Works.* Oxford: Oxford University Press.

Waterhouse, Edward (1663). *Fortescusus illustrates.* London.

Wells, Stanley and Gary Taylor, with John Jowett and William Montgomery (1987). *William Shakespeare: A Textual Companion.* Oxford: Clarendon Press.

White, R. S. (1996). *Natural Law in English Renaissance Literature*. Cambridge: Cambridge University Press.

Whitworth, Charles, ed. (2002). *The Comedy of Errors*. Oxford: Oxford University Press.

Woodhuysen, H. R., ed. (1998). *Love's Labour's Lost*. London: Thomas Nelson.

Zurcher, Andrew (2008). 'Consideration, contract and the end of *The Comedy of Errors*', in Raffield, P. and G. Watt, eds., *Shakespeare and the Law*. Oxford: Hart Publishing.

Chapter 8

Anonymous. Dir. Roland Emmerich, Columbia Pictures, 2011.

Ackroyd, Peter (2005). *Shakespeare: The Biography*. London: Chatto & Windus.

Barthes, Roland (1977). 'The Death of the Author' in *Image/Music/Text*, translated by Stephen Heath. New York: Hill and Wang, 142-7.

Bate, Jonathan (2008). *Soul of the Age: A Biography of the Mind of William Shakespeare*. London: Random House.

Bryson, Bill (2007). *Shakespeare*. London: Atlas Books.

Edmondson, Paul and Stanley Wells, eds. (2013). *Shakespeare Beyond Doubt: Evidence, Argument, Controversy*. Cambridge: Cambridge University Press.

Foucault, Michel (1987). 'What is an Author?' in Paul Rabinow, ed., *The Foucault Reader*. Harmondsworth: Penguin, 101-120.

Greenblatt, Stephen (2004). *Will in the World: How Shakespeare Became Shakespeare*. New York: Norton.

Leahy, William (2009a). 'Introduction', in W. Leahy, ed., *Questioning Shakespeare: Essays on Authorship*. Special edition of *Critical Survey*, 21.2, 1-6.

Leahy, William (2009b). 'The Shakespeare Authorship Question: A Suitable Subject for Academia?' *Discovering Shakespeare: A Festschrift in Honour of Isabel Holden*. University of Concordia Press, 5-11.

Leahy, William, ed. (2010). *Shakespeare and His Authors: Critical Perspectives on the Authorship Question*. London: Continuum Press.

Leahy, William (2013). 'I receive hate mail for questioning the authorship of Shakespeare's plays' *The Guardian*, (23 April), <www.theguardian.com/commentisfree/2013/apr/23/william-shakespeare-authorship-birthday>.

Leahy, William (2014). "'Exit pursued by a Zombie": The Vampire we Desire, the

Shakespeare we Reject' in *Studies in Popular Culture*. Volume 36.2, (Spring), 29-44.

Leahy, William (2015). 'Shakespeare's birthday: ignore the avalanche of adulation — he was a chancer of the first order', *The Conversation*, (23 April), <www.theconversation.com/shakespeares-birthday-ignore-the-avalanche-of-adulation-he-was-a-chancer-of-the-first-order-40675>.

Leahy, William (2016a). "'the dreamscape of nostalgia': Shakespearean Biography — Too Much Information (but not about Shakespeare)", in W. Leahy & P. Pugliatti, eds., *Journal of Early Modern Studies*. number 5, 31-52.

Leahy, William (2016b). 'What Shakespeare, Jesus and Mickey Mouse have in common', *The Conversation*, (23 March), <www.theconversation.com/what-shakespeare-jesus-and-mickey-mouse-have-in-common-56526>.

Leahy, William (2016c). 'Is This a Shakespeare Portrait I see before me? Well, no', *The Guardian*, (22 April), <www.theguardian.com/commentisfree/2016/apr/22/william-shakespeare-portrait-bard-400-anniversary>.

Merriem, Tom (2005). *The Identity of Shakespeare in Henry VIII*. Tokyo: The Renaissance Institute.

Potter, Lois (2012). *The Life of William Shakespeare*. London: Wiley-Blackwell.

Price. Diana (2001). *Shakespeare's Unorthodox Biography: New Evidence of an Authorship Problem*. Westport, CT: Greenwood Press.

Rudman, Joseph (2016). 'Non-Traditional Authorship Attribution Studies of William Shakespeare's Canon: Some Caveats', in *Journal of Early Modern Studies*. William Leahy and Paola Pugliatti, eds., n. 5, 307-328.

Shapiro, James (2010). *Contested Will: Who Wrote Shakespeare*. London: Faber and Faber.

Sutherland, John (2006). 'Is This a Pint I See Before Me?', *The Guardian*, 26 September, <www.theguardian.com/books/2006/sep/26/shakespeare>.

Taylor, Gary and Stanley Wells (1988). *The Oxford Shakespeare*. Oxford: Oxford University Press.

Taylor, Gary, John Jowett, Terri Bourus and Gabriel Egan, eds. (2016). *The New Oxford Shakespeare: Modern Critical Edition: The Complete Works*, Oxford: Oxford University Press.

Taylor, Gary, John Jowett, Terri Bourus and Gabriel Egan, eds. (2017). *The New Oxford Shakespeare: Critical Reference Edition: The Complete Works*, Oxford: Oxford University Press.

Taylor, Gary and Gabriel Egan, eds. (2017). *The New Oxford Shakespeare: Authorship Companion*, Oxford: Oxford University Press.

Vickers, Brian (2002). *Shakespeare Co-Author: A Historical Study of Five Collaborative Plays*. Oxford: Oxford University Press.

Vickers, Brian (2007). 'Incomplete Shakespeare: Or, Denying Coauthorship in *1 Henry VI*', in *Shakespeare Quarterly*. Vol. 58, No. 3, (Fall), 311-352.

Vickers, Brian (2008). 'Thomas Kyd, Secret Sharer', in *Times Literary Supplement*, (April 18), 13-15.

Weis, René (2008). *Shakespeare Revealed: A Biography*. London: John Murray.

Wells, Stanley (2009). 'What Was He Really Like', in *Critical Survey*. Vol. 21, No. 3, 107-111.

Wood, Michael (2003). *In Search of Shakespeare*. London: BBC Books.

Lightning Source UK Ltd.
Milton Keynes UK
UKHW02f0856220318
319763UK00006B/64/P